DISCLOSUR

Unveiling Our Role in the Secret War of the Ancients

Updated and Expanded

ISBN-13: 978-1484003404

DEDICATION AND ACKNOWLEDGEMENTS

This book is dedicated to my mother, who has gone home to be with the Lord, and to my grandparents. Mom, Grandma, and Grandpa, you always took Proverbs 22:6 seriously and to heart in raising me. I cannot thank you enough for it. I am who I am today because of you. I love you all so much!

There are many people I have in my life to thank for helping to make this book possible.

First and foremost, my Lord and Savior, Jesus Christ, who has provided me with strength, love, and direct revelation of His Holy Spirit throughout the researching and writing of this book.

Next, I thank my wife, Christina, who has been incredibly encouraging and helpful through this entire process, showing the utmost patience, love, and kindness. I can't thank you enough, sweetheart!

I also want to thank my entire family, especially those who were directly involved in my upbringing, for raising me in the Word and making sure I was always loved, even when times were tough.

There are many other people I have to thank and unfortunately, due to limited space, cannot list them all here. A very big thank you goes out to all my friends and family who have played a part in my life to get me to where I am today. I am so incredibly blessed to have you all in my life. Thank you so much!

TABLE OF CONTENTS

FOREWORD

Written by Douglas Hamp

What could be more momentous than the unveiling of the Lord Jesus Christ? A day is coming when the Lord will descend from heaven and fight against his enemies. That day will be the ultimate disclosure and all who have rejected him will instantly become believers, but it will be too late. However, for all who put their trust in the great warrior king before the day of disclosure, they are assured a place in his kingdom.

Josh Peck's Disclosure is a book that takes big ideas of Scriptures and makes them relevant for our day. He also breaks down the bigger ideas of theology and makes them easy to understand with examples of how they apply. Lastly, he addresses how the alien phenomenon could very well be the great deception that is coming upon the earth.

Foreword Author Biography

Doug Hamp graduated from the Hebrew University of Jerusalem with an M.A. in the Hebrew Bible. He specialized in ancient languages including Biblical Hebrew and Koine Greek. He is the author of *"The Millennium Chronicles"*, *"Discovering the Language of Jesus"*, *"The First Six Days"*, *"Corrupting the Image"*, as well as many others. He also teaches on a wide variety of Biblical topics through the form of PowerPoint presentations. For more information on Doug Hamp, please refer to his website at www.douglashamp.com.

PREFACE

We have all been born into a war whether we choose to believe it or not. Humanity has been caught in the crossfire and now we must make a choice. Which army will we fight for? With this book, I hope to show you what side you are currently on and help you decide for yourself what side you want to be on. To be able to make that decision for yourself, you must be properly informed. We will be getting into topics such as aliens, demons, fallen angels, hybrids, and other devices of our enemy later in this book. First, we must lay a foundation to build on.

There are things in this life we cannot understand without a solid foundation. A painter cannot learn to paint a portrait until he learns what colors are. An architect cannot design a building until he learns shapes. A novelist cannot write his first book until he learns how to spell. We find the same thing in understanding the past, present, and future as explained in the Bible. This is referred to as milk and meat teaching in Hebrews 5:12-14. The importance of a solid foundation is taught all throughout the Bible.

There is a war being fought between two ancient powers; one of light and one of darkness. The war originated near the beginning of time and is still raging around us today. The ancient powers of darkness are trying to keep this war a secret. In doing so, they hope to keep humanity uninvolved and ignorant of the truth. The truth is that this ancient and ongoing war is between God and Satan with humanity in the middle. God wants us to fight for Him. Taking the position to not fight is where Satan will use us best. To not fight for God is to side with Satan. One of Satan's favorite tactics for getting us to side with him in battle is by convincing us that a war doesn't exist. It is up to us to choose sides. There is no in-between.

Whether for darkness or light, we have all been conditioned to fight in this war from the time we were born. We find our foundation in either the teachings of Satan or the teachings of God. A solid foundation in Satan would be to let the world dictate how we believe and how we live our lives. To oppose Satan's foundation is to accept a solid foundation in Jesus Christ and allow His Word, also known as the Bible, to guide us through all aspects of life. If you have already found your solid foundation in Jesus Christ then you are off to a good start in understanding this book.

If you have not, refer to the chapter entitled *"Salvation"* and please deeply consider the information.

Once you are saved and a practicing Christian, your work is not finished. It has only begun. Salvation is just the first step. The next step is to sort out the truth from the lies, real information from misinformation, proper interpretations from misinterpretations, good behaviors from bad behaviors, and correct logic from twisted logic. In writing this book, I am hoping to lay a solid foundation of biblical information that may not be common Christian knowledge. From that foundation, I hope to build you up to the truth of what God has revealed about the age we are living in and the future.

There are many people out there who, like me, were raised in a traditional Christian background. Many churches nowadays do not teach the things I will be discussing throughout, and especially later in, this book. Remember, Satan wants to keep the Church ignorant of his devices. In doing so, he knows he will have his best chance at deceiving and destroying us. We cannot allow that to happen. It is time for us to wake up.

To be able to properly understand and accept most of this book, you may find that you have to trade some of your preconceived ideas for the revelations found in the Bible. You may have to trade tradition for truth. I only ask you to consider the information carefully and test it against the Word of God. For the benefit of the majority, I will be primarily referencing from the King James Version Bible. We should never idly accept a teaching of spiritual or biblical things without first weighing it against the Bible itself.

I hope to take you on the same journey of discovery God has been leading me through for years. This journey isn't for everyone. It will test your faith in the truth of the Word of God. If you can grab hold of the information here, compare it with scripture, and accept what God is teaching you, this can bring you to a place of deeper understanding to be able to fight beside Jesus against the works of Satan. Of course, this is not done by my words of my personal version of the truth. It is done by the revelation of God through His words of the only truth.

This book can be looked at as an information guide for the war we are involved in against Satan and the battle plans God has laid out for us in His Word. I hope this will help you on your way to a closer understanding of the Bible, the times we're living in, the war at hand, the entities involved, and what is to come. I hope this book becomes a blessing for you and I pray for everyone reading this to learn to let God be your only guiding light to the truth. I pray for you to never accept any teaching blindly, never let any man or woman stand in the place of God and His teaching, and always test the spirits and information against the Holy Word of God. Thank you and God bless.

PART 1

FOUNDATION FOR
UNDERSTANDING THE WAR

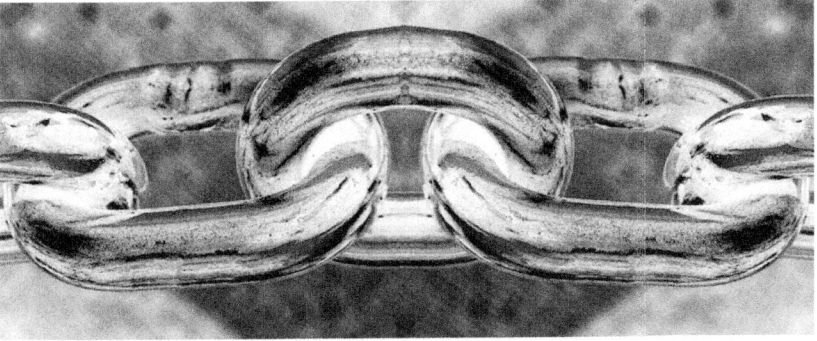

Chapter 1

INTRODUCTION

From the time I was born until the age of twelve, I was an actively practicing Baptist Christian. Within those twelve years, I can remember having many questions, just like any child. At that time, my mom and I were attending my grandparents' church and I noticed two things to be true involving my questioning. First, someone always had an answer for me. Second, the answer would always lead me to more questions. I almost have to laugh when I think back to that time. I remember feeling so frustrated when I wouldn't receive a simple answer to my questions. I realize now how frustrating it must have been for other people when their answers would not be enough to satisfy my curiosity.

The people I would question the most were my mother and grandparents. God bless their hearts for always being so patient with me. I would spend a lot of time talking with my grandma and grandpa about the Bible and God. They were always delighted to teach me something new and do their best to answer my questions. I remember how a pivotal point in my life, which would direct how I thought about God, the Bible, and church, came in the form of one of those answers.

One day, when I was about eleven or twelve years old, my mom left me with my grandparents to stay the night. I remember that night, I was stretched out on the couch, getting ready to go to sleep, and my grandmother and I were talking about God and religion. I asked her a question that had been bothering me for a long time. I asked "Grandma, how do we know the Baptist religion is right and other Christians are wrong?" She thought about it for a moment and, with all the love in the world, simply and honestly answered "I don't know". At least for the rest of that night, I was completely satisfied with the answer I received and had no more questions.

The lesson I learned from that was not only do we need to be honest with other people but we need to be honest with ourselves. If someone asks us a question about our faith or biblical facts and we are uncertain, we need to learn to be honest and tell them we don't know. If we try to come up with an answer on the spot or try to dodge the question with something else, the person asking will almost always be able to detect it. That could ruin our credibility and their view of our faith.

Learning to be humble and practicing humility are very difficult things to do. However, if we can master these skills, they also will almost always be detected and can build our credibility. Even if the person doesn't agree with our answer, if we are honest with him, he will usually have a much greater respect for us as individuals and sources of information.

If the person asks a question that we don't know but are confident we can find the answer, we must say so. We need to acknowledge our weaknesses and admit that we are human and imperfect. For example, for the longest time in my early Christian life, one of my major weaknesses was memorizing Bible verses word for word. I could usually get the basic message across through paraphrasing but if I didn't have my Bible in front of me, it was difficult to be able to recite the exact verse and remember exactly where it was located.

I found this weakness to be an extreme disadvantage when trying to witness to someone or answer questions about the Bible. To combat this weakness, beyond my own personal studies, I would be honest with the person and say that I would locate the exact verse and chapter for the next time I spoke with him. We must do our best to answer questions, even if we need some humility to do some personal studying. After all, when you think about it, the very soul and eternity of that person is at stake. If answering one question honestly is the thing that can show this person the truth, would it not be worth it to move Heaven and Earth to find the correct answer?

I believe this is one of the many reasons God wanted me to write this book. Because of the war that is currently raging, we need to be rooted in our faith, confident in our knowledge of scripture, and learn to teach God's truth honestly. We need to learn and accept the truths about our faith, even if they conflict with some traditions we were brought up in. It is so important for us to be able to set aside our own egos and pride to be able to accept what God has for us. We need to learn to lift God's Word above our own beliefs and opinions. We all have to learn to admit if we don't know something and, if it applies, admit we're wrong.

Concerning the topics discussed in this book, whether you agree or disagree, I would greatly encourage you to do your own research and come to your own conclusions. Most importantly, whatever answers you come up with, you must test them against scripture. If an answer does not fit with the Word of God, do not try and force it. There is no place in the Bible that we are told to do that. When an interpretation doesn't fit, instead of trying to redefine the Bible, we must learn to redefine our conclusions. I have had to do this countless times in my life because I, like the rest of us, am still learning.

There are many places in this book where I will say something *is* or say something is *truth.* I say these things knowing that they are speculative. There are things that I hope and pray I am wrong. The things I have discovered as truth are based on my own research and direction from God.

The fact is that none of us knows the absolute truth about everything. There are some things we know as God's absolute truth but, for some of the more fringe-beliefs, all we can really do is speculate based on the Bible and other evidence we are able to find. Given that, we must be able to admit that we could be mistaken and, if more evidence shows up that paints a clearer picture, we must reexamine our beliefs, views, and opinions.

In the first print of this book, I explained that though I recognize and identify everything I have included here as the truth, I do not know everything. I acknowledged that further study may prove certain things differently, such as things concerning the future. It is for that exact reason why I decided to put together this updated and expanded edition; now a year after the release of the first edition of *Disclosure*. This past year has been one of learning, growing, and sharpening. Not only has further study shown things differently, but a year of nearly-constant writing has given me new skills in communicating my points much more clearly.

In the first run of *Disclosure*, there were a few things I did not explain as well as I could have, which led a few to believe I was saying something other than what was intended. I now have the ability to remedy this and, with a year's worth of reader's feedback at my disposal, can make this book everything it should be. I will state again, however, that I am most certainly not infallible. There very well still could be things included in this book that even further study and growth may prove otherwise. That is why I still maintain the importance of the reader to not take my word for any of this, but instead to weigh what is written here against the word of God. As I said in the first edition of *Disclosure*, I have the utmost confidence in the Holy Spirit within me but I have little to no confidence in my own humanity. The Spirit wrestles against the flesh (Galatians 5:16-18). We must learn to forsake the flesh and be led by the Spirit.

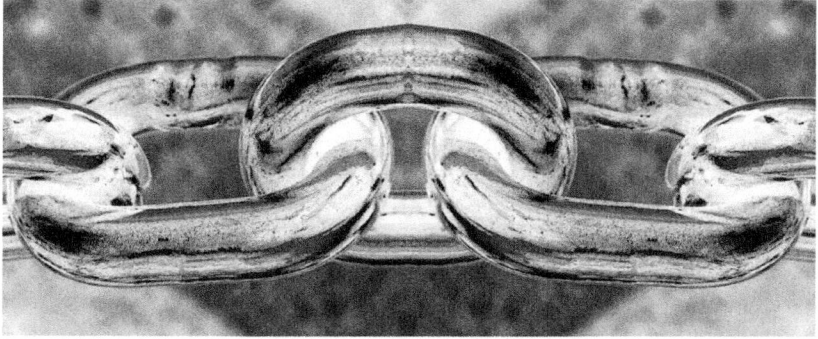

Chapter 2

SALVATION

This is where it all begins. Salvation is the beginning to discovering the truths of the Bible. When you get saved, you receive the Spirit of God and Jesus into your heart. It is the Spirit of God, known as the Holy Spirit, which becomes an internal teacher to guide you through His Word. If you try and go it alone without the Holy Spirit, most of scripture will seem confusing or ridiculous. 1 Corinthians 1:18 reads…

"For the preaching of the cross is to them that perish foolishness; but unto us which are saved it is the power of God."

There are some Christian churches that teach if you repeat a prearranged prayer, you will be automatically saved by Jesus Christ and have eternal life, even if you didn't really mean what you prayed. They will act as if the words themselves are a type of magical incantation that only needs to be repeated, not necessarily believed, to inherit salvation. Is this what the Bible teaches? If it was so easy, why wouldn't everyone simply repeat the prayer as a safety precaution, even if they don't actively believe in God or the Bible? Why would most unbelieving people find it so difficult to just say a simple prayer to ensure their eternal safety?

The first problem is that the Bible does not teach salvation comes from reciting a prearranged prayer from unbelief. In fact, there is no "salvation prayer" found within any of the books of the Bible. It is not the words spoken that saves, it is the faith behind the words. It is the belief that the words are expressing. It is true acceptance of Jesus as Savior.

There are many misconceptions as to what salvation is, what it means, and how to attain it. Unfortunately, a few churches miss the mark completely. The only place we should be looking for information concerning eternal life is the Word of God found in the Holy Bible.

BASIC LAYOUT

In the beginning, in the Garden of Eden, Satan convinced Adam and Eve to rebel against God. This rebellion is called *"sin"*. This was how sin came into the world and how humanity fell (Genesis chapters 1-3).

Since God is a perfect God, He cannot allow sin in His eternal presence. Sin is the opposite of the nature of God. Sin also causes physical and spiritual death (Romans 6:23). When Adam and Eve fell, that sin ran rampant throughout the world and all generations like a cancer. This is why all of humanity has a sin nature.

Since the sin nature ran through the very blood of every human, it was necessary for innocent blood to be shed to cleanse the sin. Animal sacrifices started because, since animals are innocent in the eyes of God, the blood would cover sin. There were different animals used in different sacrifices for different sins in accordance to God's law recorded by Moses and included in *"The Torah"* (the first five books of the Bible). Every time someone went against God's law, that person would have to offer an animal sacrifice of some kind to cover the sin. Since it was only animal blood and not human blood, it covered the sin but was not sufficient to completely cleanse it.

The only way the human sin nature could be completely cleansed would be by shedding the blood of an innocent human. It could not just be any human because every human had the sin nature. Every human's blood was infected with sin. A normal human's blood would not be sufficient to cleanse the sins of someone else.

God knew the only way for the sin nature to be defeated was to send a perfect and sinless person to be born on Earth and sacrificed for all of humanity. God knew nobody else could be properly sacrificed but Himself. God in the flesh, named Jesus Christ, was the only one in all of existence that was perfectly sinless. His blood would be innocent in the way that could cleanse the sin nature of every person who was or will be born on Earth.

When Jesus was crucified, His shed blood was the ultimate sacrifice needed to completely cleanse the sin nature of humanity. This meant that Jesus provided our salvation and completely defeated death. To prove it, He came back to life shortly after He was killed. He then ascended back into Heaven with a promise to return some day (Matthew chapter 28).

Jesus told us what salvation is and how to receive it. Without the cleansing blood of Jesus, we would die in our sins. This means we would physically die while our sin nature is still in place. The consequence of this is we cannot be with God and our sin.

The life we are given is our chance to let Jesus cleanse us and break the power of our sin nature. Death is what seals our eternity. God, being perfect, cannot reside with sin in eternity. If we die with our sin nature still intact, we have to be eternally separated from God. This is what is known as spiritual death.

HELL

The idea of Hell is an interesting topic all its own. I used to believe that Hell was a place of eternal separation from God, meaning that Hell was the only place in existence where God is not present. I used to believe Hell is merely the result of the absence of God. I had nothing biblical to back up this theory. It was just what I put together on my own as a child.

The reality is that there is nowhere in existence where God is not present in some way. Everything is His creation. Everything comes from Him. Everything is His. Right now, there is a type of veil between the physical and spiritual world. We are told many places in the Bible that man, in our present state, cannot be in the complete presence of God and live.

The entire spirit world is God's domain. When we die, we transfer from the physical world to spiritual existence. 2 Corinthians 5:8 tells us that to be absent from the body is to be present with the Lord. There is no in-between. It is the same for believers and unbelievers at the exact moment of death. This begs the question, how does Hell fit in with all of this? We read in Daniel 7:9-11…

"I beheld till the thrones were cast down, and the Ancient of days did sit, whose garment was white as snow, and the hair of his head like the pure wool: his throne was like the fiery flame, and his wheels as burning fire. A fiery stream issued and came forth from before him: thousand thousands ministered unto him, and ten thousand times ten thousand stood before him: the judgment was set, and the

books were opened. I beheld then because of the voice of the great words which the horn spake: I beheld even till the beast was slain, and his body destroyed, and given to the burning flame."

We see here a description of the characteristics of God Himself. A major component of God is fire and flame. We read that a fiery stream came from Him. We also read that in the vision, the beast, referring to the Antichrist, was given to the burning flame and his body was destroyed.

When we compare this with the book of Revelation, we discover that this is actually talking about the lake of fire which Hell is ultimately cast into. Not only will the Antichrist be cast into the lake of fire, but also the false prophet and any person who accepted the mark of the beast. From this, we can see that the fire of Hell actually comes from God Himself.

We are told in 1 Corinthians 15:42-44 that we will be given new bodies after we die if we accept Jesus as our savior. I believe it is this body that allows us to be in the presence of God in His brilliance and glory. When an unsaved person dies, they are not given a new body, but instead are sealed with their sin. This means they have no protection from the power, energy, and glory that emanates from God. This is what ultimately burns them and destroys their spiritual body. Without the covering and protection of salvation in the form of a new body, their soul will be destroyed but their spirit remains in eternal torment (Mark 9:48, Isaiah 66:24, Revelation 20:10).

Jesus said that Hell was created originally for the devil and his angels but now includes mankind (Matthew 25:41). This shows us that Hell is a created place. God is the only creator, so this means that God created Hell. Beings that do not have the protection of God and are not in right-standing with God in eternity are subject to the burning of His presence. This is why no man can see God fully in person and live. This is also why unsaved people, demons, fallen angels, Satan, the Antichrist, and the false prophet are eternally tormented. They have no protection from the brilliance of God. They do not have a body that is compatible with it. Because of this, the ultimate glory and brilliance of God destroys their unprotected soul and keeps their eternal spirit in torment forever. Since they are still eternal beings in the sense that they are not subject to complete annihilation, God created a place for them. They cannot reside with God in His Kingdom of Heaven in their unprotected and sealed state of sin. This is why God

16

created Hell; the place where the unprotected agents of sin must reside forever.

The good news about all of this is not a single one of us has to go to Hell. God has provided us with a way out. He has made the protection of a new and compatible body available to us. All we have to do is receive it. Of course, there are a lot of false doctrines, misinterpretations, and misconceptions about Hell in the world today. Sometimes it may seem difficult to sort out reality from the legends and truth from tradition. This is why we must refer to the Bible as our source for God's truth.

One of the biggest misconceptions in the world is that good people go to Heaven and evil people go to Hell. The truth is that we would all consider ourselves to be good people because everyone does what is right in his own eyes. Even Hitler thought he was a good person and doing right by the world. Clearly, we can't be trusted to judge ourselves as good or evil. That leaves the job up to God.

God loves us so much that He did not want to be eternally separated from us. The only way He could bring us with Him into eternity and still remain a just and fair God was to sacrifice His Son Jesus to cleanse our sins. If we accept who He is and what He did for us, we can claim the cleansing of the blood of Jesus for our own. After that, we live our lives for Jesus. That way, when we physically die, we can actually be with God in Heaven because our sin nature will have already been taken care of and not be sealed with us in eternity. This is eternal life. This is what is known as salvation.

Whether or not to accept Jesus' salvation is a choice we all must make. God will never force us to accept Him. If God cleansed our sins and forced it on us, He would not be just and fair and it would not be true love. The reality is that true love is by choice, not by force. We all have a choice if we want to claim that cleansing, forgiving blood for our own or if we want to reject it, keep our sin nature, and die in our sins.

RECEIVING SALVATION

God made it fairly easy for us to understand how to attain salvation and assure our acceptance into Heaven upon our death. The basic idea of the whole thing is presented in what is probably the most recognizable verse in the entire Bible. John 3:16 reads…

"For God so loved the world, that he gave his only begotten Son, that whosoever believeth in him should not perish, but have everlasting life."

We have to believe in Him. We have to believe and accept what He did for us, His love for us, and everything that makes Him who He is. We are promised eternal life if we accept and continue to live for Him. If we want salvation from Jesus, we ask Him for it, admit we're sinful, and ask for forgiveness. This should be done from our own hearts in our own words. Salvation does not come from a recital of a prearranged prayer from an empty heart.

Some may try and make salvation more complicated than what it is. If you encounter this, just remember John 3:16. The only way to Heaven is through Jesus. The only way to God is through Jesus. The only escape from Hell is through Jesus (John 14:6, Acts 13:38-39, Romans 6:23).

SALVATION MISCONCEPTIONS

There is a version of a doctrine flowing through the Church nowadays that I believe to be a big misconception. It is a version of *"once saved, always saved"*. This doctrine manifests in a variety of ways. The main one I want to address here is the version that says once you repeat some words, even if you're not sure if you really mean them, then you are saved and no matter what you do, you cannot lose your promise of salvation. It puts more emphasis in the prayer itself and not the faith and belief behind it. I see this as another doctrine that is born from misinterpretation of scripture and fitting the Bible around preconceived notions.

I will state here that I do believe the biblical version of *once saved, always saved* to be true. If you decide to accept salvation and believe in what Jesus did to provide it, you will be saved and sealed in eternity. Once you are truly saved, you are always saved. Nothing can take that away from you. However, if a person tries to merely repeat a prayer without meaning it, chances are they did not receive salvation in the first place. It must come from belief.

I remember when I was a kid in a Baptist church, at the end of each service, the pastor would ask anyone who did not know if they were going to Heaven to come up and talk with him privately. I went up almost every time. I remember my parents and grandparents would try to stop me by insisting that I was saved and I had no reason to doubt it. Still, there was something inside of me that still wasn't sure. I had this same fear all throughout my teenage years and on into early adulthood.

Until God got a hold of me and showed me what it was, I never fully understood where the fear and uncertainty came from. Once I really started living for God, He gave me a sign to show I am really Heaven-bound when I die. He also taught me where my uncertainty was coming from. I was told by other people the uncertainty was probably an attack of the enemy. I suppose in some ways it was but the enemy wasn't the root cause. He just aggravated what was already there.

The problem was, when I first received Jesus, I did not know what I was doing or what was going on. I was told to repeat a prayer and I did. The words of the prayer had no real meaning to me at the time. I was not acting of my own faith. I was just doing what I was told. After that first prayer, I continued living for my flesh and denied the spirit. I never really put God first in my life. I liked to think I was, but that was only through illogical justifications. When I had a decision to make in my life about anything, I always decided based on how it would benefit me personally. If there was a blatant contradiction to what I knew God wanted, I would justify my way out of it so I could keep doing what I wanted to do. I lived this way for years. Because of this type of living, I had an uncertainty and doubt about my salvation.

Once I learned about the true, biblical salvation that Jesus taught, I decided I needed Jesus to save me for real. This time I was properly informed and was doing it of my own free will. I faithfully asked Jesus to save me, forgive me of my sins, and come into my life. This was when I started to get serious about letting God lead my life.

After I was saved, there was a kind of transition period for a few years. During that period, my carnal life and my spiritual life were pretty much half and half. I would let the Holy Spirit lead me in the easy things but when it came to the more difficult things, I would still allow my flesh to lead me.

For example, there wasn't much resistance from my flesh when I let the Holy Spirit lead me to start going to church again, reading the Bible, get involved in Bible studies, pray with and for other Christians, and learn to praise and worship God in the way He deserves. Those were easy changes that God led me in to pave the way for the rest. I found it much more difficult to give up some of my addictive behaviors, such a smoking cigarettes, drinking alcohol, and swearing occasionally. It took longer to allow myself to be led by the Spirit concerning things I had to give up as opposed to things I needed to add.

The amazing thing I realized was the more I was Spirit-led, the more the uncertainty of salvation left me. I still had moments of weakness from time to time but they were becoming few and far between. The more areas of my life I gave to God, the more I began to receive assurance and fulfillment in a way I had never felt before.

The last battle with uncertainty began extremely subtle. Day after day, I would feel increasingly restless in my spirit. I would have thoughts of mortality and would wonder if I would really go to Heaven. I knew God had been working on me but I still didn't feel completely assured. I tried to pass off my feelings of uncertainty as an attack of the enemy but the feelings never left. My faith was wavering.

One day, I broke down and completely opened my heart to God. I was honest with Him about my doubts and feelings. I told Him I felt terrible for doubting my salvation. I did not doubt that He had the power to save and that He always makes good on His promises. I only doubted my part in it. I would wonder if I really understood what it meant to be saved, if I accepted salvation correctly, and if salvation could be lost to me. I trusted Jesus but I did not trust myself.

After I laid it all out to Him, I asked God for something I never had before. I told God I was deeply regretful for even asking because I felt I shouldn't need it to ensure my salvation. Hesitantly, I asked God for a sign. I asked Him to give me a sign to prove I was truly saved.

I had never done anything like that before and didn't know what to expect. I hoped and prayed that I didn't disappoint Him by asking because of my lack of faith. However, God knew my heart. God knew I did not doubt Him. I doubted myself. Looking back, I now believe God was actually pleased that I came to Him in honesty and humility. I believe this because He gave me the sign I was asking for.

I was lying in bed, trying to sleep for the night, when I heard something I had never heard before. I heard a single voice singing but it wasn't coming from the room I was in. The singing was coming from within my spirit, deep within my heart, inside the very core of my being. Only by direct revelation of the Spirit, I knew it was God who was singing.

I was not exactly hearing Him with my physical ears. I believe I perceived the singing through my spiritual ears. These are the ears Jesus talks about in Revelation when He calls out to those who have an ear to hear. I could not make out the words. When it was finished, I could not specifically recall the melody. However, there was no doubt in my mind or soul that it was God giving me the sign I asked for. The singing lasted for a few brief moments before fading out.

Initially, I understood what part of the experience was about but did not understand all of it. I knew it was an answer to my prayer. I knew God was allowing me to hear Him within my spirit to show me that is where He resides. He was showing me that my body truly is His temple and He does reside within me, proving I am saved. The part I did not fully understand at first was why He was singing to me. I knew of Bible verses that describe angels singing but had never heard of one that described God singing. Logically, it made sense to me that if the angels sing, God probably enjoys singing too. At the time, however, I had no biblical reference to back up that theory. I began looking up every verse I could find that had the word *"sing"* in any of its forms to find my confirmation. I knew that if the experience was truly from God, there would be a biblical confirmation of it somewhere. God led me to my confirmation.

Zephaniah 3:17 reads…

"The Lord thy God in the midst of thee is mighty; he will save, he will rejoice over thee with joy; he will rest in his love, he will joy over thee with singing."

I could not have asked for a more concrete confirmation of my experience. Before this happened, I had never read the book of Zephaniah and was barely aware it even existed in the Bible. I certainly had never heard this verse before. When I broke it down, I could see how clearly and fully it pertained to what I was going through and the sign God confirmed for me.

"The Lord thy God in the midst of thee is mighty…"

The word *"midst"* is translated from the Hebrew word *"qereb"* meaning *"the centre"* such as *"heart, inward, within self"*. I heard the voice in the midst of my being. The center of my being is my spirit, or heart, and God was saying He is mighty in my spirit.

"…he will save…"

This was the exact thing I had been worried about. I was worried that I wasn't truly saved. Through this verse, God was putting me in the right train of thought.

"...he will rejoice over thee with joy; he will rest in his love..."

God was showing me that not only was I saved, but He rejoices over me, I bring Him joy, and He loves me.

"...he will joy over thee with singing."

This was the ultimate confirmation of my experience. This was the only verse in the Bible I was aware of that describes God actually singing. God sang within my spirit as a sign of my salvation and this Bible verse was the confirmation. This proved to me that it could not have been anything else and I never need to doubt it.

God brought me through to salvation, allowed me to hear Him singing in my spirit, and confirmed the experience with His Word. Because of that experience, I never had to doubt my salvation again. Shortly after that, God taught me the true meaning of salvation and how an individual can have assurance in eternity.

TRUE SALVATION

God showed me, through His Word, the flaws with some versions of the *once saved, always saved* doctrine. Salvation isn't a prayer we recite in unbelief one time and never think about it again. True salvation will result in a progressive change of life. True salvation leads to the switch from carnal, fleshly living to Spirit-led living.

Titus 2:11-12 reads…

"For the grace of God that bringeth salvation hath appeared to all men, Teaching us that, denying ungodliness and worldly lusts, we should live soberly; righteously, and godly, in this present world."

It is the grace of God that brings us salvation. It is that same grace that teaches us to live a Godly life and shed our worldly life. Salvation brings a change of righteousness within an individual. Of course, this change is not immediate. At times, when a person receives salvation, he or she might experience an immediate change closer to righteous living. Though this is completely possible, it is not common. Typically, the transformation process takes years to really begin and will continue throughout our entire lives. Even those few who experience an immediate bump, or head start, into righteousness will still be working through the complete transformation process throughout their whole lives. Salvation does not mean an immediate and complete abolishment of the sin nature in our physical lives. Salvation is our personal and spiritual deliverance from sin and the ways of a sinful life. Matthew 24:13 reads…

"But he that shall endure unto the end, the same shall be saved."

Accepting Jesus is the first step but there is another component to the salvation process. We must hold on to Jesus and endure with Him our entire lives. If we let Him go, easily deny Him, and live carnal and flesh-led lives, it could be possible salvation wasn't truly received in the first place (Revelation 3:1-6).

Romans chapter 11 tells us that if we accept salvation through Jesus Christ, we are added to His family like the branches of a tree. We are also told that those same branches can be cut off and thrown in the fire. Romans 11:22 reads…

"Behold therefore the goodness and severity of God: on them which fell, severity; but toward thee, goodness, if thou continue in his goodness: otherwise also shalt be cut off."

This tells us that we have the ability to fall away or remain in the goodness of God. One interpretation of this passage states that if we fall from God, He will show us His severity and cut us off from Him. This can be further supported with Matthew 7:19…

"Every tree that bringeth not forth good fruit is hewn down, and cast into the fire."

Clearly, it isn't enough to just be a good person or repeat a salvation prayer without belief and continue leading carnal lives. We must be saved and give our lives to Jesus. If we remain in His goodness and continue to lead our lives by His Spirit, we have nothing to worry about.

There is a passage in the Bible that used to terrify me before I fully understood it. This passage illustrates that there are people who may believe they are saved yet are not going to Heaven. The passage is Matthew 7:21-23, which reads…

"Not every one that saith unto me, Lord, Lord, shall enter into the kingdom of heaven; but he that doeth the will of my

Father which is in heaven. Many will say to me in that day, Lord, Lord, have we not prophesied in thy name? and in thy name have cast out devils? and in thy name done many wonderful works? And then will I profess unto them, I never knew you: depart from me, ye that work iniquity."

These are very sobering words that Jesus spoke. Jesus is telling us that the mere act of calling out to Him is not enough. He is telling us that calling His name and using it to prophesy, cast out devils, and do wonderful works is still not enough to enter the Kingdom of Heaven.

Jesus is speaking about people who know how to use His name and can even prophesy and cast out devils. The thing that blows my mind is there are Christians today who don't believe in modern-day prophecy or demon possession. In this passage, Jesus is talking about unsaved people who believe in and practice those very things. At first glance, it could seem those unsaved people are spiritually stronger in the works of the Holy Spirit than much of the Christian Church today. How can this be? How can any of us know if we are going to enter the Kingdom of Heaven?

Jesus answered that question by how He closed this passage. Jesus said *"...I never knew you: depart from me, ye that work iniquity."* The works of the people that Jesus was talking about were considered iniquity. There is power in the Holy Spirit, without doubt. Jesus has the ultimate authority over the enemy due to what He did on the cross.

There are many facets to this but what it boils down to is the purposes of the works. If the person half-heartedly prayed to accept Jesus and learned the power of His name but tried to use it for personal gain, such as to personally empower himself, make people believe he is a powerful and holy man, or make money by selling products and increasing offerings, then there is a serious problem. That person would not be doing things in the name of Jesus for Jesus' or the Church's benefit. The person would be doing these things for personal gain. This would fall in line with the Pharisees of Jesus' day as a biblical example.

If a person is using the power of the Holy Spirit only for personal gain, he does not know Jesus and his works would be considered iniquity. However, if a person truly accepts Jesus as his savior, learns the power of His name and the Holy Spirit, and uses that power for God's true purposes, then that person's works will be counted as worthy resulting in true blessings. That is the difference between someone who is truly saved and someone who isn't.

It is not the works of a person that result in him being saved. The good works of a person are the result of being saved. A saved person will want to do the work that God calls him to do, not primarily for his own personal gain but for the benefit of the Church. When God looks at the works of a person, He alone judges if it is from a right heart or not. If it is, that person's works will have good results for the Church (himself included, more than likely, unless it is a completely sacrificial act), or what is known as *"good fruit"* in Matthew 7:15-20. If the works are done from a heart that is not right with God, then those works will not yield good results for the Church but could still result in personal gain. That is the point Jesus was making in the previously stated passages.

That doesn't mean we will go to Hell if we commit one sin after we are saved. It depends on our relationship with Jesus and our reaction to sin in our lives. Do we allow sin to take control and bring us into more sin resulting in living a life led by the flesh, or do we repent and allow God to get us back on the right track? God knows we will sin but we must have a repentant heart. Revelation 2:4-5 reads...

"Nevertheless I have somewhat against thee, because thou hast left thy first love. Remember therefore from whence thou art fallen, and repent, and do the first works; or else I will come unto thee quickly, and will remove thy candlestick out of his place, except thou repent."

REPENTING AND ASKING FOR FORGIVENESS

One specific version of the *once saved, always saved* doctrine typically teaches that once we recite the words, we are saved and we no longer need to repent or ask for forgiveness. This is not the biblical salvation that Jesus taught. I see this more as a weak attempt at a spiritual insurance policy. If we commit a sin against God, we must do the honorable thing by admitting our mistake and changing our behavior.

Acts chapter 8 tells the story of Simon, a person who accepted Jesus as His savior and received salvation (verse 13). After he was saved, Simon saw the power of the Holy Spirit through the apostles. Simon wanted this power as well but went about it the wrong way. Simon offered money to the apostles in exchange for the power of the Holy Spirit. Acts 8:20-22 reads...

"But Peter said unto him, Thy money perish with thee, because thou hast thought that the gift of God may be purchased with money. Thou hast neither part nor lot in this matter: for thy heart is not right in the sight of God. Repent therefore of this thy wickedness, and pray God, if perhaps the thought of thine heart may be forgiven thee."

This shows that we need to still ask for forgiveness and repent, even after we are saved. This also shows that God looks at a person's heart to decide if they are forgiven or not. If someone is truly repentant, God will forgive him. If a person is not repentant, God will judge his heart.

We cannot take the stance that, because we are saved, we have no real sin in us. We cannot admit and agree that we commit sins while saying we don't need to ask for forgiveness. 1 John 1:8-9 reads...

"If we say that we have no sin, we deceive ourselves, and the truth is not in us. If we confess our sins, he is faithful and just to forgive us our sins, and to cleanse us from all unrighteousness."

Many in the Church would teach that this passage only refers to unsaved people and is a plea for them to receive salvation through Jesus. This is a common misconception. When we look closer at how John worded this passage, we see that this is not just a plea to unbelievers. Consider a verse written just before that passage. 1 John 1:6 reads…

"If we say that we have fellowship with him, and walk in darkness, we lie, and do not the truth."

In both of these passages, the plural form is used. John uses words such as *"we"* and *"us"*. This shows that John was including himself in these passages. This gives the passage new meaning. This was a message to believers.

This supports the belief that it is impossible for us to be truly saved, yet continue to lead sinful and unrepentant lives without any kind of transformation. We are not able to transfer our minds to do the will of God without repentance. This is further illustrated in 1 John 2:1-29. Being that passage is the entire chapter, I will not copy it all here. However, I will suggest that you read through it to gain further understanding of repentance, forgiveness, and true salvation.

There is also a Bible verse that is commonly misquoted with half of it usually left out. Romans 8:1 reads…

"There is therefore now no condemnation to them which are in Christ Jesus, who walk not after the flesh, but after the Spirit."

This verse is used many times to support false versions of the *once saved, always saved* doctrine. The teachers of this false version will typically only quote the first half of this verse, not put as much emphasis on the last half, and try to say it is teaching there is no condemnation for anyone who has accepted Jesus Christ. That is not what this verse is saying.

This verse is saying there is no condemnation for those who have accepted Jesus Christ *and* who live their lives by His Spirit and not the carnal flesh. We can't just say we accept Jesus as our savior and expect to be able to continue our sinful lives. True salvation will create a progressive change in life and thinking. We have to walk after the Holy Spirit within us and stop walking after our flesh. There are other references of this in the Bible, such as Mark 9:43-48 and Galatians 1:6-9, as well as many more.

It is important for us to look at the fruit, or the result, of a matter to judge if it is of God or not. In my personal experience, the fruit of this version of the *once saved, always saved* doctrine is weak, confused pseudo-Christians who have no real reason to turn away from their sin because they do not realize they are doing anything wrong. It creates so-called Christians who feel they have a license to sin. They typically have to twist scripture, usually while not realizing they are doing so, to confirm their belief that it is acceptable to remain in sin. I understand this because I was in that category for much of my life.

When we look at the result of the *once saved, always saved* doctrine that says we must be Spirit-led, however, we find more Christians who are confident in their salvation. It creates assurance in eternity. It brings about a stronger faith that makes us stronger warriors for the Kingdom of God. It keeps us on the path of righteousness through a healthy fear, respect, and acknowledgment of the truth of God. It brings us fulfillment in our lives and a closer relationship with God in our walk. It teaches us how to properly discern God's Word and interpret the Bible. It brings all of the salvation Bible verses into clearer focus.

Before I fully understood biblical salvation, I was terrified with the feeling that I might not truly be saved. I had no way of knowing for sure. It wasn't until I realized the truth of salvation that I gained the proper perspective. When I realized the possibility that a person who believes he is saved may not be in reality, all the fear I had completely left me. I know at first that may seem backwards and should be the other way around. It seems like the possibility of not having salvation should bring fear.

Being a false version of the true doctrine, it only brought about a false kind of comfort and a very real fear. Once I traded the false version for the real doctrine, the fear completely left me and the true comfort presented itself. I was no longer afraid because I finally understood the truth and how to deal with it. Knowing the truth is what released me from my prison of fear and brought in the comfort of the Holy Spirit. I learned a powerfully important and life-changing lesson from that whole experience. No matter what it is or how it may seem before we understand it, the truth does set us free.

BE RID OF GUILT, CONFUSION, AND DOUBT

One struggle that every honest Christian has is trying to stay away from sin. When we commit a sin against God, we usually go through a process that brings us back to where we began. It is a chain of events that can be best illustrated with a list.

1. Sin – This is the first stage when, for whatever reason, we commit a sin of some kind.

2. Guilt – We feel guilt, directly following or some time later, after the sin has been committed.

3. Confusion – This is the point where the guilt can become so great that we become confused as to the reason why we sinned in the first place. We feel that, because we are saved, sin shouldn't have that kind of power over us.

4. Doubt – Confusion breeds doubt. This can manifest in many different ways. We sometimes justify the reasons and doubt the severity of the sin. In extreme cases, we can begin to doubt our salvation and right-standing with God.

5. Repentance – This is the point where I believe the Holy Spirit comes in, allowing us to deny our own logic and talk to God about the sin that was

committed. We set ourselves aside, accept what we've done for what it is, and repent. Repentance includes apologizing to God, asking Him to forgive us, and asking Him for the strength to change our behavior.

This is a cycle that usually comes back around full circle. After repentance, many times we will find ourselves committing that same sin again later. This adds even more guilt, confusion, and doubt. We look at ourselves and see no difference in our behavior compared to the behavior of an unbeliever. The only real difference we see is the aftermath of the sin. We know, however, that our salvation is not found in the aftermath of sin. Eventually, this can lead us to wonder if we are really saved.

This cycle, this five-step process, is not the way God wants us to handle our sin. A perfect example of this can be found in the seventh chapter of the book of Romans. Paul wrote in Romans 7:17-20...

"Now then it is no more I that do it, but sin that dwelleth in me. For I know that in me (that is, in my flesh) dwelleth no good thing: for to will is present with me; but how to

perform that which is good I find not. For the good that I would I do not: but the evil which I would not, that I do. Now if I do that I would not, it is no more I that do it, but sin that dwelleth in me."

This passage can be a bit confusing in its wording as to the point Paul is trying to make here. In cases like this, I like to go to another translation of the Bible that I trust for additional clarity. The New Living Translation of the Bible puts the same passage this way...

"So I am not the one doing wrong; it is sin living in me that does it. And I know that nothing good lives in me, that is, in my sinful nature. I want to do what is right, but I can't. I want to do what is good, but I don't. I don't want to do what is wrong, but I do it anyway. But if I do what I don't want to do, I am not really the one doing wrong; it is sin living in me that does it." (1)

Paul is making a distinction and a separation here. He is saying that there is a difference between the flesh and the spirit. In the flesh, or the physical body, there is nothing good or Godly because it is infected with sin. That is why we still physically die, because sin causes death.

Paul is also saying that the sins he commits are not really committed by him but are committed by the sin-nature in his body. This is what it means to be born again as a new creature. Before accepting Jesus Christ as our Savior, it was us personally who sinned. Now that we are saved, it is our physical body that sins, not our saved selves. Paul did not wish to sin but he found himself sinning anyway. This passage, and really all of chapter seven of the book of Romans, really helps us round out the definition of salvation.

Salvation is our spiritual escape from the consequences of sin. The consequence of sin is death. There is a physical death and a spiritual death. We all die a physical death because none of us can completely stop sinning and we have all sinned in the past. The damage to our physical being is already done. However, there is still hope for our spiritual being to not have to suffer death, or what is known in the Bible as the second death.

When we accept Jesus and decide to live for Him, He comes into our spirit and, in a sense, pushes out the sin-nature that once resided there. This means that when we die, since we will be separated from our physical body, that sin-nature is confined to our body and will not be able to follow us into the afterlife. Because of this, we can reside with God and His brilliant glory in eternity instead of being separated from Him due to our sin.

Paul realized the distinction between his spirit and his physical body. Since Paul was saved, he was no longer living for himself, meaning he was no longer living to please his physical being. Once he accepted Jesus, Paul moved into a frame of mind that allowed him to want to serve God instead of his own desires. Paul knew this would not result in him never sinning again. Such a thing is impossible. The difference is the sin-nature, instead of running rampant throughout his entire being, was now confined to only his physical body.

The whole point is that there is a difference between living in sin and sinning in life. Living in sin is what a person is before they are saved. Sinning in life is something we all do, no matter what. We cannot abolish the sin-nature in our bodies but, if we ask and allow Him to, Jesus can abolish the sin-nature in our spirits.

As Christians, we should try to limit our sins the best we can and, when we make a mistake and commit a sin, repent. Before we were saved, our physical existence in our body was all we knew. After we were saved, God revealed something new to us. Now we reside in our spirits with God instead of in our bodies, alone with sin.

Of course, this does not give us a license to sin. If we look at this as an excuse to sin then we have missed the idea of salvation completely. Just because we will sin does not mean we should think it is acceptable to sin. If we do, then we are potentially inviting sin back into our spirit and pushing Jesus out. That could absolutely compromise our salvation.

We must not allow sin to run our lives. We do not live to sin. We live to serve God. When we sin, instead of going through the entire five-step process every time, we should immediately repent and move on. Anything between sin and repentance is a hindrance, a distraction, and unnecessary.

We are not our body, we are our spirit. Salvation is giving our spirit to Jesus and leaving our body to the sin-nature. It is banishing our sin-nature from our spirit, leaving it confined to our physical body. Our physical body will die but, if we are saved, our spirit will not have to endure death. This is the meaning of eternal life. We move out of our body of sin and into our spirit with Jesus. In Romans 7:24-25, Paul said...

"O wretched man that I am! who shall deliver me from the body of this death? I thank God through Jesus Christ our Lord. So then with the mind I myself serve the law of God; but with the flesh the law of sin."

CONCLUSION

Salvation is a matter of the heart and cannot be attained through just trying to be a good person, doing good things, or by repeating an empty prayer. We all have sinned. We all have gone against God in some way at some time. Because of that blemish of sin, we have not achieved perfection and cannot be on the same level as a perfect God. We are not perfect and do not have the ability to save ourselves so, thankfully, God provided a way for us.

God wants us to be with Him when we die but He will not force it on us. God is a gentleman. He wants us to choose Him by our own free will. We can choose to accept Him one day and choose to reject Him the next. Either way, we are deciding our own eternal destiny. If you accept Jesus, this is only the beginning of an incredible relationship between yourself and God.

We have to be honest with others about what salvation is and not sugar-coat it. We cannot allow ourselves to preach the wrong version of the *once saved, always saved* doctrine. This version results in weak Christians who are unable to turn away from sin and recognize the truth. It results in Christians who may not even be saved, which can lead to major hindrances within the Church. We have to emphasize the importance of prayer, righteous living, and the Lordship of Jesus Christ.

On that same point, we are not here to condemn others. God wants us to help others accept salvation. God wants us to grow the family of His Church and expand His Kingdom. We can only do that by being honest about what salvation is. We are also commanded to go out into the world to preach the gospel (Mark 16:15). We are not told to just timidly invite someone to church and hope the pastor's message sticks. We have to go out there and do the work in complete love and honesty.

We aren't supposed to teach someone to accept salvation and then never talk about it again. We are supposed to tell others of what we have, how it works, and how they can have it too. If someone doesn't want to accept it, that is his choice and you cannot force it on him. He may accept it later in life. You merely talking to someone about Jesus can plant a seed of faith that could later grow into an acceptance of Jesus.

If you are reading this and have not accepted Jesus Christ as your savior, I would ask you to at least consider it. This should not be done by my words alone, but by the words of Jesus and the Bible; God's personal message to you. We are naturally built to have a relationship with God in our hearts. When we don't have it, we have instead an emptiness within ourselves that cannot fully be explained. We try to fill it with other things of this world and it may get our minds off of it for a while but it is not a lasting solution. Those things usually end up being negative forces in our lives. Since that emptiness is there because God is not, only God can fill it.

Salvation is a simple thing that people will sometimes try to overcomplicate. Sometimes people will try and overcomplicate it in their own minds to justify a way out of accepting the truth. It can be difficult to get over the fact that if we accept salvation, we are also accepting that we are being held accountable to someone else more powerful than us. The truth about this Person; this God that holds us accountable, is if we accept Him, He wants us to live for Him instead of ourselves.

Though He expects this out of us, He also realizes it is an ongoing process. He does not expect an immediate and complete transformation. When you receive salvation, you are accepting a God of complete love and total forgiveness. You are accepting a Father that will never deny you, never betray you, and no matter what, will always love you. All you have to do is receive His free gift of salvation and live for Him.

God leaves it up to us to make the first move. The Bible says in the first part of James 4:8...

"Draw nigh to God, and he will draw nigh to you..."

God will not force Himself into our lives. We have to make the first move. We don't have to rush it or change who we are. God made you who you are for a reason. You are completely unique and God does not want you to change that. God only wants to help you in your life to be the best version of yourself you can possibly be.

God loves you and He wants to show you how to love Him too. Don't feel bad or confused if this love doesn't come right away; it may take some time. Salvation is our first introduction to God. He doesn't expect us to immediately fall in love with Him. It is a process that can take time and God understands.

Out of His love for you, Jesus made salvation simple to understand. Quite simply, salvation is a free gift from God and our only way to Heaven, so why not accept it? After all, this is one of those situations where you have nothing to lose, but you have everything to gain.

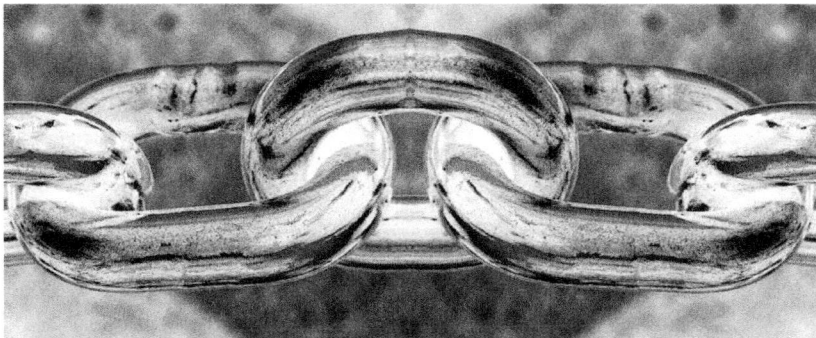

Chapter 3

SEEKING THE TRUTH

In this chapter, I would like to show you some things that have greatly helped my research and Bible study. When I first started, there were many bad habits that impeded my search for the truth. It wasn't until I recognized and removed those habits that I was able to see the Bible in God's true light, which in turn has strengthened my faith.

God showed me different methods to seek out the truth in His Word. He taught me how to use the Bible to form my thoughts, opinions, and theories instead of using the Bible to support my preconceived notions. He taught me how to refrain from twisting scripture. God gave me tools to use in Bible study and proper research. This chapter is all about providing you with the same tools so you can seek out the truth as well.

TRADITION AND SCRIPTURE

Throughout my studies of scripture, I have found many examples of traditional accounts conflicting with what the Bible actually teaches. For example, it is traditionally taught that Adam and Eve ate an apple and that was basically what encompassed the first sin. In reality, the Bible never says exactly what type of fruit was eaten. We read in Genesis chapter 3 that it is referred to only as *"fruit"*. In Genesis 3:7, it says Adam and Eve sewed fig leaves together to make aprons to hide their nakedness. The only indication we can speculate from this account is that the fruit was more than likely a fig, not an apple. At the very least, we can say there is more evidence pointing toward the fruit being a fig than it being an apple. This is just one example of many where traditional teaching conflicts with biblical teaching.

Another example of a traditional teaching is what is sometimes known as *"divine translation"*. Basically what this means is that, though the texts of the Bible were originally written in Hebrew and Greek, our English translation of the Bible is perfect. This means that, when the original texts were translated to English for the King James Bible, God made it to be translated perfectly with no mistakes or errors. This teaching goes on to say that since the original Hebrew and Greek texts are exactly equal with the English translation, it is not important to learn the original languages or use a concordance to find out what is in the original texts.

I will say that I do agree with some of this, but only to a certain point. I do believe, within the original Hebrew and Greek texts, there are no mistakes or contradictions in the Bible. Minor things might come through a bit hazy or specific may become lost in translation, but these can be discovered easily enough by looking at the original languages. I have had many supposed contradictions brought to my attention and have never seen anything that was a legitimate problem with the Bible. These apparent contradictions are usually a misunderstanding of the texts or a problem with the interpretation of the verses in question. Many times it's a result of taking a verse out of context by not reading what the entire chapter is saying. It is easy to misinterpret a verse of the Bible if it is read in that way.

While I agree with certain aspects of the divine translation viewpoint, I do disagree with others. I do believe it is important for us to discover what the original languages say and how they were translated. Not every Hebrew or Greek word can be translated perfectly to English. This does not mean there are problems with God's Word. When we think about it logically, God's Word does not reside only in the English-translated Bibles. God's infallible Word resides within all properly translated Bibles. God's Word is not the specific words themselves, but the ideas, messages, and teachings they convey. God's message to us transcends all language barriers. A language's letters and words are only tools used to carry that message.

The fact is that Greek, Hebrew, and English are different languages and sometimes certain revelations can be lost in the translation. A great example of this is the word *"love"* in the New Testament. There are actually three Greek words that were all translated to our English word *"love"* in the Bible. While these three Greek words are each representing a type of love, they are still more different than we might imagine. This shows us that Greek words do not always translate perfectly to English without losing any of the meaning. No matter what Greek word for *"love"* is used, it is still a form of love and still literally means love. The translation of those Greek words into the English word *"love"* is still correct, though when we look to the original Greek, we see the deeper meaning of the words.

The three Greek words used for *"love"* in the Bible are *"agapao"*, *"storge"*, and *"phileo"*. They each represent a different type of love. The word *"agapao"* is used for the highest form of love, such as the perfect love of God. This is the word used in John 3:16, which reads...

"For God so loved the world..."

The word *"storge"* is used for the love within a family, such as for a brother, sister, mother, or father. An example of this is found in Romans 12:10, which reads...

"Be kindly affectioned one to another with brotherly love; in honour preferring one another."

Lastly, the word *"phileo"* is used for more of a strong liking, such as the love shared between close friends.

In the John 21:15-17 account we can see how knowing the real meanings of these Greek words can add insight to what is being said. In the passage, Jesus asked Simon Peter three times if he loved Him. The first two times Jesus asked, He used the word *"agapao"* and both times Simon Peter used the word *"phileo"* to answer Him. Finally the last time Jesus asked, He used the word *"phileo"* and Simon Peter answered with *"phileo"*. To fully understand this concept, we need to look at the conversation as it is written. With the definitions of *"love"* that I have included, John 21:15-17 reads...

"So when they had dined, Jesus saith to Simon Peter, Simon, son of Jonas, lovest (agapao – perfect love) *thou me more than these? He saith unto him, Yea, Lord; thou knowest that I love* (phileo – friendship love) *thee. He saith unto him, Feed my lambs. He saith unto him again the second time, Simon, son of Jonas, lovest* (agapao – perfect love) *thou me? He saith unto him, Yea, Lord; thou knowest that I love* (phileo – friendship love) *thee. He saith unto him, Feed my sheep. He saith unto him the third time, Simon, son of Jonas, lovest* (phileo – friendship love) *thou me? Peter was grieved because he said unto him the third time, Lovest* (phileo – friendship love) *thou me? And he said unto him, Lord, thou knowest all things; thou knowest*

that I love (phileo – friendship love) *thee. Jesus saith unto him, Feed my sheep."*

I believe that Simon Peter was grieved because the third time Jesus changed the word from God's perfect love to the more human friendship kind of love. I believe it grieved Simon Peter to know he did not have God's perfect love for Jesus because he desperately wanted to know that kind of love. Simon Peter was honest with Jesus, though, and told Him the level of love he was capable of at that time. Simon Peter was only human and could not feel for Jesus the perfect love of God. This is, after all, speaking of the love between Jesus and God.

This account begs the question, with us all being human and flawed, can any of us experience that perfect love for God that He has for us? Are any of us fully able to reciprocate the same level of love God shows us? Was Jesus showing how to move from human love to perfect love by telling Peter to feed His sheep? Can loving Jesus at least enough to do His work grow into a more perfect love? Or, in this human existence and fallen world, is *"phileo"* the strongest love we can feel for God without direct intervention of the Holy Spirit? Without looking to the original Greek language, these questions would never be asked, as the proper definitions of *"love"* in the Bible would never be realized. It is definitely something to think about.

When we look at what the Greek really says about this particular story, we can see how the true meaning of one word translated from the original language can give us a more accurate insight into what was being said, what is being taught, and what we are supposed to take away from it. This is just one example of many I will share throughout this book that shows the importance of understanding what was written in the original languages of the scriptures. To utilize this, you do not need to learn the Hebrew or Greek language. You can simply pick up a concordance, such as the Strong's Exhaustive Concordance of The Bible. Though it's not perfect and infallible, I do recommend this concordance because it is simple to use and has all the valuable information needed for this type of study. For those who want to utilize an online source, I would suggest www.blueletterbible.com and www.biblehub.com.

GOING TOO FAR

In this section, I want to present some examples of what I would define as going too far. I do not present these certain beliefs to judge or criticize; only to inform. While I do believe the logic behind the beliefs presented here is flawed, I certainly do not hold myself to a higher position against someone who may hold these beliefs. If for nothing else, I hope to at least present some new options to think about and research thoroughly.

When using something to help us understand scripture better, it is important for us to keep the ultimate authority of God's Word with the Bible and not with a concordance, notes from a study Bible, or any other such tool. I have seen good men who love Jesus fall into a pattern where they will look up a word, mistranslate or misinterpret, and try to force the rest of the Bible to fit around their theory. Of course, with instances like this, the problem doesn't arise with the tools at our disposal, but arises with pride found within a person. Pride can be responsible for keeping a person from properly discerning the information found within tools such as other Bible translations, concordances, or even appendices found within a Bible.

Sometimes, when we take a word found in our English Bible back to the Hebrew language, we find that there are multiple words presented as possible translations. When this happens, we must put the Bible before our own thinking, test scripture against scripture, and define the word properly. We must not let our own theories dictate how we decide to translate a word if it doesn't line up with the rest of scripture.

For example, there are Christians who believe the six days of creation were not six literal days, but six thousand years, or six different evolutionary ages. In my humble opinion, there are numerous biblical contradictions with this theory and I see it as an attempt to marry the evolution theory with biblical facts. I am not necessarily talking of the Christian theory of Old Earth Creation that excludes evolution. I do not take issue with Old Earth Creation. I take issue with trying to marry the theory of evolution within the creation story of Genesis. Many times, when this is attempted, the idea of Old Earth Creation is used as a backdrop. I do see a possibility that there may have been an expanse of time before the first day of creation, but that is an entirely different topic altogether.

The belief everything was created in six thousand years originates from a misinterpretation of 2 Peter 3:8, which states…

"But, beloved, be not ignorant of this one thing, that one day is with the Lord as a thousand years, and a thousand years as one day."

Christians will equate this back to the creation story in the book of Genesis and say that each day spoken of represents one thousand years. The problem here is they are only looking at the first part of the verse, *"…one day is with the Lord as a thousand years…"*. If this was all it said and nothing more I might be able to at least consider the possibility. However, when you consider the second part, *"…and a thousand years as one day."*, we come to an interesting conclusion. These two parts of the same verse seem to contradict themselves. If we were to believe the six day creation actually happened in six thousand years, we would equally have to accept that the thousand year reign of Christ on Earth in Revelation 20:6 is only going to last one day.

We have to test scripture with scripture. We know from scripture that God created everything. This includes the very notion of time. God is also all-powerful. This means He can move throughout time as He pleases. One major misconception is that God is bound within time just like the rest of us. This verse, 2 Peter 3:8, is teaching otherwise. It is saying that for God, one of our days can be as long as a thousand years, and a thousand of our years can be as quick as a single day. God is outside of time. He would have to be. If He weren't, it would mean there was something out there that is more powerful than God, and we know this to be impossible. God can bend time at His will, He can lengthen days or shorten days, and He can travel within time and space to be in more than one place at one time. He is not bound by time like we are. 2 Peter 3:8 illustrates that fact for us.

For the belief that the creation happened in six ages, the problem originates with a possible misinterpretation of a single Hebrew word. Sometimes, when you take an English word back to the original Hebrew language, you will discover that the English word could mean many different things in Hebrew. This happens with the English word *"day"*, which was translated from the Hebrew word *"yom"*. While it is true that one of the possible definitions for the word *"yom"* is *"age"* as well as *"day"*, to find the accurate definition, we have to look at the words in the context they were written in. For example, Genesis 1:5 reads…

"And God called the light Day, and the darkness he called Night. And the evening and the morning were the first day."

Each of the six days of creation was written about in this way. First it says what God did and then it says the number of the day. God even defines what a day is in the creation story for us. For each of the six days, the texts say *"the evening and the morning"*. A thousand years would consist of hundreds of thousands of evenings and mornings. An age would consist of even more. The only span of time found with the definitions for the Hebrew word *"yom"* that consist of one evening and one morning is a single, literal, twenty-four hour period; one single day. Of course, there are other interpretations that have answers for this within Old Earth Creation. As stated earlier, I don't take issue with these other interpretations as long as they do not include evolution; I personally would have to see more evidence and biblical support before making an absolute determination.

What is also important to bring up is the idea that if the Bible were talking about six different ages, you would have death before sin, as Adam brought sin into the world and sin is the reason for death (Romans 5:12). If this is true, this could potentially be a huge contradiction. There are a lot of reasoning on both sides of the fence. It can get incredibly confusing. When I encounter this, I am reminded of 1 Corinthians 14:23, which states…

"For God is not the author of confusion, but of peace, as in all churches of the saints."

To further illustrate how this concept of original languages can be taken too far, there are Christians and pastors out there who preach that there were more than eight people saved from the flood and aboard Noah's ark. Of course, with Biblical passages such as Genesis 7:13, 1 Peter 3:20, and 2 Peter 2:4-5, it is very difficult to believe there were more than eight people saved from the flood. To make this theory fit in with scripture, I have had Christians tell me many different things like the flood was not worldwide, or it was eight "adamic" souls saved; that it makes sense if you only add one word to the Bible, even up to saying that the Bible has this whole Noah story wrong can't be trusted as an accurate source of information from God. This is what happens when a person gives more authority to their own logic than to the Word of God.

As for their source of this type of misleading information, some will cite other pastors, others will cite sources such as the Companion Bible or other study bibles, and some just will not reveal their reasons for believing this. As a quick side-note, while I do believe there is some valuable information containing in the appendices of the Companion Bible, I do not believe all of the information should be blindly accepted and believed, as is the case with any text outside of the Bible itself. This type of information needs to be tested against scripture to find out if it is accurate or not. We must lift the Bible itself above any study notes or appendices that might be included.

REASONS FOR IMPORTANCE

While certain beliefs, such as the age of the earth or how many people were spared from the flood, may not be salvation issues, it is still important to know the facts in our Bibles and what God's Word says. For example, 2 Peter 3:3-7 reads…

"Knowing this first, that there shall come in the last days scoffers, walking after their own lusts, And saying, Where is the promise of his coming? for since the fathers fell

asleep, all things continue as they were from the beginning of the creation. For this they willingly are ignorant of, that by the word of God the heavens were of old, and the earth standing out of the water and in the water: Whereby the world that then was, being overflowed with water, perished: But the heavens and the earth, which are now, by the same word are kept in store, reserved unto fire against the day of judgment and perdition of ungodly men."

We are living in the last days and I believe this passage defines it for us perfectly. This is a big reason why, though maybe not salvation issues, we need to know what is in our Bibles.

We are told here that in the last days there will be scoffers walking after their own lusts. These scoffers will ask where Jesus is and, if He is real, why hasn't He returned yet? They will say everything on earth now is as it has always been. They will deny biblical truths about the heavens, the earth, and the flood without doing any real research of their own, hence the term *"willingly ignorant"*. They will also deny God's earthly, prophetic, and eternal judgment.

The really disturbing fact is not only that we have people like this today, but that we have Christians like this today. There are Christians within the body of Christ who have allowed themselves to deny the very facts found within the Bible. They have become *"willingly ignorant"* by refusing to believe in things like the flood, Hell, or the soon return of Jesus. They will twist scripture and misinterpret Bible verses to fit their own theories and opinions instead of allowing their theories and opinions to come from the Bible itself.

That is why it is so important to know these seemingly insignificant facts. Just because they may not be salvation issues does not mean we shouldn't know the truth. If that were the case, Jesus' entire ministry; everything Jesus ever said and even the things Jesus' followers said, would have only been about how to get saved and nothing else. The plain and simple truth is the reason these facts are so important to know is because God wants us to know the facts and the truth about them.

As if that wouldn't be enough, there are other reasons why we need to know the truth about these seemingly insignificant biblical details. It is important for witnessing, for teaching, and for our own understanding of what truth is. We are even told in 1 Peter 3:15 to *"...be ready to give an answer to every man that asketh you a reason of the hope that is in you...".* Of course God wants us to give the most honest and truthful answer we can.

While we all have different beliefs about different things, some major and some minor, there is not a single one of us that has all the answers and knows every single bit of the truth. We must recognize this so we don't become arrogant in our thinking about our beliefs. Pride like that makes it easier to fall into twisting the scriptures to fit what we think is truth. From there, it is even easier to start denying the Word of God without realizing we are doing so.

Arrogance, pride, ego, and being closed-minded with our own beliefs are all extremely slippery slopes. We need to learn to be honest with ourselves. We need to show humility to other people and, most importantly, to God. It is important we safeguard our hearts and know in our minds what is biblically right, but also be open-minded to what other people have to say.

What I have found to be true is that, most times but not all, an answer can be found in the Bible for just about any common question. It only depends on where we want to look. An example of this can be found in, what I have heard referred to as, the most confusing verse in the Bible.

Describing the exclamation of Jesus at the moment of His death, Matthew 27:46 reads…

"And about the ninth hour Jesus cried with a loud voice, saying, Eli, Eli, la'ma sabach'thani? that is to say, My God, my God, why hast thou forsaken me?"

The reason some people find this verse is so perplexing is it sounds like, even if for only a moment, God forsook Jesus. There are many explanations and speculations by a wide variety of pastors and Christian Church leaders to explain this. The most popular explanation teaches that God turned His back on Jesus because, at the time, Jesus was carrying all the sins of the world and God couldn't face Him. For many, this explanation is difficult to accept since one of the promises of God is to never leave or forsake His children (Hebrews 13:5).

For a long time, I could not fully explain what was going on in Matthew 27:46. The problem was, at the time, I was not letting scripture define itself. I was seeking the knowledge of other people instead of seeking the knowledge and wisdom of God. I only had one of three Bible passages needed to fully understand why Jesus said what He did in Matthew 27:46. I had the beginning, but I did not have the middle or the end.

We read that, after He gave His exclamation in Matthew 27:46, Jesus was given a sponge full of vinegar to drink from. We can use this as a connection point. When we compare Matthew's account to John's account, we can find the same story with a bit more information. We read in John 19:29 that Jesus was given the sponge of vinegar. Next, in John 19:30, we read...

"When Jesus therefore had received the vinegar, he said, It is finished: and he bowed his head, and gave up the ghost."

Now we have the beginning and end of Jesus' words for this passage. It started with Jesus saying *"My God, my God, why hast thou forsaken me?"* and ended with Him saying *"It is finished"*. Now we only need the middle to bring this all together and make sense of it.

The book of Psalms, in many ways, can be considered a book of prophecy. There are many psalms telling of God's words, the last days, and even Jesus Himself. Psalm 22 is a prophetic psalm telling about the Messiah. The entire psalm is important and should be read in entirety but, for our purposes here, I am mainly going to focus on the first and last verses. Psalm 22:1 reads...

"My God, my God, why hast thou forsaken me? why art thou so far from helping me and from the words of my roaring?"

The last verse in the chapter, Psalm 22:31, reads...

"They shall come, and shall declare his righteousness unto a people that shall be born, that he hath done this."

Now it begins to make sense what Jesus was really saying. Jesus wasn't in doubt and God did not forsake Him. Jesus was fulfilling prophecy. To confirm this is what was happening, He quoted the words of David in Psalm 22. Jesus began by quoting the first line of the psalm, word for word. He ended by fulfilling the last line of the psalm *"...that he hath done this"* by saying *"It is finished"*. This was not a moment of weakness or doubt in Jesus' life. This was a moment of great strength and a proclamation of fulfilled prophecy.

Before I began allowing scripture to define scripture, I never would have been able to make that connection on my own. I remember that I would listen to pastors admit they had no idea what it meant, even calling it the *"most confusing verse in the Bible"*, and it discouraged me from trying to find the answer for myself. I figured if a pastor three times my age with thousands of hours of Bible study couldn't figure it out, I didn't have a chance. I was wrong.

I had to allow God to show me instead of relying on my own intellect and study. Getting a hold of that revelation, to let God lead me through my studies, completely transformed how I learn and read the Bible. Since that time, there has been nothing but benefits. The confusion I once had has significantly diminished.

God had to show me the difference between truth and tradition. I had to learn to trade my preconceived notions for His truth. The more time and effort put into it, the easier it is to do but it was not always like that. In the beginning, I found it very difficult to shed some of my traditional beliefs, even if I found out they conflicted with the Bible. I had to learn to let the Bible, and only the Bible, be my guiding light to the truth.

The first time I heard the fruit in the Garden of Eden was not an apple, or at least the Bible doesn't say it was, it did not seem right. I was sure I knew what the Bible said. When I finally looked it up on my own, I realized I was wrong. Admitting I was wrong was difficult, but I knew I couldn't keep believing and telling people something if I knew it wasn't biblically true. We must fight against our own pride and lift the authority of the Word of God above our own ego.

CONCLUSION

To be a Christian and remain in the will of God, there are many things we must not allow ourselves to become involved in. We must not let any traditional teaching that doesn't line up with the Bible dictate our beliefs. We must not let our own pride or fear dictate our beliefs. We must not let misinformation of any kind dictate our beliefs. God is the only one who should be allowed to have that kind of control in our lives. Only He can guide us to the truth.

God works in many ways to give us information. He uses His own words recorded in the Bible. He uses people in our lives, such as pastors, teachers, family members, friends, or even strangers. He uses various teachings through media such as television, radio, and books. He even will reveal the truth to us by speaking to our own hearts, guiding our souls, and stirring our spirits. God can be an amazing source of information and a wonderful teacher if we allow Him to do so in our lives. With such an amazingly powerful, lovingly honest, and completely trustworthy God at our disposal, why would we want to rely only on our own understanding to teach us?

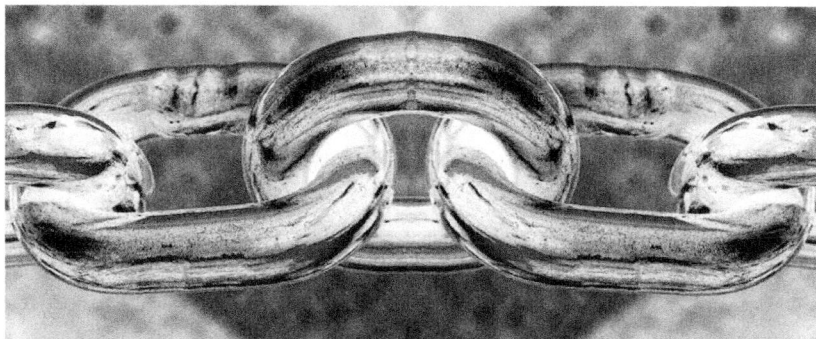

Chapter 4

PLACES AND NUMBERS

The idea behind this chapter is to give you some examples of truth and tradition to help you understand the rest of this book. I will begin where God began with me. To understand certain things of the ancient war, last days, and prophecies, God began by showing me how there was a difference between traditional teaching and biblical teaching. Traditional teaching is what you receive from a source that tells you what the Bible says and interprets it for you, such as from a preacher. Biblical teaching is the raw, uncut, truthful teaching you get directly from God and the Bible without an intermediary. Biblical teaching is solid, trustworthy, and foundational whereas traditional teaching, unfortunately, can be subject to mistakes and misinterpretations.

Of course, not all traditional teaching is bad. It is a wonderful thing to go to church and listen to a pastor, but everything being taught about the Bible should always be tested by the Bible. It is increasingly important to learn to compare every teaching with the Word of God. True biblical teachings will always agree with other true biblical teachings. However, sometimes traditional teachings disagree with other traditional teachings.

I can clearly remember the first time I heard a pastor teach something that directly challenged the traditional Christian beliefs I held. This was during a time I was not actively attending church, back when my wife Christina and I were dating. Christina called me one day close to Christmas. She told me her father had invited me to their church. She urged me to go with her and told me I would not be disappointed. After a while of explaining to me how their church was different than my previous experiences, I decided to go.

I didn't immediately notice anything different or unique when we entered the small church building the next Sunday morning. The only thing that stuck out to me was the congregation room contained chairs instead of pews. After about twenty or thirty people entered the room and found their seats, I heard Christmas-themed music begin to play. After we all sang a few familiar hymns and carols, the music stopped and the pastor took his place behind the podium in the front of the room. It wasn't long until things became a bit different from what I was used to.

I expected the same basic Christmas message about the birth of Jesus, the Virgin Mary, and the three wise men. For a short while, that's exactly what the message was. After the pastor had been talking for a few minutes, however, I witnessed something I had never seen in a church before. A member of the congregation interrupted the pastor with a thought of his own.

You must remember, I was born and raised in a traditional Baptist family, church, and lifestyle. There is absolutely nothing wrong with the Baptist faith, but with it comes certain things that are just not done in church, such as interrupting the pastor while he is giving his sermon.

Even though the interruption I witnessed was done respectfully, I was still a bit shocked.

I don't know how I expected the pastor to react to being interrupted by a member of his own congregation but I know I did not expect what ended up happening. After the interruption, the pastor quietly smiled, looked around the room to the rest of us, and said with absolute sincerity, "That is an excellent point. Does anyone else have anything to add?" There was not a drop of sarcasm in his tone.

I was shocked by the patience of this pastor. A couple more people added other thoughts and after a few minutes the pastor continued with his message. The entire service carried on in this manner. I quickly realized this wasn't only a sermon, this was a discussion. I felt as if I was in the midst of a large scale Bible study where everyone was free to share their own personal beliefs and ideas without fear of judgment. It was wonderful.

The thing that surprised me the most about this particular sermon was what the pastor talked about next. He made mention that there were some contradictions between what is traditionally taught in most churches and what is actually in the Bible. He began to describe examples from the traditional Christmas story. I was intrigued about what he was saying but didn't really know what to think about it until he had us open our Bibles. To my surprise, everything he was talking about was correct. Right there, in my Bible, were chapters and verses that told the Christmas story with some majorly different details than the traditional story I had heard since childhood. I remember thinking to myself that if the traditional Christmas story could have certain details wrong, what other traditional versions of biblical stories might have the same problem?

THE WISE MEN

In the traditional account of the birth of Jesus, three wise men followed a star to meet Mary and Joseph in the manger with the newborn baby Jesus. This is where they gave Jesus gifts of gold, frankincense, and myrrh. However, when we look at the biblical account of this part of the story, we find that the traditional account is a combination of two different biblical stories with some filler details not found in the Bible.

When we have heard a story many times, and even when we read a story many times, such as the biblical Christmas story, it is easy to read over small details without noticing their true meaning. To sort through the confusion and find the true details, we must look carefully at what the Bible really says. Matthew 2:1-2 reads…

"Now when Jesus was born in Bethlehem of Judaea in the days of Herod the king, behold, there came wise men from the east to Jerusalem, Saying, Where is he that is born King of the Jews? for we have seen his star in the east and are come to worship him."

Matthew 2:11 reads…

"And when they were come into the house, they saw the young child with Mary his mother, and fell down, and worshipped him: and when they had opened their treasures, they presented unto him gifts; gold, and frankincense, and myrrh."

When we look at the details of this story closer, an inaccuracy found in the traditional story becomes apparent. The Bible does not state that there were three wise men. In fact, the Bible does not give a specific number to how many wise men were actually present at this time. The Bible does say, however, that there were three gifts presented to Jesus. This is where the confusion originates.

It is traditionally assumed that, because three gifts are mentioned, there were three wise men to present these gifts. The truth is that the Bible doesn't disclose how many wise men were present or how much of each gift was given to Jesus. Because the Bible uses the plural word *"men"*, we know that there were at least two wise men, and one could have been holding two of the gifts, or they each could have divided up one of the gifts.

Another possibility is there could have been many more than three wise men. Since the Bible doesn't tell us how much of each gift Jesus received, it is possible that more than one wise man offered Jesus any of the three gifts. For example, if there were thirty wise men, ten could have given Jesus gold, ten could have given frankincense, and ten could have given myrrh. The Bible isn't specific enough about the number of wise men for us to be able to say accurately how many were present.

I know this may seem like a small and insignificant detail. You might be asking yourself, is it really important how many wise men there were? Is it really a problem if someone wants to teach there were three? While I do believe the number of wise men is not a salvation issue and in those regards isn't a top priority in a person's beliefs, I do believe it is our responsibility as Christians to be accurately informed about every detail in our Bible. Clearly, this is a lifelong pursuit because of the amount of information contained in the Bible.

One of the reasons I put so much importance on knowing the truth concerning these seemingly small details is because of the amount of scrutiny and criticism Christianity receives. If we want to be successful at reaching the lost and presenting the gift of salvation, we need to be able to answer any question a person may have. Sometimes it does not take any more than one inaccurate detail for someone to believe the Bible is full of errors and Christians can't get their own facts straight.

Imagine you were considering becoming a Christian and you had a basic understanding of the traditions of the biblical Christmas story. Now imagine you had read the story directly from the Bible and found these inaccuracies. Now you go to your Christian friend who had been witnessing to you and ask him why the Christmas story in the Bible is different than the Christmas story traditionally told. When your Christian friend cannot provide you with an answer or tries to make up one on the spot when it's clear he wasn't aware of the inaccuracies either, it would be really easy for you to think "If he has something as basic as the birth of his own Savior wrong, how can I believe he is not wrong about the rest of Jesus' life and my salvation?" It's that easy to inadvertently lead someone astray. Something as small as one incorrect detail can become another person's excuse for not accepting Jesus.

It is exceedingly important that we know our Bible to the best of our ability, but we also have to be honest about our personal limitations. This can be difficult at times. Just remember that a person's eternity might be hanging in the balance. It is important to be able to tell someone honestly and with love that we may not have all the answers to everything, but the answers we do have are absolute, true, and we can back them up with the Bible. Just like my grandmother all those years ago, we can't be afraid to simply say "I don't know".

LOCATION

Let's look at verses 1 and 2 of chapter 2 in the book of Matthew again. The first verse states...

"Now when Jesus was born in Bethlehem...there came wise men from the east to Jerusalem"

This verse tells us that Jesus had already been born when the wise men came to Jerusalem to ask about His location. This is further shown to be true in the second verse which states…

"Saying, Where is he that is born King of the Jews?"

The words used here, *"that is born"*, signifies past tense and is showing that Jesus had already been born by this time.

We read in verse 7 that King Herod asked the wise men what time the star signifying Jesus' birth appeared. Next, we read in verse 8 and 9 that Herod sent the wise men out to find Jesus and when they departed they saw the star over where Jesus was. The first step in understanding this is to figure out how long it would take someone in biblical times to travel from Jerusalem to Bethlehem. When we look at a map, we see that Bethlehem is only about five miles away from Jerusalem.[1] It is possible that the wise men made this journey within one day, but the Bible does not say for sure how long they took in their travel from Jerusalem to Bethlehem.

Next, we read in verse 11…

"And when they were come into the house, they saw the young child with Mary..."

When we compare this part of the story with account of Luke 2:7, we read...

"And she brought forth her firstborn son, and wrapped him in swaddling clothes, and laid him in a manger; because there was no room for them in the inn."

It is clear in the book of Luke that when Jesus was born, He was laid in a manger. However, we read in the book of Matthew that the wise men saw Jesus with Mary in a house.

When we take the word *"house"* back to the original Greek language, we discover that the word used was *"oikia"*, which is defined as *"properly residence (abstract), but usually (concrete) an abode (literal or figurative); by implication a family (especially domestics):-home, house, household"*.[2] The word for *"house"*, used in Matthew 2:11, literally means a family house. This describes the house that Mary, Joseph, and Jesus lived in long-term.

We can solidify this teaching by finding the definition of the Greek word used for *"manger"* in the original manuscript of the book of Luke. The word used for *"manger"* in Greek is *"phatne"* from the word *"pateomai"* meaning *"(to eat); a crib (for fodder):-manger, stall"*. We see that two different words meaning two very different things were used. This shows us that Matthew 2:11 and Luke 2:7 were speaking of two different events and locations. We can see now that the wise men did not meet Jesus and Mary in the manger. The wise men met them in their family home.

Now, that is not to say that Jesus, Mary, and Joseph were alone in the manger. We read in Luke 2:8-19 that shepherds had heard of the miraculous birth from the angel of the Lord and went to see the newborn Jesus in the manger. It does not say the shepherds presented gifts, but it does say the shepherds told of what the angel of the Lord had said about Jesus. Given this information, we can see how the story of the shepherds and the story of the wise men became meshed with one another. The shepherds were at the manger when Jesus was born and the wise men were at the family house later on. The closer we look at the biblical account and all the details involved, we see how further the traditional story strays from the truth.

AGE

When we look to the Bible to find information about when exactly Jesus was born, we find some interesting facts that conflict with what is traditionally taught. We are taught that Jesus was visited by three wise men on the day He was born, which we have just discovered is not exactly what the Bible teaches. We have learned that the Bible does not say there were three wise men and does not say they met Jesus in the manger. So, does the Bible teach us anything else about the birth of Jesus that conflicts with tradition? To discover the answer to that question, we must start at the beginning.

Concerning the age of Jesus throughout various periods of His life, we are first traditionally taught that Jesus was born in the manger on December 25th, Christmas morning. When we look to the Bible and do a small amount of investigation, we can see that this is not the case. Zacharias, the father of John the Baptist, was a priest in the temple. We read he was *"a certain priest, of the course of Abia"* (Luke 1:5). We read later that before John's birth, when Zacharias was attending to his duties at the temple, the angel Gabriel visited him and told him that he and his wife, Elisabeth (who, according to Luke 1:36, was also

Mary's cousin), would have a son named John. Gabriel then gave various prophecies concerning John's future life and ministry. After that, the Bible says when Zacharias was finished with his duties, he went back home and Elisabeth conceived a child with him (Luke 1:8-23). We read in the next few verses that John was in the womb for six months when Jesus was conceived (Luke 1:24-41, confirmed in Luke 1:36). From this, we see that John the Baptist was six months older than Jesus Christ.

If we can find when John was conceived, then we can add six months and find out approximately when Jesus was conceived. After that, all we have to do is add nine months and we have the approximate date of the birth of Jesus. The key to discovering this is John's father, Zacharias, and his priestly duties.

Luke 1:5 states that Zacharias was of the course of Abia. We can find more information on this in 1 Chronicles 24 where it lists the courses and duties of the priesthood that served in the temple throughout the year. From there, all we have to do is line up the course of Abia and find what time of year Zacharias would have been serving in the temple.

The Companion Bible has an extensive appendix on this, showing historically that the course of Abia (or Abijah) would have been taking place and finishing around mid-June.[3] We know based on scripture that John was conceived after Zacharias' temple duties were complete. If we add nine months, we come up with the middle to the end of March for John's birth. We have also learned, based on scripture, that John was six months older than Jesus. By adding six months to March, we come up with September as the month of Jesus' birth, approximately near the end of the month. Interestingly enough, if we back this up nine months, we do come to the end of December as the conception of Jesus Christ. This clearly shows that Jesus was not born on December 25th but He was conceived around that time.

To further confirm this fact, we can look at the part of the account that tells us about the shepherds who visited Jesus when He was born in the manger. If it was in the cold month of December, the shepherds would not have been out with their flock because the weather would not have permitted it. We also know from the Bible that Jesus was thirty three and a half years old when He was crucified. Again, all we have to do is a small amount of math and we come to the same month of September for His birth.

There are also various historical evidences showing that the census that was going on when Jesus was born would not have been in the winter months. More than likely, the census would have taken place in the fall months. This would probably be done for various reasons such as to allow easier travel for everybody involved. It would have been more difficult back then to travel long distances during the cold of winter.

CONCLUSION

With these simple and familiar examples, it is plain to see how easily a traditionally told story can stray from the original. When we hear something taught, especially from a person of authority such as a preacher or pastor, we usually take what he says as the unquestionable truth. We normally do not think to look at the original source of information to see if the story was told correctly. This is a mistake. It is good for us to learn from others but it is even better to learn for ourselves. Learn, then confirm.

So many different traditional teachings have twisted what the Bible says and we tend to believe it. We should not follow man's teaching blindly. The only one we are permitted to follow blindly is God. If a man is truly led by God and is leading the right path, we should follow him, but first we have to compare his leadership with God's Word to make sure it is true. We should not just take someone's word for it. We should not refuse to test him to spare his feelings. Most importantly, we must be educated so we can tell the difference between what is God and what is not. We owe it to God and to ourselves to live our lives according to the right direction. As it says in Hosea 4:6; a verse I will quote often throughout this book…

"My people are destroyed for lack of knowledge: because thou hast rejected knowledge, I will also reject thee…"

Instead of rejecting knowledge, we need to embrace it together. Instead of blindly following someone and blindly rejecting another, let's hear them both out and test what they say against scripture. Instead of relying on another person to teach us once a week, let's rely on God to teach us every day. If we take the first step and draw near to God, we are promised He will draw near to us (James 4:8). I think it's time we all take Him up on His offer.

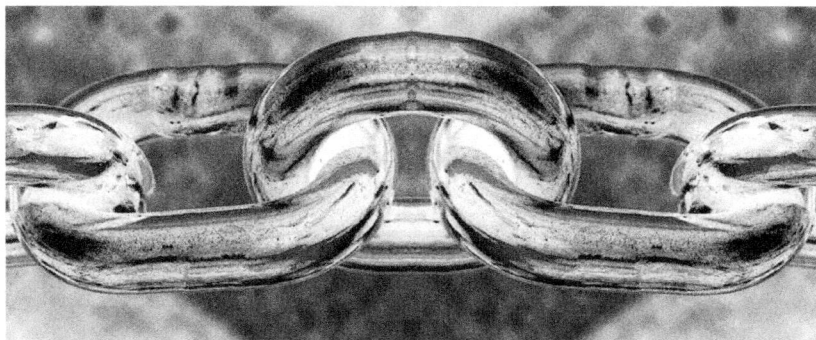

Chapter 5

THE HOLY TRINITY

To understand how to claim victory in the war, we must understand our Great Commander and His nature. Now, possibly more than ever before, there seems to be a great deal of confusion within the Christian Church concerning the Holy Trinity. Some Christians maintain that God the Father, Jesus, and the Holy Spirit are three separate entities while others believe they are all the same and interchangeable. Each side has a collection of a few Bible verses they use to support their opinion without coming to a common agreement.

I have always been in favor of the Trinity belief, meaning I believe that God the Father, Jesus, and the Holy Spirit are all one Being; separate yet equal. Growing up in a Trinity Baptist church, I was given the same basic collection of verses to support this belief. I was not aware there were other Christians in the world who believed otherwise. It wasn't until I was a little older that I discovered there were a lot of Christians out in the world with their own collection of Bible verses who did not believe in the Holy Trinity. After I came to that realization, I had to take a step back and really think about the reasons for my beliefs. Besides my traditional teaching and a few Bible verses, I really did not have a good reason to believe one way or another. It was then that God led me through some research of my own to discover the truth.

I found out the problem was that I was not looking at the whole picture of what the Bible was teaching. Having a few stand-alone verses and some basic reasoning would not be enough to support that I knew the truth. My Christian brothers and sisters who did not believe in the Holy Trinity had the same tools at their disposal supporting their beliefs. I had to find out what the books and chapters of the Bible were actually saying as a whole instead of only relying on those stand-alone verses. I had to compare the two testaments, old and new, to find the biblically universal truth. Most importantly, I had to cast my own ego and logic aside and let the Bible speak for itself.

ELOHIM

We find an interestingly worded verse very early on in the Bible. Genesis 1:26 reads...

"And God said, Let us make man in our image, after our likeness..."

We can draw two important conclusions from this section of the verse. First, God is referred to in English as the singular form *"God"* and next in the plural form *"us"*. Second, God created man in His image and after His likeness.

Let's first look at the word *"God"*. In Genesis 1:26, the Hebrew word used for *"God"* is *"elohim"*. This is the same word used throughout the majority the book of Genesis when referring to God. There are only a few times that a different Hebrew word is used, such as when is used the singular derivative, *"eloah"*, or the proper name, *"YHVH"*. The word *"elohim"* used for God in Genesis

1:26 is actually a word in plural form. The definition found in the Strong's Exhaustive Concordance is as follows...

"H430 - elohim plural of H433 (eloah); gods in the ordinary sense; but specifically used (in the plural thus, especially with the article) of the supreme God; occasionally applied by way of deference to magistrates; and sometimes as a superlative:- angels, exceeding, God, gods, godess, godly, great, very great, judges, mighty." (1)

From the original Hebrew, the word *"God"* is in plural form. This allows us to further understand why it says *"let us"*. From having a basic knowledge of the Trinity, we can say that God is referred to in the plural form because God is a tri-part being, meaning He is one God consisting of three Persons.

Of course, this being the nature of the existence of God, it is impossible for us to fully understand this with our finite minds. To help accept and support this fact, we can look to Isaiah 55:8-9...

"For my thoughts are not your thoughts, neither are your ways my ways, saith the Lord. For as the heavens are higher than the earth, so are my ways higher than your ways, and my thoughts than your thoughts."

I have encountered Christians who, despite knowing that God is above all understanding, will try and explain Genesis 1:26 with their own logic. One of the most desperate attempts I have heard of this states that the *"us"* mentioned was referring to God and all the heavenly hosts. They will use the fact that one of the possible translations for *"elohim"* is the English word *"angels"*. While it is true that there are times throughout the Bible the word *"elohim"* is used in reference to other spiritual beings, this is not what we are dealing with in our example from Genesis. This is a perfect example of what can happen when scripture is not compared with scripture.

The verse is explaining how God created man. To assume that the angels participated in the creation process would be to make angels equal with God, at least in creative power. It would be to say that God needed the angels to help create man. It would eventually lead to the thought that if God created the angels, it could not be that God needed the angels to create man, so God must not have created the angels. It sounds very confusing, but that is where this kind of logic can lead.

Also take into consideration the fact that the verse says man was created in God's image and likeness. This could not include the angels as we are not created in the image and likeness of angels. There are angels that look very different than us. Each one of the four living creatures of Ezekiel 1:5-14 are described as having all sorts of things that man does not have. Examples of this include four faces, wings, and what looked like the feet of a calf. The angel mentioned in Revelation 10:1 has pillars of fire for feet, a rainbow on his head, and was clothed with a cloud. No human being has these qualities, thus we were not created in the image and likeness of angels. We were created only in the image and likeness of God Himself.

Also consider that the word *"elohim"* is used throughout most of Genesis to describe God. If the angels were included in this, then equal credit, prayer, and even worship would have to be given to the angels. This would be a complete contradiction to biblical teaching because we are told not to worship angels (Colossians 2:18, Revelation 19:10, and Revelation 22:8-9). This further proves that the Hebrew word *"elohim"* in this verse is not referring to angels or any other heavenly hosts. It is referring to God in singular and plural form, meaning God the Father, Jesus, and the Holy Spirit.

Jesus was literally God in the flesh. We can look at some of God's other names to show He and Jesus are the same person. There is a prophecy of Jesus in Isaiah 7:14 in which He is called *"Immanuel"*. This prophecy is confirmed in Matthew 1:23. This verse even interprets the name *"Immanuel"* (or *"Emmanuel"*) for us as *"God with us"*.

There is another prophecy in Isaiah 9:6 with a list of names concerning Jesus. Among these are *"...The Mighty God, The everlasting Father, The Prince of Peace."* Here, we are specifically told that the Messiah, Jesus Christ (or The Prince of Peace), is God. This is confirmed in Isaiah 46:9 when God says *"...for I am God, and there is none else; I am God, and there is none like me."*

If Jesus Christ was a separate entity from God, He would have been *like* God. Jesus Christ was not only *like* God. Jesus was, is, and always will be God. This is why Jesus said in John 10:30 *"I and my Father are one"*. This would have been a misleading statement if Jesus and God are separate entities. Either Jesus lied or Jesus was exactly who He said He was.

OTHER COMPARITIVE VERSES

We can further prove that Jesus was and is God by comparing scripture with scripture in the book of Revelation. In Revelation 1:11, Jesus said…

"…I am Alpha and Omega, the first and the last…"

Later, in Revelation 21:6, God said…

"I am Alpha and Omega, the beginning and the end."

Jesus and God are describing themselves in the exact same way. Either one of them is being misleading, or Jesus and God are the same person.

Jesus has His name written on His own vesture and thigh as *"KING OF KINGS, AND LORD OF LORDS"* in Revelation 19:16. With God being the ultimate King and Lord, for Jesus to say this means one of two things. Either the Bible is putting Jesus above God, which would be an extremely misleading contradiction, or Jesus is God, completely validating Him in making that claim.

Also consider that if Jesus was not God, wouldn't it be breaking the first commandment to worship and pray to Him? We are not to put any other gods before the Almighty *(Exodus 20:3)*. Therefore, if Jesus was not God, Jesus certainly would not put Himself above God. Jesus would also rebuke anyone worshipping or praying to Him. If this were the case, Jesus' followers would have known it. If Jesus was not God, worshipping and praying to Jesus would have been considered a serious sin and breaking the first commandment, which would have been an obvious and basic understanding to any follower of Jesus. Following this logic, that should mean the Bible would be absent of a description of any sincere follower of Jesus worshipping or praying to Him. Speaking of the wise men meeting Jesus Christ for the first time, Matthew 2:11 reads...

"And when they were come into the house, they saw the young child with Mary his mother, and fell down, and worshipped him: and when they had opened their treasures, they presented unto him gifts; gold, and frankincense, and myhrr."

Acts 8:59 reads...

"And they stoned Stephen, calling upon God, and saying, Lord Jesus, receive my spirit."

In these short verses, we find even more support for the fact that Jesus was and is God. First, the wise men fell down and worshipped Jesus and, according to the Bible, nobody but God is worthy to be worshipped. Second, at the moment of his death, Stephen prayed to Jesus. Stephen called upon Jesus to receive his spirit. If Jesus was not God, this would be considered a sinful act. It is illogical to believe such a mistake could happen from a devoted servant and follower of Jesus, especially when we're told in verse 55 of the same chapter that he was full of the Holy Ghost.

We can even see how Acts 8:59 is worded to prove Jesus and God are the same entity. Stephen, *"calling upon God"*, said *"Lord Jesus, receive my spirit."* How could Stephen have been calling upon one person yet talking to another? How could Jesus receive a spirit if He was not God? Stephen was praying to the same person, the one and only God, the Lord Jesus Christ.

We can also consider the account describing the time Satan tempted Jesus in the wilderness. To combat Satan, Jesus quoted scripture. There were three temptations by Satan and three scripture quotes by Jesus. When Satan tempted Jesus to turn stones to bread, Jesus replied in Matthew 4:4 by saying...

"...It is written, Man shall not live by bread alone, but by every word that proceedeth out of the mouth of God."

Since Jesus was speaking here and was the one being tempted, He was referring to Himself within this verse. The mouth of God and the mouth of Jesus are one in the same. If it were not so, this would not have had any effect on Satan and would have not deterred him from this course of temptation. Instead, since Jesus was God in the flesh, Satan had to try a different tactic.

Satan tempted Jesus to throw Himself off of the temple and command the angels to catch Him to prove He was who He said He was. In Matthew 4:7, Jesus replied by saying...

"...It is written again, Thou shalt not tempt the Lord thy God."

Once again, it would have been nonsensical for Jesus to quote this commandment if He were not God. Jesus identified Himself as God and reminded Satan of the commandment against tempting Him. If Jesus was not God, this quote would have had no effect and would not have deterred Satan in tempting Jesus to throw Himself off of the temple. Instead, since Jesus was God in the flesh, Satan had to try a different tactic yet again.

Satan showed Jesus all the kingdoms of the world and told Him that He could have them all if He would worship him. Jesus replied in Matthew 4:10 by saying...

"Get thee hence, Satan: for it is written, Thou shalt worship the Lord thy God, and him only shalt thou serve."

Satan left after Jesus said that. Again, Jesus was identifying this quote with Himself. Only God is worthy of worship and servitude. Jesus is God, so we worship and serve Jesus. If Jesus was not God, it would be sinful and a violation of God's law to serve and worship Him. You cannot have one without the other. It is all or none. There would be so many contradictions, misleading statements, violation problems, and most of all, confusion found within the Bible if Jesus Christ was not God in the flesh. We must remember that God is not the author of confusion (1 Corinthians 14:33).

WE ARE TRI-PART BEINGS

Reading Genesis 1:26 again and knowing that God created man in His likeness and image, we can take this thought process further. Though both are included, this does not only mean that we were given the same types of emotions God has or that we may physically look how God looks in Heaven. There is a much deeper truth found here. 1 Thessalonians 5:23 reads...

"And the very God of peace sanctify you wholly; and I pray God your whole spirit and soul and body be preserved blameless unto the coming of our Lord Jesus Christ."

We can see here that we are all made of a spirit, a soul, and a body. We were created as tri-part beings, just as God is a tri-part being made up of Father, Son, and Holy Spirit.

Another way to illustrate this is to look at 1 Corinthians 3:16-17, which reads...

"Know ye not that ye are the temple of God, and that the Spirit of God dwelleth in you? If any man defile the temple of God, him shall God destroy; for the temple of God is holy, which temple ye are."

This passage is referring to the ancient holy temple of the Jews in which God Himself dwelt within once a year. The comparison of ourselves to the Jewish temple makes sense when we have a basic understanding of what it consisted of. The wealth of information the Bible gives about the temple could easily fill an entire book of its own but for our purposes here we will just look at a basic layout of the construction.

In the Old Testament, we read that the Jewish temple was made up of three parts. There was the Outer Court, Inner Court, and the Holy of Holies. Exodus 27:9-19 speaks of the layout of the Outer Court, which is representative of our physical bodies. In 1 Kings 6:36, we read a short description of the Inner Court which represents our souls. In 1 Kings 6:16, we can find a short description of the Holy of Holies which is a representation of our spirit.

The Holy of Holies contained the Ark of the Covenant and is the place where God Himself would come to meet with the priest. Now we have a High Priest who forever dwells within our very spirit if we have invited Him to do so. That Great High Priest dwelling within us is Jesus Christ Himself (Hebrews 4:14-16, Romans 8:9-11).

NECROMANCY

In Deuteronomy 18:10-12, God gives us a list of things which are abominations to Him. Among these is necromancy. A basic definition of the word *"necromancer"* is a person who communicates with the dead. The law in Deuteronomy 18:10-12 was given by God to man because He does not want us attempting to communicate with the dead.

An interesting event concerning this can be found in 1 Samuel 28:6-20. The passage states that Saul consulted a witch to try to speak with Samuel, who had died. Saul and the witch encountered a type of demon known as a familiar spirit posing as Samuel. The demon spirit, while having seemingly special knowledge and information, was not actually the spirit of the deceased Samuel. Saul, nor the witch, ever tested the demon spirit against God and was thus frightened and confused.

We can compare this to certain events in the life of Jesus. We are told throughout the Bible that Jesus Christ was absent of sin. He could do no wrong in the eyes of God as He led a perfect and sinless life. The main reason for this is that Jesus and God are the same entity. We can prove this fact further if we look at the transfiguration from a different angle while keeping in mind the law against necromancy.

In Matthew 17:1-9, we are told that Jesus took Peter, James, and John up to a high mountain and was transfigured. During the transfiguration, Moses and Elijah (or Elias, as translated from the Greek) appeared and spoke with Jesus. Peter then asked Jesus if they could make three tabernacles in that spot; one for Jesus, one for Moses, and one for Elijah. While Peter was talking, God spoke through a cloud in the sky and said *"This is my beloved Son, in whom I am well pleased..."*, referring to Jesus. After that, Jesus took the disciples down from the mountain and told them not to tell anyone of what happened until after He had been resurrected.

We can make some interesting observations supporting the fact that Jesus is God from this passage. First, by God's own law, man is not allowed to speak with the dead. Only God (and I suppose other dead people) can talk with the dead without breaking this law. If Jesus was only a man and not God Himself, He would have been breaking God's law against necromancy by speaking with Moses. This would be considered a sin in God's eyes which would prohibit Jesus from living a sinless life and being the Messiah. Conceivably, it would be allowed for a man to speak with Elijah since he has not yet died in the technical sense, but no man would be allowed to speak with Moses, since he did actually die. Given this fact, the only way Jesus could have spoken with Moses and remained sinless is if He was God Himself.

108

Peter knew the law against necromancy. That is why he did not attempt to speak with Moses. Peter instead spoke directly with Jesus and asked only His permission to build the tabernacles. Also, while Peter was speaking, God told them that Jesus was His son and He was pleased with Him. This confirms the fact that Jesus was God in the flesh because God would not have been pleased with Him if He were only a man and had broken His law against necromancy.

I believe this is, at least partly, why Jesus told the disciples not to tell anyone of what happened until after He had been raised from the dead. Some of the Jewish people would have come to the same conclusion of necromancy if they did not believe Jesus was God. In their belief, this would have been a direct violation of God's law. They would have come against Jesus in anger to punish Him, more than likely by death, and it was not yet time for that. Jesus still had more work to do.

I believe when we look at this account from a Jewish law perspective, we can come to one of two conclusions. Either Jesus was not who He said He was and He was nothing more than a man who, at least once, engaged in necromancy, or He was God in the flesh and allowed Peter, James, and John to participate in a wonderful and miraculous occurrence. Given what the Bible says, to deny Jesus is to deny the very nature of God Himself. Jesus was not a necromancer. Jesus was and is God.

TIME

An issue that some Christians have against the Trinity belief is how the Bible describes Jesus' relationship with His Father, God. They bring up the point that Jesus prayed to God all the time. If Jesus was God, wouldn't He just be praying to Himself? To answer this question, we have to look at the nature of God and His creative process.

In Genesis, we read that God created everything. There is nothing that exists in any form that was not created by God except for God Himself. This would include time. God created time. We are bound by time. Everything bound within time has a beginning and an end. God has no beginning and has no end which is why He has described Himself as the Alpha and Omega (Revelation 22:13). God Himself *is* the beginning and the end.

God is not bound by time like we are. That is how He can be in more than one place at one time. It is how He is able to hear every prayer ever prayed to Him and answer accordingly. It is also how we are able to have a personal relationship with Him. Time is just another of God's creations.

To try to gain a clearer understanding of this, think of this in terms of a wedding video. When you are videotaping a wedding home movie, you walk around and let people say things into the camera for the bride and groom, usually well-wishing and various jokes. You go to the bride and groom to get their reaction to the whole experience. You sometimes will ask if they want to say anything into the camera for their future-selves, perhaps for when they watch this video again on their first anniversary. The groom might say something into the camera like "Hi future-self, if you're watching this and it's a year later, I hope you're still married and treating your wife well".

Now, as the groom is saying that, he has no idea what the future is going to be. He doesn't know for sure what life is going to be like a year into the future. However, by the time he watches the video again in a year, he knows exactly what that year brought and knows what has happened. He is able to listen to himself from the video and receive the message he gave to himself a year ago. His past-self had no idea of the future or what would happen. His future-self has all the information concerning his time and knows far more than his past-self ever could.

Even though, in that scenario, the groom is always bound by time, by using human terms, we can apply this to Jesus' relationship with God to gain a better understanding. God the Father is not bound by time at all. God was born in the flesh as Jesus Christ and while He was on earth, He was bound by the constraints of time.

Now here is where it gets a bit tricky and deep. Since God is not bound by time, He can be in more than one place and more than one *time* whenever He wants. He is in all times and all places at once. That is His nature. So when He was born as Jesus Christ, He still existed in Heaven, outside of the constraints of time.

Think of this in terms of the wedding video. Think of the past-groom as Jesus, the future-groom as God the Father, and the video itself as all of God's creation. They are both the same person but the future-groom has more information, is able to receive messages from his past-self, and is even able to rewind and fast-forward to experience any time within that video.

Of course, this is not a perfect example to represent the nature of God. There are no perfect examples in human terms. The main problem with any illustration like this is we are talking about God, not a man who is bound by time. God would be able to answer back to the past-groom in the video and even give him information about the future. If we look at this in terms of God, the Trinity begins to make sense, at least from a theoretical standpoint. Since we are human, we can never fully understand the nature of God completely. However, I do believe we can obtain a basic understanding.

God was born into the earth and time as a man named Jesus Christ. While God existed within time as Jesus, He also existed outside of time in Heaven. The earthbound God; Jesus Christ, had certain restrictions since He was bound within time with the rest of humanity. God, the Father in Heaven, had no restrictions. Jesus was a man, bound within time, who had to communicate with God in Heaven the way we all do, by prayer.

Being within the confines of time and a human body, Jesus did not experience the absolute freedom of God in Heaven. While still being God, though in the flesh, Jesus had certain advantages He would not have had if He were just a man, such as miracles, healings, special knowledge, and wisdom. Jesus did not have access to all of the information in existence while on earth as He did in Heaven. In Matthew 24:36, Jesus said that nobody knows the day or hour of His return, but only the Father.

In the wedding video illustration, this is comparable to how the past-groom did not know the things of the future-groom but the future-groom knew the things of his time and the past. As I said, this thinking can be very deep and involved, but it is not impossible to understand the basics. You can find more information, explanations, and illustrations about God, time, and the Trinity in the book *Mere Christianity* by C.S. Lewis, especially Book 4, entitled *"Beyond Personality: Or First Steps In The Doctrine Of The Trinity"*[2].

Jesus, God, and the Holy Spirit are all a single entity and have been so eternally. So, if Jesus was never created, would it make sense that Jesus existed, was active, and even participated in certain events before His own birth? Another way to ask, was God ever in more than one place at one time in the Old Testament?

In Genesis 19:24, speaking of the destruction of Sodom and Gomorrah, we read…

"Then the Lord rained upon Sodom and upon Gomorrah brimstone and fire from the Lord out of heaven;"

If we can accept that this is not a typo found within the Bible and can accept this passage as an accurate account of past events, then this passage gives us a very interesting detail usually left out in the traditional telling of the Sodom and Gomorrah story. God on earth rained brimstone and fire down from God in Heaven. God was on Earth and in Heaven at the same time. Many believe verses like this are referring to the pre-incarnate Jesus, meaning this account describes Jesus before He was ever born into an earthly body. I tend to agree with this belief. However you look at it, this verse, as well as others, clearly supports the Trinity belief. For an excellent teaching on this, I would highly suggest Dr. Michael Heiser's presentation entitled *The Jewish Trinity* on YouTube. I also get into this idea much deeper in my book *Quantum Creation* (www.ministudyministry.com).

Everything we are dealing with here describes the very nature of God. Concerning His own name, God said in Exodus 3:14 *"...I AM THAT I AM...".* This is, at least in part, showing that everything to God is His own present tense, outside of time itself, no matter if it is past, present, or future for us. This is also showing that the very nature of God is absolute. He is what He is and that's it. Jesus further supported and explained His relationship with God and time by saying *"...Before Abraham was, I am"* in John 8:58. This is showing us that Jesus did exist before Abraham's time but, even more than that, He is saying that our past is still His present while being outside of time. He now presently exists before Abraham was created.

CONCLUSION

The whole issue of God and time can be incredibly difficult for us to wrap our minds around because we are, in fact, only human. All we know is our existence of being bound within the flow of time. We can't imagine the intricacies of how something like two types of timelines can exist within each other and how the reality of God can integrate with the dimensions of physical existence. To fully understand this would be to fully understand God's nature.

God has given us enough information and mental ability to get by, but we cannot fully understand the nature of God with the mind He has given us. We can at least gain a base understanding of His relationship with time and with Himself. The rest comes by faith. We can know enough to understand that God is not bound in time like us. If He was, it would lift time above God, meaning there would be something out there more powerful than God Almighty. God is all powerful, omnipresent, and eternal.

God did something absolutely beautiful and amazing for us on the cross. To not understand the basics of it, to not even accept that God Himself did it but instead someone else, is to do a great disservice to God, His sacrifice, and ourselves. Philippians 2:5-11 explains this beautifully and shows what the God of everything did for each and every one of us personally. It reads…

"Let this mind be in you, which was also in Christ Jesus: Who, being in the form of God, thought it not robbery to be equal with God: But made himself of no reputation, and took upon him the form of a servant, and was made in the likeness of men: And being found in fashion as a man, he humbled himself, and became obedient unto death, even the death of the cross. Wherefore God also hath highly exalted

him, and given him a name which is above every name: That at the name of Jesus every knee should bow, of things in heaven, and things in earth, and things under the earth; And that every tongue should confess that Jesus Christ is Lord, to the glory of God the Father."

Within that passage are many undeniable facts proving that Jesus is God. If Jesus is not God, how could He have the form of God without it being wrong to be equal with God? Who could be equal to God but God Himself?

We are even told in Hebrews 6:13 that when God made a promise to Abraham, He had no one He could swear to, so He had to swear by Himself. If Jesus is not God, yet is equal with God, why didn't He swear by Jesus? How could Jesus have a name above every name? How could He have every knee in Heaven bow to Him? This means, if Jesus is not God and God is in Heaven, God Himself would bow to Jesus according to that passage. See how that theory doesn't fit and where that type of logic can lead? God is Jesus and Jesus is God in the flesh. Simply put, God Himself died for you.

I do not believe this matter of the Trinity is a biblical mystery hidden from us. I believe God wants us to know Him and is clear in the Bible of His nature. God is what He is and that's it. We can take it or leave it. It is good for us to try to understand Him, but we must not try and change Him with our biblically-opposing beliefs and theories. The nature of God is exactly how it is eternally and will not change. To try to understand the Trinity is to try to understand the very nature of God Himself. To deny the Trinity is to deny the reality of the nature of God. We must lift God above our own beliefs and views to accept His truth, the only absolute truth, and cast our limited human understanding and opinions aside. Our prejudices, doubts, logic, and everything else; we must lift God above them all.

PART 2

LIVING AND FIGHTING IN THE LAST DAYS

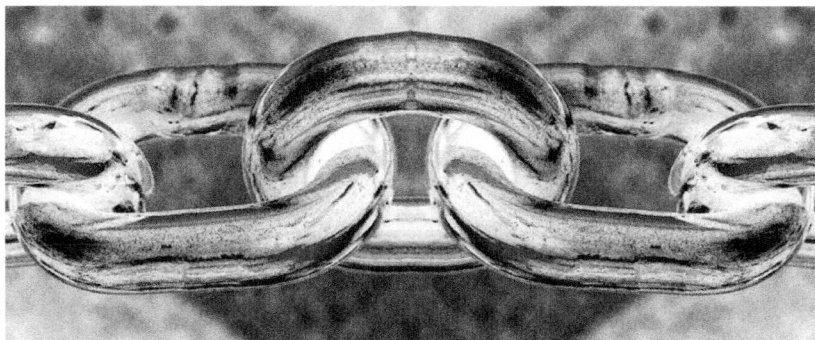

Chapter 6

FORGIVENESS

Learning to live in these, the last of the last days, is becoming increasingly difficult. We are living in times that are completely unique and have no comparison in history. We went from horses and carriages to space shuttles to the moon in under a hundred years. We now live in a time when a constant flow of information and entertainment is available at our fingertips via the internet and television. It is becoming easier to be distracted with the things of the world and more difficult to focus on the things of God. Because of this, we are losing the very ideals and spiritual tools we need to get through life. One of the most important tools we are losing more and more with each passing conflict is forgiveness.

Forgiveness is our "get out of jail free" card. When we forgive, we escape the prison of resentment, anger, and bitterness toward the person who wronged us. The feelings caused by an absence of forgiveness are poison to our bodies, minds, and souls. Refusing to forgive, or forgiving improperly, ends up doing more damage to ourselves than the person who is in the wrong. To properly forgive someone requires humility. Since not one of us is sin-free, forgiveness needs to be an act of love and understanding.[1]

The problem is, many times, we get forgiveness confused with trust. We believe forgiving and forgetting go hand in hand. The reality is, if we properly forgive someone of something, we are no longer holding that person accountable for that action in that instance. If the person continues to do the same thing over and over again, we should still forgive them, but that doesn't mean we have to remain a victim. At that point, trust has been broken and we should follow the biblical steps to handle it correctly. For example, if someone keeps breaking into your house night after night, steals your possessions, and gets away without leaving any clues as to his identity, you should still forgive him in your spirit between you and God, but you should also call the police and buy a new lock for your door.

Forgiveness in no way shows weakness. It actually shows great strength because it is one of the most difficult things we can learn to do. It is reflecting the personality and nature of God. Forgiveness can even be a strong witnessing tool and testimony.

To recap, forgiveness is…

1. Our escape from hurt in our hearts.
2. Different than trust.
3. A great feat of strength.
4. A reflection of the personality and nature of God.
5. Something we can utilize to reach the lost.

At the end of this chapter, I will share a personal story that encompasses these five things. God showed me what forgiveness is, the importance of it, the power behind it, and how to put it into practice. The best resource we have for things like this is the inerrant Word of God. If anyone knows about forgiveness and is in a position to teach its principals, it's Jesus Christ. He died the worst death imaginable to forgive every one of us, individually, if we choose to accept Him. That is how important forgiveness is to God. One of the most applicable skills to our lives we can learn is to make forgiveness just as important in our own lives as it is to God.

THE TWO FORMS

Forgiveness can be a verb and a noun. For example, if you say *"I forgive you"*, it is a verb. If you say *"I grant you forgiveness"*, it is a noun. In the New Testament, these two forms are used quite frequently. For the verb form, there are three Greek words used. For the noun form, there is only one Greek word used.

The noun *"forgiveness"* comes from the Greek word *"aphesis"* and means *"freedom"*. When you grant someone forgiveness, you aren't only granting them freedom, but you are granting yourself freedom. We can see this illustrated in the book of Acts. Speaking of Jesus, Peter said in Acts 5:31…

"Him hath God exalted with his right hand to be a Prince and a Saviour, for to give repentance to Israel, and forgiveness of sins."

Jesus has provided us with a freedom from our sins. He has lifted that weight of sin off us and set us free. If Jesus has given us freedom, we should be doing the same for other people, especially fellow Christians.

If a Christian brother or sister wrongs you, there is a biblical way to handle it, but the most important thing to realize is that if they truly are a Christian, God has already forgiven their sins. God already forgave the sin that was committed against you. If God already forgave it, it is not an option for us to still hold it against that person. To do so would be to try and undo Jesus' work on the cross for that person. We need to forgive, provide freedom, and be set free ourselves.

The English word *"forgive"*, in verb form, can be translated from three different Greek words. The first one is *"aphiemi"* meaning *"to send forth"*. This is the most common translation. We can see its application in the Lord's Prayer, found in Matthew 6:9-15. It reads...

"After this manner therefore pray ye: Our Father which art in heaven, Hallowed be thy name. Thy kingdom come. They will be done in earth, as it is in heaven. Give us this day our daily bread. And forgive us our debts, as we forgive our debtors. And lead us not into temptation, but deliver us

from evil: For thine is the kingdom, and the power, and the glory, forever. Amen. For if ye forgive men their trespasses, your heavenly Father will also forgive you: But if ye not forgive men their trespasses, neither will your Father forgive your trespasses."

Every time the word *"forgive"* is used here, it means *"to send forth"*. When someone wrongs us, we must take their sin and send it away, out of our hearts and our minds. If we keep it within ourselves and do not send it forth, it will breed feelings of contempt and resentment.

The longer we hold it in, the worse it will get. It is like leaving a piece of fruit on your kitchen table. After the first couple of days you probably won't notice much change, but after a few weeks your entire house will be filled with an awful stench, fruit flies and other bugs will have invaded your house, and the mold content in your kitchen will create a health risk.

This is the same in our bodies. When we let unforgiveness fester, we are filled with terrible feelings, our minds are invaded by painful thoughts, and the stress of all of the negativity will begin breaking down our bodies in a very unhealthy way. Forgiveness is essential to our physical, mental, emotional, and spiritual health. God feels so strongly about this that He says if we won't forgive others, He won't forgive us. That is a pretty powerful and sobering statement that we should all take to heart. We need to send forth, out of ourselves and others, the sins against us.

The next Greek word used for the verb form of forgiveness is *"apolyo"* and is only used in one place for the words *"forgive"* and *"forgiven"*. It means *"to free fully"* and *"let die"*. It is really interesting that this translation of the word is only used in one place in the New Testament. It is used in Luke 6:37 which states…

"Judge not, and ye shall not be judged: condemn not, and ye shall not be condemned: forgive, and ye shall be forgiven:"

Jesus is saying that if we can free others fully of their sins against us and let those sins die, then God will do the same for our sins against Him. Jesus performed the ultimate demonstration of this on the cross. He took all of the world's sins upon Himself and died, thereby letting the sins die with Him and freeing us fully of their condemnation and power over us. If we want to claim this full freedom and have sin dead within us so it holds no power, we must learn to forgive.

The last Greek word used in the New Testament to describe the verb form of the word *"forgive"* is *"charizomai"* and means *"to grant as a favor i.e. gratuitously, in kindness, pardon or rescue"*. We see this used in 2 Corinthians 2:10-11 which reads…

"To whom ye forgive any thing, I forgive also: for if I forgave any thing, to whom I forgave it, for your sakes forgave I it in the person of Christ; Lest Satan should get an advantage of us: for we are not ignorant of his devices."

Paul is saying that he is providing a service by forgiving. In fact, he is rescuing those he is forgiving from Satan. If we don't forgive, it opens a crack for Satan to slip into our lives and the Church. Satan can and will use that as his advantage to breed all sorts of negativity and separation.

Forgiveness is such a powerful tool of spiritual warfare because it fills in all of those little cracks that Satan can slip into. To not forgive is to give Satan a legal right to be in your life. We are told how to keep him out and if we choose not to follow it, then he has every right to be in our hearts and minds to bring about destruction. We must not give him that right. He doesn't deserve it. Instead, forgive others. Give Jesus the right to be in your heart so He can bring peace and wellbeing.

FORGIVENESS AND TRUST

There are two Bible passages concerning forgiveness and trust that, at first glance, may seem to contradict. In reality, these two verses describe a very important distinction. First, Matthew 18:15-17 reads...

"Moreover if thy brother shall trespass against thee, go and tell him his fault between thee and him alone: if he shall hear thee, thou hast gained thy brother. But if he will not hear thee, then take with thee one or two more, that in the mouth of two or three witnesses every word may be established. And if he shall neglect to hear them, tell it unto the church: but if he neglect to hear the church, let him be unto thee as an heathen man and a publican."

Second, Matthew 18:21-22 reads...

"Then came Peter to him, and said, Lord, how oft shall my brother sin against me, and I forgive him? till seven times? Jesus saith unto him, I say not unto thee, Until seven times: but, Until seventy times seven."

In the first passage, it seems like Jesus is saying to give someone three chances with different methods to make things right. In the second passage, by using simple math, it seems as if He is saying to do it 490 times. So what is going on here?

These two passages describe a clear distinction between forgiveness and trust. In the first passage, Jesus gives us clear instructions on how to handle someone who wronged us. First we talk to them privately. If that doesn't work, then we bring in a couple of people to hear everything out. If that still doesn't work, then we take it to the church. If the problem still cannot be resolved and the person in the wrong will not correct their behavior, then we are told to treat them as an unbeliever. At that point, we just need to stay away from them. This is a matter of trust.

Though we should still forgive that person, as outlined in the second passage, it doesn't mean we have to trust them. There comes a point when we need to remove harmful people from our lives. If we don't, they could cause us to focus on them and their problems instead of our relationship with God. They can cause all sorts of division within our lives. The problems we experience with that person could cloud our minds and become a massive distraction. We still need to forgive that person, for our wellbeing as well as theirs and for the protection of the

Church from Satan, but that doesn't mean we should trust them in our lives.

The first passage describes how to deal with trust while the second passage describes how to deal with forgiveness. In the second passage, Peter asked how often to forgive and threw out the number seven. Jesus told him not to only forgive seven times, but to forgive *"until seventy times seven"*. At first read, this may seem like an odd way for Jesus to word His response but when we understand the meaning behind what He is saying, it makes perfect sense.

Seventy times seven equals 490, meaning Jesus is saying here to forgive until 490. Of course, Jesus doesn't expect us to carry around calculators and keep track of every time someone sins against us. It's just a principal. We're to do it over and over again.

To prove this, we have to look to the book of Daniel. Comparing scripture with scripture and allowing the Bible to interpret itself, we discover why Jesus worded it using the word *"until"* which, as I said before, at first glance seems to be a strange way to word it. We are informed, in Daniel 9:24, there will be *"seventy weeks"* until the return of Jesus to set up His millennial kingdom on Earth. Here, a week is referring to a set of seven years. There are seventy sets of seven years, or seventy times seven. Therefore, Jesus is saying to forgive *"until seventy times seven"* or, in other words, until He returns to set up His kingdom. This occurs after the tribulation. Sixty-nine of these weeks of years are already finished and passed. We are just waiting for the last week, the last set of seven years, to begin.

That is the difference between forgiveness and trust, between forgiving and forgetting. We should always forgive, but upon forgiving, we need to follow Jesus' instruction on how to deal with the problem. If you follow what Jesus said and the person still will not change, then you have to respectfully remove them from your life so they don't get in the way of your relationship with God. You don't need the distraction of someone who wants to put themselves before God and allow pride to dictate how they get through this life. God has more important things for you.

FORGIVENESS IN REAL LIFE

Throughout my life, God has really taught the importance of putting forgiveness into practice. Learning the principles is easy but putting them into practice is a whole other situation. Sometimes the idea of applying the principles of forgiveness into real life can seem downright impossible. God taught me how necessary it is to learn and how possible forgiveness can be through Jesus Christ.

From the time I was a kid, I had always been taught about forgiveness from my family and church. There was one member of my family specifically who constantly tested the rest of my family's strength in forgiveness. This person was verbally and physically abusive while taking no responsibility for his actions. I do not wish to divulge personal information about this person, such as name or position in the family, so from here on out I will be referring to him as "the abuser".

I didn't fully understand the depth of what was going on while I was growing up because the abuse had always been there for me to witness. When I was twelve years old, however, the abuse spilled over into my personal life and I understood it firsthand. When my mother found out, she decided the best thing to do was to move out of the house because it was owned by members of the abuser's side of the family.

To my understanding, the abuser's side of the family did not condone his actions but they continued to allow him in their lives. This made my mother extremely uncomfortable. She felt, if she allowed me to continue my relationship with that side of the family, it could open a door for the abuser to reenter my life. She knew she could never drop me off at any of their houses with any degree of confidence in my safety. She knew if the abuser decided to visit the house I would be visiting, the family would possibly invite him in. My mother was not willing to take that chance.

My safety was first on my mom's list of importance. She cared more for my safety than for sparing someone else's feelings. She felt that if the abuser's side of the family cared as much for my safety as she did, there would be no way they would continue allowing the abuser in their lives. To be on the safe side, my mom had to make the incredibly difficult judgment call of removing me from that part of the family.

After my mother and I moved out of our house and in with my stepfather, members of the abuser's side of the family would call and ask to speak with me. They still loved me and wanted to maintain a relationship. Much to my surprise, my mom made the decision to tell me to get on the phone with them and tell them that I did not want anything to do with them anymore.

At the time, it really hurt me to have to do that. I didn't fully understand the potential danger of having them in my life. I loved them so much and to tell them I didn't want them in my life was one of the most difficult things I've ever had to do. I didn't want to lie to them but I trusted my mom and did what she said. After that, we didn't receive any more phone calls from that side of the family.

The whole experience, at least for a while, caused me to feel like I was living a lie. Though it was incredibly painful, I never resented my mom for making that decision. Years later, I was able to better understand.

I was twelve years old when my mother and I broke ties with the abuser's side of the family. I wasn't allowed to call or write anyone who still allowed the abuser in their lives, which was basically everyone on that side of the family. After I grew up and could better understand her reasoning, I gained more respect and love for my mother than I ever had before.

My mother had refused to take a chance with my safety. She knew that if I kept a relationship with anyone on that side of the family, even just over the phone or by letter, it would progress to deeper involvement. She knew I would eventually want to go and visit them or have them come and see me. She knew that would open the door to potential danger. She knew she would have to shut that door and it would end up hurting me all over again. The last thing she wanted was for me to hurt any more than I already was but she had to make sure I was informed to the potential danger surrounding that side of the family.

My mom was always open and honest with me about the events that caused us move. I was twelve years old, uprooted from the life I knew and loved, and had to start a brand new life with a new father-figure, new house, new friends, new school, and new problems. It was a lot to have to deal with at that age and my mom wanted to make sure I wouldn't struggle to hold onto my old life. She knew it would only cause me more pain.

Because of the magnitude of the situation and how much it tore up our lives, the other side of my family that remained in my life; my mom, grandparents, and stepdad especially, found it very nearly impossible to forgive the abuser and his side of the family. When I was old enough to understand everything, I also found it impossible to forgive. That lack of forgiveness festered in me and lashed out in unusual ways.

My mom, stepdad, and grandparents did the absolute best they could in regards to the devastation the abuser wrought upon our family. My mom was always there for me to talk to. My grandparents were there to cheer me up and make me laugh. My stepdad, who had been in the air force and worked in law enforcement, was always there to keep me in line and out of trouble. Of course, me being a teenager at the time, I did not see what he was trying to do or understand his motivation. His methods came across to me as cold, overly strict, and mean. It wasn't until much later that I realized he was acting out of love.

By the time I was an adult and out on my own, I had let the unforgiveness in my heart fester so much that it clouded my view of God. I never denied Jesus or forsook His gift of salvation, but I definitely wasn't living for Him. I was living for myself. It was rare I ever considered how God felt about how I was running my life. I was involved in all sorts of addictive behaviors and my life was spiraling out of control.

Despite a few rough patches, I kept a pretty good relationship with my mom, but I had a terrible relationship with my stepdad and barely ever spoke with my grandparents. I lived that way for years. Then one day, I called to speak with my mom and my stepdad answered the phone. When I asked for my mom, he said he would have to call me back. About an hour later, I heard a knock on my door. I opened the door and to my surprise, it was my stepdad. He looked at me with tears in his eyes and told me the unthinkable. My mother had passed away.

I later found out that she had passed away from congestive heart failure the night before I called to speak with her. Apparently, she had passed away in her sleep. My stepdad told me that the doctor said it would have been sudden and painless.

My mom had passed away about twelve years after we moved away from the abuser and his side of the family. In that time, I had not talked to any of them. Within those twelve years, I developed a lot of feelings of resentment for the abuser, but not so much for the rest of his side of the family. They were easier for me to forgive.

At my mom's funeral, two of the members of the abuser's side of the family arrived to pay their respects and attempt to reunite with me. I was actually really happy to see them. They informed me that the abuser had left the family to follow his own desires and I would not have to worry about coming into contact with him.

Throughout the following days, weeks, months, and years, everyone on that side of the family worked together with me to pick up where we left off. Even though no one said my mother was wrong in her decision to take me out of that side of the family, they still all forgave her with complete understanding. No one faulted her. No one tried to tell me she was wrong. They understood why she did it, as did I, and they apologized for allowing it to get to where she was put in that position. I forgave them and we worked on being a family again.

The other amazing thing was, shortly after my mom died, my stepdad called me and apologized for how our relationship had been up until that time. He explained that he was acting out of love but was sorry for not making it known to me earlier. I apologized to him also for putting him through everything I did in my teenage years and for the lack of respect I showed him. He quickly forgave me.

He then asked if I could forgive him too and if we could just start over again. He explained that he did not want us to drift out of each other's lives. He wanted to be there for me and help guide me through life as a real father should. Hearing him open and honest with me like that completely annihilated all the negative feelings I had for him. I forgave him.

We both worked out our differences and established a foundation for a relationship. All the hard work and mutual respect completely paid off. I was able to let him direct me through things in my life. It led to me putting in more of an effort with my grandparents and appreciating the relationship we had. Their influence, as well as my stepdad's, led me to stop living for myself and start living for God. Just having a relationship based on mutual respect with my stepdad showed me that God can change hearts. Today, my stepdad is the most influential person in my life and I love him as a son loves a father.

A few years later, one of the members of the abuser's side of the family was talking to me about forgiveness. She was a Christian. I looked up to her for her spiritual knowledge and wisdom. She asked me if I could ever forgive the abuser for everything he put me and my family through. I told her that I knew I should but I didn't know how or if it was even possible. I told her how I held so much hate in my heart towards him for so much of my life that I didn't know if I could let it go. I felt as if it was a part of me and I didn't think he was worthy of my forgiveness. This was when my real lesson on forgiveness was first presented, to me from God, through this family member.

Throughout the next couple of years, she taught me what true forgiveness was and why it was so important to practice it. She explained to me that if I did not fill my heart with forgiveness, it could leave room for other things, like hate and resentment. She told me those things are like poison to our bodies.

She also explained that, though forgiveness is something every Christian should practice, it did not mean I should trust him again. She said trust like that would have to be built up again, if I decided I wanted to go that route. She said the best thing to do would be to leave it with Jesus and let Him, instead of my resentment, guide my heart.

It took a lot of prayer from the two of us before God would finally get through to me. He showed me that I was able to forgive, even though I thought it was impossible.

Because I asked Him and allowed Him to work in my heart, He took out all those horrible feelings of hate and replaced them with forgiveness and love.

God showed me I had the power to forgive the entire time, I just didn't want to because of my own pride. I felt that I had the right to not forgive because the abuser never apologized, asked for forgiveness, or gave any indication he had any remorse whatsoever. I felt the abuser didn't deserve forgiveness or mercy on my part. God showed me that was not my decision to make. God decides who is forgiven, not me, and for my own physical, mental, emotional, and spiritual health, I had to let go of my bitterness. Once that happened, I finally felt free.

A year or so later, the abuser contacted me via email and apologized for all of his destructive actions. I told him that I had already forgiven him but it didn't mean I trusted him or condoned what he did. I told him we would have to have some serious talks before I could ever consider inviting him back into my life. I told him he would have to work to build trust back up, if it was even possible. I also told him that I would be leaving all of it up to God and His direction.

At that time, I was married and my wife was pregnant with our daughter. I told the abuser that I would not risk my wife or child's safety just to spare his feelings. He said he understood and would be honest with me about everything. He never tried to excuse his behavior. He didn't put the blame on anyone else but himself. He took full responsibility for what he did and never tried to make me feel pity for him. He told me he was getting professional help and it was showing him what kind of harm he had caused in other people's lives. All of this set him on the path toward an attempt to build trust back up.

Obviously, this is not something that happens overnight. It takes a lot of intervention from God. I decided, with God and my wife, to never put that man in a position where he would have the chance to hurt any one of us in any way. He understood this and never gave us grief about it.

Because of our willingness to forgive, though we have been cautious with what we do and say around him, there really has been nothing but benefit from our standpoint. From this situation, I realized how I can use my forgiveness as a witnessing tool and a testimony. I no longer have those feelings of betrayal and resentment in my heart. All of my anger problems are gone and my stress levels are nearly nonexistent. I feel stronger. I can feel more of a reflection of the nature of God within me. I have been able to be a better husband and father. I can get over problems easier and have learned how to handle personal issues with family. I have learned when to forgive and trust someone and when to forgive and remove someone from my life. I have learned how to forgive without putting anyone in danger.

Most importantly, it gave me a deeper relationship with God. It strengthened my trust in Him and love for Him. I now have a powerful testimony to pass on to others who might be going through something similar. It has made it easier for me to follow God, claim the things He has for me, and do the work He assigns to me. Simply put, when all the negative feelings were expelled out of my heart, it just made more room for God and His love.

CONCLUSION

It is so important we learn how to forgive in these last days. We need everyone we can get in our lives that will be a benefit to us, the Church, and the advancement of

God's Kingdom. We need to learn to forgive always but to follow Jesus' instructions on how to know who to trust and keep in our lives.

Time is too short to waste with people who do not have what is best for the Church and its members at heart. We should not put people in a position where they can hurt us, especially if they haven't proven they are trustworthy enough to be in our lives. God has more important things for us to be doing in the world.

Family is an absolutely essential thing to have in life, but family is not limited to biology. Family is the close-knit people in your life that have proven they love you and are trustworthy. They will make mistakes, as we all do, but when they make them they will work it out with you the way Jesus has instructed. They will also forgive you when you make a mistake against them.

Family is the group of people you can learn and grow in God with. If they aren't believers, they are people who will listen to what you have to say and, at the very least, not become a hindrance to your relationship with God. Family is loving and strong. Family forgives and learns to trust each other. Most importantly, family is an invention of God.

Let's trust that God knows what He's talking about and follow His direction. Let's be done with the negativity in our hearts no matter what the situation. Let's not let Satan in our hearts. Let's make more room in our hearts for God. Let's embrace forgiveness.

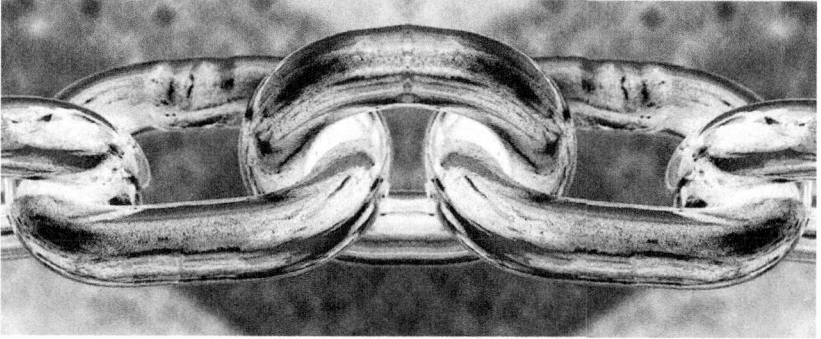

Chapter 7

DISTRACTIONS

Learning how to identify distractions in our Christian life can be a humbling, yet spiritually rewarding, skill and practice. Looking back to my teenage years, I had so many things distracting me from God that I became too dense to notice it. It is rare that anyone falls into distractions willingly and with full knowledge of the spiritual consequences. Allowing ourselves to become distracted is usually done out of ignorance.

Distractions can come in many different forms. Most times they are easily dismissible. Even though they are laid out in the Bible, it is easy to say things like *"The*

Bible doesn't really mean it that way", or *"If God meant it like that, why wouldn't He just say it like that?"*, or even *"Well, that word isn't even in the Bible"*. I understand this all too well, for there was a time in my life when I said each and every one of those things to my Christian brothers and sisters who were trying to get me back on the right path.

At the time, I saw them as intrusive and felt they should mind their own business and let me live my own life. I didn't really understand what was happening until I opened myself up to God, asked Him to tell me what He expected out of me, and allowed Him to change my heart. It was difficult enough to merely accept His truths about what I was doing and not twist scripture to suit my own needs, but putting them into practice was a whole other issue. However, as long as I allowed Him, God always led me through it.

After a few years of working on myself and becoming more obedient to God, I found myself wondering when I would be finished. I wondered how much work I had left to do. I wondered when I would be good enough to not have to worry about constantly improving myself and be able to just live out my Christian life. My answer was *"not in this lifetime"*.

It's not an answer of hopelessness but a definition of life. We are all flawed and we can never achieve perfect obedience to God. No matter how long we live, there will always be something we need to work on. There will always be something to improve within ourselves. We can't dismiss or be blind to this fact. Also, we can't let this fact be our excuse to not try to improve. It was mine for many years.

I remember that I lived life with the view of *"I'm saved and I'm going to Heaven. What I do before then doesn't really matter"*. Of course, just like the vast majority, I had certain lines that I wouldn't cross. Not crossing those lines was my definition of being a good person.

I never denied Jesus. I never killed anybody. I was even able to abstain from premarital sex. The problem was these were only some of God's expectations. Also, I wasn't actively staying away from committing these actions for God's sake but for my own. I didn't consider crossing these lines because I didn't want to risk my salvation, I didn't want to go to jail, and I didn't want an STD or, at the time, a baby to have to be responsible for. I didn't stay away from those things because I knew that was what God wanted. I stayed away from them because I knew that's what I wanted.

After God gave me a base understanding of my flawed logic, He began to show me other things I had in my life that were enjoyable to me yet displeasing to Him. With most of them, I was able to twist scripture to make it acceptable for me to continue what I was involved in. God showed me a different way of looking at it.

Basically, if something wasn't automatically seen as good; if I had to explain myself and justify any certain action as being acceptable, it probably wasn't worth doing. God started having me look at my actions and the things I was involved in a simpler way. Were they helping God or were they helping me? Were my actions helping the advancement of His kingdom, or were they helping my own enjoyment and entertainment? Were they Godly actions, or were they personal distractions? I learned that this type of self-examination is not only important for our walk with God, but also to be able to get through life in these last days without being destroyed by the enemy.

We are constantly being bombarded by attacks and distractions from the enemy. If we don't learn to recognize them for what they are, we won't have the knowledge to overcome and keep them from governing our lives. We need to have the knowledge of the truth of these distractions. We must be able to recognize what things are destructive and what things are constructive. We need knowledge of when to abstain and how to not overindulge. We need the knowledge of how to recognize the truth for what it is, even if it means we have to change something about ourselves.

A lack of knowledge of the truth is like poison to our lives and spirituality. God takes this very seriously. Remember what Hosea 4:6 says...

"My people are destroyed for lack of knowledge: because thou hast rejected knowledge, I will also reject thee, that thou shalt be no priest to me: seeing thou hast forgotten the law of thy God, I will also forget thy children."

IDOL WORSHIP

When we think of idol worship, we normally think of a small statue set upon an altar surrounded by the smoke of burning incense with a person praying to it. This is, of course, a form of idol worship, but is it the only kind? What does the Bible say about it? What does God consider an idol?

One Hebrew word used for the English word *"idol"* is *"semel"* meaning to *"resemble; a likeness"*. An example of this can be found in 2 Chronicles 33:7 which reads...

"And he set a carved image, the idol which he had made, in the house of God, of which God had said to David and to Solomon his son, In this house, and in Jerusalem, which I have chosen before all the tribes of Israel, will I put my name forever."

In the New Testament, a Greek word used for the English word *"idols"* is *"eidolon"* meaning *"an image i.e. for worship"*. An example is found in Romans 2:22, which reads...

"Thou that sayest a man should not commit adultery, dost thou commit adultery? thou that abhorrest idols, dost thou commit sacrilege?"

A translation of the English word *"worship"* (or *"worshippeth"*) from the Greek word *"sebomai"* meaning to *"revere i.e. adore"* is used in Acts 19:27 which states...

"So that not only this our craft is in danger to be set at nought; but also that the temple of the great goddess Diana should be despised, and her magnificence should be destroyed, whom all Asia and the world worshippeth."

We learn from all this that idol worship can be something as severe as honoring a false god or can be something seemingly mundane, such as revering or adoring an image or a resemblance of something or someone else. What this shows is that an idol can be anything that gets in the way of our worship of God.

To gain more understanding, we can put this into modern-day terms. An image can be anything from a television screen to a computer monitor to a poster on our wall or a picture in our minds. There doesn't have to be an outward display of worship, such as bowing down and praying, because adoration and reverence can be accomplished without taking part in such displays.

If there is anything in our lives that we put before God in any way, we need to recognize it, work on it, and let God guide us out of it. We need to recognize the potential harm to our spiritual lives that idol worship can cause. We have to get outside of our preconceived notions of what idol worship is and let the Bible define it for us.

How many times have we stayed home from church to watch a game? How many times have we freely declared publicly that we love a certain song or artist yet are too embarrassed to proclaim our love for Jesus Christ? How many times have we let our own imaginations, fantasies, goals, and ideas for what our lives should look like drive how we choose to live instead of allowing God that right and respect?

I am not saying any of this from a judgmental standpoint. I am preaching to myself here as well. I had been guilty of this plenty of times throughout my life and it took a lot of patience from God to pull me out of it. I am not saying that we should never watch television, listen to music, or have imaginations and goals. I am saying that we should never put those things before our God who provided a way to have them in the first place. There is nothing in this world that is really ours. Everything we have, even our very lives and families, are out on loan from God. He gave them to us, so we must not love the gift more than the giver. We need to have the knowledge of what the Bible is saying about certain things so we do not fall into temptation, deception, or sin. If we put God first in our hearts above all else then we will never be guilty of the sin of idol worship.

SORCERY

More than likely, if asked, the vast majority of Christians would say that they absolutely do not participate in sorcery. However, just like the idea of idol worship, this is another one of those terms that biblically may mean something other than what our preconceived notions tell us. When we think of sorcery, most of us would picture some form of witchcraft, devil worship, or occult practices. In many ways, we would be right and should steer clear of those things, but the biblical definition of sorcery has an added feature that many of us overlook or are not aware of.

The English word *"sorceries"* sometimes comes from the Greek word *"pharmakeia"* meaning *"medication"* and is where we get our word *"pharmacy"* from. This does not mean medication in the healing and medicinal sense. It means it in the mind-altering sense, such as taking medication, or drugs, to get high. This is further proven by looking at the English word *"sorcerers"*, at times translated by the Greek word *"pharmakeus"*, meaning *"a drug; druggist or poisoner"* and is where our word *"pharmacist"* comes from. We can look to the Bible to put this into context for us. Revelation 9:20-21 reads...

"Neither repented they of their murders, nor of their sorceries, nor of their fornications, nor of their theft."

Revelation 21:8 reads…

"But the fearful, and unbelieving, and the abominable, and murderers, and whoremongers, and sorcerers, and idolaters, and all liars, shall have their part in the lake which burneth with fire and brimstone: which is the second death."

Revelation 22:14-15 reads…

"Blessed are they that do his commandments, that they may have right to the tree of life, and may enter in through the gates into the city. For without are dogs, and sorcerers, and whoremongers, and murderers, and idolaters, and whosoever loveth and maketh a lie."

It is clear that God takes this very seriously. So seriously, in fact, that it is equal with murder and idol worship, in that the consequence is the lake of fire. Thank God we have a Savior that forgives all sins so we can escape that horrific consequence.

Again, these passages do not refer to a medically-licensed pharmacist whose goal is to heal people by providing medicine within the confines of the legal system. The reference here would be comparable to drug dealers working outside of the law to make money by getting people high. This can even refer to legal drugs that are taken recreationally, such as narcotic painkillers or even marijuana (depending on the state).

Of course, there are many ways to try and find loopholes or justify this. For example, I have talked with people who would try to redefine what is and what is not a drug. I cannot count how many times I have heard *"Marijuana is natural, God created it, so it's fine"*. If we all lived with that type of logic, the human race would have died off millennia ago. There are a lot of God's creations that can kill us if we are not cautious. Snakes and spiders are natural things created by God, but if we drink the poison of certain kinds, we could easily get very sick or even die.

Another excuse I have heard a lot is *"Marijuana is not a drug"*. If anything that alters the body is considered a drug, such as nicotine, alcohol, or even caffeine, then marijuana would absolutely fall into that category. Attempting to change the definition of something does not change reality.

I have also heard people say they need things like marijuana or heavy narcotics because they have headaches or stress. The thing is that, most times, the actual drug abusers go first to the drugs that will get them high. They do not seem interested in the medications that will not cause them to be high. I have heard over and over things like *"Those other medications won't work on me"* or *"I tried everything and nothing else works"* but will still admit they enjoy getting high. They sometimes will even get defensive about their privacy when they are told their enjoyment is influencing their decision making.

Again, I am not taking a judgmental stance against anyone. I am preaching to myself here as well. My goal is not to be a buzz-kill or be preachy with all this. I just know firsthand the level of damage this type of thinking and these types of activities cause. I was involved in it for years and would have never been able to get out of it by myself. God had to help me and I had to learn to let Him. The type of justification-logic I had when I was trying to convince myself that God was okay with it or that it wasn't too big of a deal would have ruined my life without God's direct intervention. These things will be a huge distraction and will keep anyone imprisoned in the addiction if they indulge in it.

I would even include alcohol in this. Alcohol use can be an incredibly addictive behavior and the ramifications physically, emotionally, mentally, and spiritually have, for the most part, been downplayed by our culture. I used to think that because Jesus drank wine, it would be okay for me to drink alcohol, even to the point of getting drunk and passing out. That is how the justification-logic works. I was never thinking of the fact that Jesus was not a fall-down drunk stumbling around Israel. He was always sober in body, soul, and spirit.

It is an easy concept to grasp if we don't waste time kidding ourselves or giving in to misleading justifications. The word *"wine"* in the Bible is generic and can mean anything from grape juice to wine comparable to what we have today (1). You have to look at the context to find out what is being said. For an example of the word *"wine"* meaning a type of grape juice, Isaiah 16:10 states...

"...the treaders shall tread out no wine in their presses..."

This is referring to grape juice. You cannot ferment the grape juice into wine until after it comes out of the winepress. It would be impossible to tread out alcoholic wine in the presses. This is the same type of drink that is referred to when Jesus turned the water into wine at the wedding in Cana (John 2:1-11). When Jesus was told that he kept the good wine for last, this was referring to grape juice, as fermented grape juice was considered inferior (2).

Jesus lived a sinless life, meaning He always obeyed God and His Word. Proverbs 23:31-32 states...

"Look not thou upon the wine when it is red, when it giveth his colour in the cup, when it moveth itself aright. At the last it biteth like a serpent, and stingeth like an adder."

This is referring to grape juice when it becomes fermented. Other passages tell us that alcohol (referred to as *"wine"* or *"strong drink"*, depending on context) is poison (Deuteronomy 32:33), is not even to be given to our friends or families (Habakkuk 2:15), and can get in the way of our inheritance of the Kingdom of God (1 Corinthians 6:10). We cannot take alcohol use lightly.

All of that being said, I don't believe God will strike us dead if we have a beer or glass of wine with dinner once in a while, but we need to keep what we are doing in check. We need to realize when it is becoming a problem, even if only a supposedly small one. We need to realize people will use what you do as their excuse. Even our children could think that, because we drink once in a while, it is acceptable for them to do it too. The difference is they probably won't have as much restraint as we might have to know when to stop.

With all of the potential danger and negativity that can come out of drinking alcohol, it is probably better to just stay away from it all together. You may not think it is hurting anyone, but is it legitimately helping anyone? Is it setting a good example? Is it something that is helping you and those around you have a closer relationship with God?

When it comes to alcohol abuse and overindulgence, we all should be staying away from it. When it comes to occasional, legal, and responsible alcohol use, then to each his own, but it is best to keep in mind that just because something is not a problem now, it doesn't mean it never will be. It is also best to consider what God says about things like that. Proverbs 20:1 states…

"Wine is a mocker, strong drink is raging: and whosoever is deceived thereby is not wise."

We all have the power to deceive ourselves. It can be a really easy habit to fall into if we aren't careful. We all have to learn to be honest with ourselves and each other.

Concerning things like this, we have to realize that, though certain things may not be visibly hurting anybody, they certainly are not helping. Indulging in drugs, or any type of addictive behavior that is contrary to the will of God, can be harmful by setting a bad example to others. If you are a Christian and are doing these things, as I was at one time, you are basically telling everyone that God is okay with it.

At times, other people will look at what Christians are doing and use that as their excuse to do the same thing. It certainly made it easier for me to justify doing drugs when I would see Christians that I respected doing it first. The really difficult thing is, once you decide to get out of it and quit, you don't have those same Christian friends there to back you up and help you. That is how you know they are not putting God first. Their addictions are first in their hearts and their lives.

The *"pharmakeia"* spirit is running rampant throughout our country and the world. The enemy wants to distract us away from the things of God. The Bible makes it clear that God has a plan for you. His plan most certainly does not involve you getting high or drunk, even occasionally, just so you can have a good time socially or relax by yourself.

There are so many lives all across America, as well as other countries, that have been destroyed by drug addiction. Have you ever heard of someone's life, not just mood, actually improving because of an addiction? Will using drugs get you any other respectable career besides drug-dealing? Will it improve your chances at a successful family and marriage?

You might be able to use drugs for a while in spite of these things but will eventually catch up with you. God will not bless addictions like that. If we are not honest with ourselves, we will not know if we have a problem because we will always assume that a problem does not exist. This is another example of how a lack of knowledge can bring our destruction.

CONCLUSION

As I said before, I don't mean to sound preachy, strict, or judgmental. The last person in the world that has a right to judge people with addictions is me. I just understand how difficult it was for me to get out of addiction.

When I was indulging in addictive behaviors, I never saw the destruction it brought to my life. I never even acknowledged I had a problem with addiction. I was so good at convincing myself there wasn't a problem that I never would have seen it had it not been for God. He showed me a lot of mercy and patience. It took years for me to finally start listening to Him, and when I finally did, the realization of what I was doing hit me like a truck.

I noticed all of the time that I was wasting on myself when I could have been spending it attaining the goals God had waiting for me. I saw all the opportunities I had missed and people I had alienated. I saw how powerfully and effectively I had been deceived.

We are living in dangerous times. We are living in what is commonly referred to as *"the last days"*. God gave us clear instruction as to what we need to do to make it through this period in time while keeping our bodies, souls, and spirits intact.

God told us how to not risk our physical lives or spiritual eternity. If we waste time on ourselves through distractions, such as the ones mentioned in this chapter as well as many many more, we will not have time to get ourselves right with God when the time of His return arrives. Everything is ramping up in the world to something unimaginable and we need to be prepared for it the best we can. We are told that biblically prophetic things are going to come exponentially faster and we will not be able to fully see the end until it arrives. By then it will be too late.

I have made so much of an intense effort to get the facts in this chapter through to you because of how important the information is for the time we are living in. We need strength in the Church. We need to learn to be honest with ourselves in our self-examinations. We need to be able to properly define what the distractions are so we know what we need to remove from our lives.

If you are involved in any of these distractions, I don't look down on you or judge you and neither should any Christian. I want to help you. I want to teach you the things that God taught me. Everybody needs to be given a chance and I hope you will take this as your own. However, you don't really need me to give you that chance because God has had it waiting for you all along.

Trust God and there is nothing He won't help you with. Learn from Him and there is nothing He won't teach you. Love Him and there is nothing that will keep Him from loving you. God wants to help you. All you have to do is let Him.

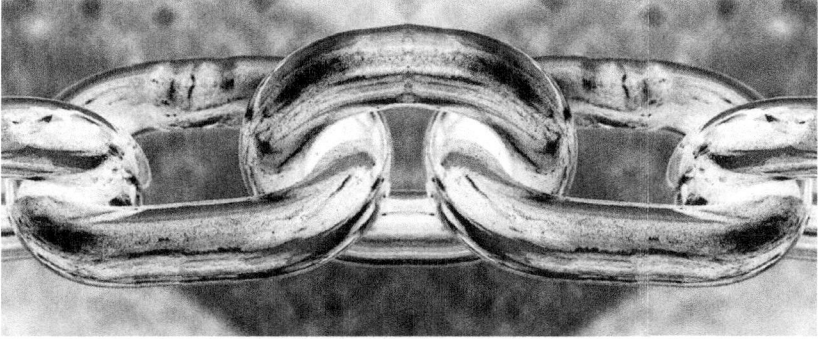

Chapter 8

RACES AND LIFESTYLES

Before anything else, I must express how blessed I am to have had the upbringing of my family and church. While I may not agree with all of the traditional doctrines, I was brought up in a family church environment of love and unity. I never had to question if the church loved God or if my family loved me. Even after my mother and I decided to not attend the Baptist church anymore, the church and my grandparents still rallied around us in prayer and support in our walk with God.

When I became older and more mature, I realized that family does not always have to hold the same beliefs to still love each other. We were always one in Jesus regardless of denomination. Even though there are some fringe-beliefs I have now which are completely different than from what I was raised with, I still love the people and church I was brought up in. My core doctrinal beliefs are the same and always will be. I will never deny Jesus as my savior, who was born of a virgin, died for the sins of the world, was resurrected, and is going to return to Earth in the near future.

The other beliefs I write about in this book are from my own research of the Bible through the guidance and direction of God. As God has done in my life, I am laying a foundation with these beginning chapters that is leading somewhere deeper. If I started the book out with end-time prophecy, I would have lost many of you and confused the rest. God has used my entire life to teach me the things I have written in this book and the only reason I was able to accept it was the foundation He gave me first.

I am so incredibly blessed that those who raised me took time to instill what it truly means to love. When I was young, the people in my life may have held beliefs that were not socially popular, and even some I would not agree with today, but they always put love above all else. They never made anyone suffer in any way because of their beliefs. I was always taught that God is a God of love and He does not want people to suffer, but instead come to repentance.

There are some self-proclaimed Christians in the world who have protested and proclaimed their biblical beliefs in horrific ways. While, in some cases, I may hold the same doctrinal beliefs as some of these individuals, I do not always agree with their methods. I am thankful that my mother, grandparents, and church taught me the biblically correct way to exercise and practice my beliefs without bringing hate into it. After all, why would any of us want to tarnish the love we have in our hearts for God with such an ugly thing like hate?

There are two main issues that cause a lot of controversy throughout the Church. The way some Christian groups choose to handle these issues are, in my opinion, appalling. It is important to discuss these issues to understand certain things that will come into our future. It all leads back to prophecy.

Both issues, in my opinion, are clearly outlined in the Bible as to what is right and what is wrong. I am not as concerned with the opinions of the issues as I am with how they have been handled. We need to fight our battles in the way God teaches.

I have no problem expressing how I feel about things or taking a stand against anything God says is wrong, even if it isn't socially popular. However, I will not stand with a group who does this out of hate in their hearts and not out of love from God. I believe that these groups, while trying to stop certain behaviors, are perpetuating existing problems, creating new issues, giving God a bad name, and making the Bible into something it isn't.

INTERRACIAL MARRIAGE

I believe there are some serious misconceptions and biblical misinterpretations about interracial marriage. The "old fashioned" viewpoint of marriage is that it should be between a man and a woman within their own race. As a child, when I asked about friendship and marriage, the way it was explained to me was something along the lines of "Well Josh, you should be friends with whoever you want if they are a good influence on you. As far as marriage, people should probably marry within their own race but sometimes you just can't help who you fall in love with."

I never fully understood how it would be possible to marry someone who is within our race when most of us, especially in America, are already mixed in some way throughout our ancestries. Also, if we are to be equally kind, loving, and accepting of all people, I would wonder why that would not include marriage. Did God tell us not to marry outside of our race? If so, where is it in the Bible? When I asked my family these questions throughout my early years, time and time again, I was directed to the biblical account of the tower of Babel.

The story of the building of the city of Babel and the tower can be found in Genesis 11:1-9. We learn that after the flood, everyone in the world spoke one language and settled in the land of Shinar. They decided to build a city and a tower that would reach into the sky. The Lord then came down to see what they were building. Genesis 11:6 reads...

"And the Lord said, Behold, the people is one, and they have all one language; and this they begin to do: and now nothing will be restrained from them, which they have imagined to do."

The word *"restrained"* here is from the Hebrew word *"basar"* and can mean to be isolated, fenced, or withheld.

The word *"imagined"* comes from the Hebrew word *"zamam"* which basically means to plan in a bad or evil sense. God is saying here that, because they were building this city and tower, nothing would be withheld from them and they would accomplish all the evil they had planned. We can compare this with 2 Thessalonians 2:6-9 which reads…

"And now ye know what withholdeth that he might be revealed in his time. For the mystery of iniquity doth already work: only he who now letteth will let, until he be taken out of the way. And then shall that Wicked be revealed, whom the Lord shall consume with the spirit of his mouth, and shall destroy with the brightness of his coming: Even him, whose coming is after the working of Satan with all power and signs and lying wonders,"

There is something withholding, or restraining, the full amount of wickedness and evil of Satan. This Restrainer, when it is time to do so, will let loose the enemy in the last days. In the Genesis account of the city and tower, God said that all people were one. They were of one language, all gathered in one place, and had a common type of religion. Illustrating this is the fact that they were of one mind by working together on one thing that was in defiance of God.

When God saw what the people were doing, He said that nothing would be restrained from them, meaning the Restrainer would be let loose and all the evil of Satan would pour out upon the earth. It was not yet time for this because it was not yet the last days. Due to this, God scattered the people of the world and gave them different languages. This could have also been how other religions could have started.

This account does not mention anything about people's races. Many traditional teachings say that this was when all the races of the earth were created and when the continents drifted apart. Before this, they were all one race which is why God said in Genesis 11:6 *"Behold, the people is one"*. This is a possible scenario but it is not biblically provable in an absolute and concrete way. It is a theory. The traditional teachings say that God did not want people marrying outside their own race and that's why he scattered them and gave them different languages. This teaching completely misses the whole point of the biblical account of Babel.

The problem was the entire world was gathered together and working on something that was in defiance against God. If God had not stepped in to stop it, this could have turned into the one-world government we read about in the book of Revelation. There was something about building that city and tower that was going to let loose the Restrainer before the appointed time. God scattered the people of the earth and gave them different languages to ensure they could not become a one-world government before the appointed time.

Seeing that the Babel issue was more of a governmental/political problem that angered God, we can see why He had to scatter everyone and give them different languages. He did not want the Restrainer let loose before the appointed time. God had to put up barriers that He knew we would not be able to easily break down. Now, thousands of years later, we are breaking down those barriers.

The scattering of the people of Babel had to do with a worldwide political system being implemented on the people of the earth in a way that is an insult to God. It had nothing to do with what race marries what other race. Using the city and tower of Babel story to say God does not want us to marry outside of our race is a misinterpretation of what happened and a misconception of what that account has for us to learn. The lesson has nothing to do with race. The lesson has to do with the evil that ensues from a worldwide effort for all humans to govern themselves without God. (For more information on the tower of Babel, please refer to the chapter entitled *"Spirit of Antichrist"* under the heading *"Nimrod"*)

Another issue brought up by some traditional teachers is that God told the ancient Hebrews in Deuteronomy 7:3 that they were not allowed to marry anyone from the surrounding countries. The traditional teachers will say that, since the ancient Hebrews couldn't marry outside of their race, we should not either. That is a great example of the problems and false teachings that can come up when someone reads a single Bible verse without reading the context it is found in.

When someone takes a single Bible verse out of context, they can make it mean all sorts of things. This is how the Word of God can be twisted to fit one's own personal beliefs and traditions. We should never make the Bible fit our beliefs. We should make our beliefs fit the Bible.

The surrounding verses of Deuteronomy 7:3 are saying that God did not want them marrying outside of their own people because of all the idol worship and beliefs in false gods that ran rampant throughout the surrounding lands. The Hebrews, sometimes called the children of Israel, were a chosen people by God. He did not want them straying away from Him. It all makes perfect sense when we read Deuteronomy 7:3 with the very next verse. Deuteronomy 7:3-4 says…

"Neither shalt thou make marriages with them; thy daughter thou shalt not give unto his son, nor his daughter shalt thou take unto thy son. For they will turn away thy son from following me, that they may serve other gods: so will the anger of the Lord be kindled against you, and destroy thee suddenly."

Here, God gives the law and the reason for the law. God did not want His chosen people to be spiritually corrupted by the inhabitants of the surrounding lands. I also believe there is strong biblical evidence that there were Nephilim in those lands and God absolutely did not want His people to mix with them. (For more information on this, refer to the chapter entitled *"The Nephilim"*)

This account had nothing to do with human racial issues. It was a spiritual matter. God had big plans for His people and He did not want them turning away from Him. Further evidence is found in Exodus 12:48, which reads...

"And when a stranger shall sojourn with thee, and will keep the passover to the Lord, let all his males be circumcised, and then let him come near and keep it; and he shall be as one that is born in the land: for no uncircumcised person shall eat thereof."

This verse is from a passage that is talking about eating at Passover but the point of race is still made. If a person was willing to convert and follow God, then he was considered to be the same as a native-born Hebrew. God does not discriminate by race. It does not matter where you are from, it only matters if you are following God or not.

Another fact proving this point is that Moses had an Ethiopian wife. Moses was not from Ethiopia, so for him to take an Ethiopian woman as his wife would have been an interracial marriage. The account in chapter 12 of the book of Numbers explains how Aaron and Miriam spoke against Moses because of this interracial marriage. God stepped in on Moses' behalf and expressed His anger toward Aaron and Miriam for speaking against Moses.

The issue Aaron and Miriam had with the marriage was racial and God showed them how wrong they were. God was so angered by their words that He gave Miriam leprosy. Aaron saw that they had acted foolishly and begged God to release them from their sin. It wasn't until Moses prayed to God on Aaron and Miriam's behalf that Miriam was healed but even that was a long and grueling process. Moses asked God to heal Miriam. God said to shut Miriam out of the camp for seven days. God said, after the seven days had passed, that she would be healed and could be let back into the community. This account makes it incredibly clear how God feels about racism.

There is no problem with interracial marriage found in the Bible. There is, however, an issue with interfaith marriages. This sometimes gets confused with interracial marriages by the Church. We are told not to be unequally yoked with unbelievers (2 Corinthians 6:14), meaning not to be personally and deeply attached to someone who is not a Christian, such as in marriage.

When we marry or even have a deep connection or friendship with someone outside of our faith, it can easily cause strife and even a falling away from God. It is better to marry someone with whom you can share your beliefs, grow your faith, and strengthen your relationship with God. It can be someone of any race and long as Jesus Christ dwells in their spirit.

God created us all equal. We all come from the same created man and woman. We are all children of Adam and Eve. We are all one big family. God does not discriminate against race. God does not look at skin color. God looks at the heart. He wants us to have a relationship with Him, regardless of race. If you fall in love with someone who you can worship, learn about, talk to, and love God with then He can bless that, regardless of race.

We are all created by God and all live within the same reality. We are all under the same curse of the world and grace of God. Jesus came to save us all, Gentile and Jew, and we who have accepted Him are to become His spiritual bride in Heaven (Revelation 19:7). In the eyes of God, there are only two types of human beings in the world; believers and unbelievers. Race has nothing to do with it.

LIFESTYLES

One of the biggest controversies hitting the church is over the issue of homosexuality. It has been debated as a religious issue, a social issue, a political issue, and everything in between. It seems that, within the Church, no one is exempt from the opinions of others. Generally speaking, Christians who take a stand against homosexuality are accused of being intolerant and hateful while Christians who do not take a stand are accused of being secular and weak.

Most Christians know of a bible verse or two that speaks against the act of homosexuality with a lot of opinions and human thinking to back them up. Much of the rest of the world will downplay the sin and ask why Jesus never spoke of it if it was such a big deal. It seems there are no winners or losers in this ongoing debate.

In the day of age we live in, with issues such as this, it can be increasingly difficult to know what is right, what is wrong, and how to handle either one. If we have an opposition to something, are we supposed to say nothing because it is an unpopular view? On the other hand, are we supposed to act aggressively to the point that other people have to suffer for our own beliefs? With things like this, it is best to shed our carnal humanity and look at what the Bible says. We can trust the Bible, being His Word, to clear up how God feels and what He wants us to do.

In Leviticus 18:22, while speaking with Moses and describing His laws for the children of Israel, God says…

"Thou shalt not lie with mankind, as with womankind: it is abomination."

Later, in Leviticus 20:13, God reveals the punishment to the children of Israel for committing this sin is death. In our world and with no basis to work from, this would seem exceptionally harsh. This is another example of the dangers of taking a verse without looking at the rest of the Bible for context and explanation. What we have to do is come to the realization of who this law was meant for and why God put it in place.

This law shows the expectation of God and discloses to us something He considers a sin. We also learn the punishment for that sin. The fact is, the punishment of death for the sin of homosexuality was only intended for the Israelites of that time. This is why the Church nowadays is not permitted by God to go around killing homosexuals.

If we study the Bible, we find that even the children of Israel were not permitted to go out into the world and kill homosexuals. This was a punishment only for the Israelites within their own land. So the question comes up, why would God have such a strict punishment for the children of Israel but not for the rest of the world? Wouldn't this prove Him to be an unfair God?

In answering these questions, there is one main thing to remember. The children of Israel were God's chosen people set aside to bring forth the Messiah who would save the entire world. This was such an important and delicate goal and one that Satan was constantly trying to get in the way of, that God had to set the children of Israel to a stricter moral standard than the rest of the world at that time. God judges us all by the same standards but, to make sure we would have a chance to escape Hell, He had to make sure Satan would not interfere with the birth of the Messiah.

Jesus taught that *"...whomsoever much is given, of him shall be much required..."* (Luke 12:48). God gave a long list of laws and expectations to Moses for the children of Israel. The issue of homosexuality was only one of them. This is not to downplay the importance of such an issue, but to show how much God really expected out of the Israelites. God knew if He was not as strict as He was with them, it would have been increasingly easier for them to fall away from Him, take part in practices of people worshipping false gods, and make it impossible for the Messiah to be born.

Another question often asked is, if the topic of homosexuality is so important, then why didn't Jesus speak of it throughout His ministry? There are three main points to think about in answering this question. First, to ask a question in that way assumes that Jesus' teachings were more important than the rest of the Bible. That is as if to say, *"Jesus did not speak on a certain topic, so that negates the importance of that topic throughout the rest of the Bible"*. If we take on that viewpoint, we would have to say sexual relations with animals is acceptable as well because Jesus did not speak against it. Of course, this is not the case. The reality is that when it comes to the Bible, it is all or none. It is not reasonable to pick certain parts of the Bible to live by and agree with while disregarding the others. To do so would to be going against the Bible itself.

The second point comes from the Bible itself. John 21:25 says…

"And there are also many other things which Jesus did, the which, if they should be written every one, I suppose that even the world itself could not contain the books that should be written. Amen."

We do not know for sure that Jesus did not speak against homosexuality. This verse tells us that there were many things Jesus did that were not included in scripture because it would have been too much to write down. Knowing this, we cannot say with any degree of certainty that Jesus did or did not speak about homosexuality. We do know, however, that He certainly did not encourage it because that would have gone against the will of God.

Jesus was in complete agreement with God concerning every issue. John 5:45-47 reads…

"Do not think that I will accuse you to the Father: there is one that accuseth you, even Moses, in whom ye trust. For had ye believed Moses, ye would have believed me: for he wrote of me. But if ye believe not his writings, how shall ye believe my words?"

Jesus lived in accordance to the law God gave Moses (Galatians 4:4) and, while the Bible does not say if He openly and outright condemned homosexuality, He did make it clear how God feels about marriage. Matthew 19:4-5 reads…

"And he answered and said unto them, Have ye not read, that he which made them at the beginning made them male and female, And said, For this cause shall a man leave father and mother, and shall cleave to his wife: and they twain shall be one flesh?"

This brings us to the third point. We have to keep in mind who Jesus was primarily talking to. Jesus was teaching and preaching to the Jews. They would have already known and had access to all of God's expectations through His original teachings and writings, such as the Torah (the first five books of the Bible). It was this list of expectations, commonly referred to as the Law of Moses, which Moses gave to the children of Israel generations earlier. The Jewish people, especially the Pharisees (the religious leaders of the time), would have already known what God thought about issues such as homosexuality.

This could be a main reason why Jesus did not bring it up in His ministry, or at least why it was not recorded in the four gospels. It was already spoken about in scripture. God already made it known how He feels about homosexuality. If it wasn't a question at the time or if it wasn't an ongoing issue in the land, there would not have been a major reason for Jesus to repeat what was already taught. Saying it once should be enough for us to understand His will.

Moving on from the topic of Jesus' ministry, here is another point to consider about the issue of homosexuality from a biblical perspective. In the days of Noah and Lot, there were Nephilim in the surrounding lands. The Nephilim were created out of the unholy union of fallen angels and mankind. This union was completely against the will of God. (For more information, refer to the chapter entitled *"The Nephilim"*)

In Jude 1:6-7, we read of the Nephilim account and it being compared to Sodom and Gomorrah. The fornication sins of Sodom and Gomorrah are explained here as *"...going after strange flesh..."*. The account of homosexuality and the account of fallen angels mating with humans are referred to in this way simply because it is one kind of flesh that was never meant to be with another kind of flesh. Homosexuality is a kind of shadow, or spiritual representation, of the unholy union of fallen angels and human women that produced the Nephilim. This is why He looks at the act as an abomination.

I will stop and say right here that God does not hate homosexuals and if someone is saying that, it is my belief they are not representing Christianity. They are expressing their own prejudices. Biblically speaking, God does hate sin but He loves all of us despite our sin. Jesus died as a sacrifice for all sin so that everyone can be saved (John 3:16).

We Christians need to realize that if Jesus loves all people, we need to love all people too, regardless what their individual sins might be. We do not have to, and should not, condone any sin whatsoever. We should be working on ourselves continuously to become more Christ-like while trying to help, yet not force, others to do the same thing.

It is good to take a stand with God against sin but we should not act in a manner that is fueled with hate and anger. We need to reach people through love, understanding, and prayer. We do not need to be protesting at funerals, speaking evil things while saying they're from God, and making everyone's lives worse. This is no solution and is only giving Christianity a bad name to those who don't know the God of the Bible.

The Bible does not say "Homosexuals are going to Hell" or "God hates homosexuals". The Bible says all who reject Jesus will go to Hell, but all who receive Him and give his life to Him will have everlasting life (John 3:16). He makes salvation available to the whole world because He is a God who loves everybody (John 3:16). What Jesus did, the great sacrifice God made, was enough to cover the sins of the entire world for all time (this would include homosexuality).

This begs the question I have heard over and over again, can a homosexual be saved? The answer is yes! Salvation is not only for heterosexuals. There is only one prerequisite for salvation and that is Jesus Christ. If a homosexual accepts Jesus Christ as his Lord and Savior and decides to live for Him instead of a life of sin, then absolutely yes, he will be saved (again, John 3:16).

CONCLUSION

The fact of the matter is that we live in tumultuous times. We need as many Christian brothers and sisters as we can get to help us fight in this war against Satan. We need as many people as we can have to lean on when things get rough and rejoice when we are blessed. Ultimately, we want as many people to share in God's Kingdom as possible.

If you have a personal conviction to only marry within your race, then you are absolutely justified in doing so, but that does not allow you to condemn others for not making the same choice. If you have a personal conviction against witnessing to homosexuals, then you have to ask yourself what the reason is. If it is because they are involved in a life of sin, well who isn't? Besides perhaps the unpardonable sin, does God pick and choose what sins He will forgive and what sins He won't? Isn't God powerful enough to forgive and change any sin?

Jesus' beautiful gift of salvation is the only chance any of us have to be released of the sin controlling our lives. It's also our only shot at an eternal life with God. Salvation depends on a person's willingness to shed their life of sin and accept a Spirit-led life. We have to be able to give everyone that chance and let them decide for themselves. We should never want to deny someone their chance at salvation, regardless of what sins that person might be caught up in.

It is an act of love to share the gospel with each and every sinner. Homosexuals are no different. You should share the gospel with them and tell them how to get saved. If they don't accept it, then you can walk away in love knowing you at least tried and maybe even planted a seed for later. If they do accept it, then get them saved, explain to them what a Spirit-led life is and how to live one, and let God decide if they really meant the salvation prayer in their hearts or not.

God is the ultimate judge with those kinds of things, not any one of us. We don't get to decide who goes to Heaven and who goes to Hell. We must give people a chance to choose for themselves. We need to show people what true love really is, not show them how hateful and ugly we can be. Lastly, if for some reason you really believe that there are certain people who just can't be saved, even though that is a completely unbiblical view, would it really hurt to at least try?

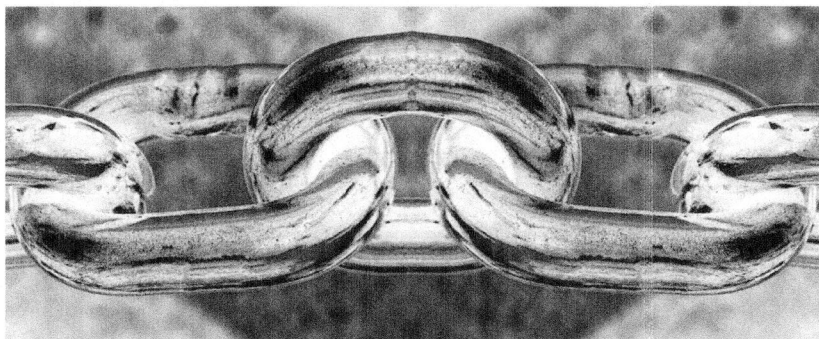

Chapter 9

GIFTS OF THE HOLY SPIRIT

Upon receiving the Holy Spirit, the followers of Jesus were equipped with certain gifts. From the very first demonstration, the validity of the gifts was attacked by the enemy. Today nothing has changed. We as Christians still have a right to claim these gifts and Satan is still attacking their validity.

Jesus gave us these gifts for a reason. We are to use them to expand the kingdom. They are also vital in getting through these last days without falling into deception or being defeated by spiritual attacks. Satan doesn't want us to have these gifts because they exhibit the power of God. The gifts of the Holy Spirit have power over Satan. One of Satan's oldest tricks is using unbelief and doubt to get what he wants and fulfill his wicked plans. After all, if you don't believe the gifts exist, you won't be pursuing them, and Satan will know in which areas you are defenseless.

There are nine specific gifts of the Holy Spirit found in 1 Corinthians 12:8-10. Listed in order of mention, they are...

1. Wisdom
2. Knowledge
3. Faith
4. Healing
5. Miracles
6. Prophecy
7. Discerning of spirits
8. Tongues
9. Interpretation of tongues

Though in this chapter we will be mainly focusing on the nine gifts of the Holy Spirit, I believe it is important to note there are also nine fruits of the Holy Spirit, as outlined in Galatians 5:22. The fruits of the Holy Spirit are...

1. Love

2. Joy

3. Peace

4. Longsuffering

5. Gentleness

6. Goodness

7. Faith

8. Meekness

9. Temperance

The fruits of the Holy Spirit describe characteristics that the Holy Spirit brings into people who have Jesus in their hearts. The gifts of the Holy Spirit describe certain abilities that the Holy Spirit makes possible for people who have Jesus in their hearts to perform. As Christians, it is our personal responsibility to get a hold of all these things and put them into practice. We are going to need them in these last days. We need them to be able to survive and do everything God calls us to do.

Though the fruits of the Holy Spirit are important to know and attain, I am mainly going to be focusing on the nine gifts of the Holy Spirit in this chapter. The reasons for this are that the gifts of the Holy Spirit can be used as defensive and offensive weapons against Satan, they are not all commonly taught throughout the Church, and there has been a wide range of attacks from the enemy. These attacks come in the form of controversy and doubt, many times by fellow Christians, as to the legitimacy, power, and interpretation of each of these gifts. We need to have a proper understanding of each and every one of these gifts for the profit of the entire Church.

I am going to outline various explanations of the gifts in this chapter. It is important to keep an open mind for some of these, as the definitions might contradict with certain traditional teachings. This is why, instead of blindly following what we are traditionally taught, we need to follow God as our Teacher and the Bible as our textbook. For easier reference and better understanding, I am going to break down this chapter by going through each gift of the Holy Spirit and its meaning. I won't spend a lot of time on the ones that are mostly self-explanatory. The majority of people will already have a basic understanding of what those gifts are.

WISDOM

The word *"wisdom"* comes from the Greek word *"sophia"* meaning *"wisdom (higher or lower, worldly or spiritual)"* and can be compared with *"phronimos"* meaning *"thoughtful i.e. sagacious or discrete".* Having wisdom means to know how to handle situations in life without letting ourselves get in our own way. It means bowing to God's will over our own. Wisdom is knowing how to properly use the information we have. Wisdom does not just mean *"smart"* or *"knowledgeable".* Wisdom is to know how to use knowledge. You can have knowledge without wisdom but you cannot have wisdom without knowledge.

Solomon, quite possibly the wisest man to have ever lived save for Jesus Christ, was blessed by God with His wisdom. Using that wisdom, Solomon wrote many things in the Bible that are still applicable today. The book of Proverbs can be looked at as a basic manual to get through life the best way possible.

Just as it was with Solomon, for us to have wisdom today means to have a deeper relationship with God and an understanding of His will. This is why wisdom is so crucial. Wisdom of God is not something we can just learn on our own. It must be put in us by power of the Holy Spirit. We should be continually trying to cultivate our wisdom. The best way to do this is to read and put into practice the wise writings of the scriptures, such as in the book of Proverbs, and ask God for His direction.

KNOWLEDGE

The word *"knowledge"* comes from the Greek word *"gnosis"* and means, quite simply *"knowing (the act)"*. Having knowledge is just partaking in the act of knowing. It means to have facts or information. The gift of knowledge from the Holy Spirit is God presenting His knowledge to you for purposes in accordance to His will. Here is a good definition of knowledge in regards to the Holy Spirit gift...

"The Word of Knowledge is simply the Holy Spirit transmitting His specific knowledge to you on something that you would have no ability or means to be able to know about with your own limited intelligence and knowledge levels. It is supernatural knowledge and insight being given directly to you by the Holy Spirit Himself, not by your own mind or your own intelligence levels." (1)

Knowledge and wisdom go hand in hand. Knowledge is the information and wisdom is to know what to do with it. You can have all the knowledge in the world, but if you don't know how to connect with people and teach, you will never be able to share that knowledge. The ability to connect with others comes from wisdom. Having the information to teach is knowledge.

We need to allow God to teach us. God can give us extremely valuable knowledge if we allow Him. For example, God gave me all of the knowledge included in this book. It took wisdom from God to decide to actually write a book and make it available to anyone interested.

Knowledge is important to fight in this war and overcome the battles. We must have knowledge of God first and foremost but we must also have knowledge of our enemy. The more knowledge we have about Satan and his angels, the better off we will be in our defenses.

FAITH

The word *"faith"* comes from the Greek word *"pistis"* meaning *"persuasion, i.e. credence; moral conviction (of religious truth, or the truthfulness of God or a religious teacher), especially reliance upon Christ for salvation; abstractly constancy in such profession; by extension the system of religious (Gospel) truth itself: - assurance, belief, believe, faith, fidelity."*

I included the entire entry from the Strong's Exhaustive Concordance because I think there is a lot of good information in there. Faith is a type of persuasion about the things of God. I think this is interesting because, especially with the attacks the enemy throws at us, a lot of times what we see in our day to day life seem to contradict with what we believe God's truth is.

For example, there is pain and death in the world, yet the Bible says God is loving and kind. How can that be? The simple, go-to answer for many Christians when they don't know an answer is to say *"just have faith"*. While I basically agree with that idea, it does not do much to answer the person's question. The answer, short and simple, is because we live in a world that became broken, sinful, and full of evil when Satan convinced Adam and Eve to rebel against God. Because God is a just and honest God, He will fix what Satan has done to the Earth when the time for that comes, but for now Satan has free reign over the Earth and its inhabitants. However, in the meantime, because God loves us, He gave us a way out of the power and claim of the enemy; salvation in Jesus Christ.

That is where the true faith comes in. We have faith that Jesus will make good on His promise to save us and bring us to Heaven with Him in the afterlife. We have faith that Jesus will work in our lives and get us past the trappings of Satan and his angels. We have faith that we can lean on the understanding God has provided for us as described in His Word. When we need it and if we allow it, God also gives us a supernatural faith to be able to overcome the most trying times in your life. He does this by power of the Holy Spirit.

HEALING

The word *"healing"*, as used here, comes from the Greek word *"iama"* meaning *"a cure"*. I find this interesting as the definition is *"a cure"* and not *"to cure"*. The healing gift of the Holy Spirit is a gift of a cure. The cure comes from God and has nothing to do with us. This affirms my belief that this gift is not merely the ability to cure, such as with a doctor, but it is a supernatural representation of God's creative power.

The gift of healing, or the gift of a cure, has nothing to do with an individual's own capabilities or pursuits.

While I have a great respect for the people practicing in the medical profession to keep us alive and healthy, there really is nothing supernatural about it. If a person wants and is driven enough, he can study hard and learn everything he needs to know to become a practicing doctor, whether with God or on his own. However, I don't believe that someone can attain the gift of healing, or any such gift, from the Holy Spirit if they do not know Jesus Christ as their savior.

I believe miracles can and do happen. I also believe God can do whatever He wants whenever He wants, but for something to be a true gift of the Holy Spirit, one must have the Holy Spirit. The gift of healing is not just a personal gift for practicing medicine and being an exceptional doctor. The gift of healing is a direct manifestation of God's creative power through a person who has the Holy Spirit.

I am not saying that every supposed miracle of healing on television is a true representation of the Holy Spirit, as some of them have been proven to be faked, but I also do not believe every single one is fraudulent. Though some Christians will claim that this, as well as some of the other gifts of the Holy Spirit, is really a manifestation of the devil, the fact is that miraculous healing through power of the Holy Spirit absolutely happens. Before you decide to get too skeptical, remember what Jesus Christ said about this matter. Matthew 12:22-32 reads…

"Then was brought him one possessed with a devil, blind, and dumb: and he healed him, insomuch that the blind and dumb both spake and saw…but when the Pharisees heard it, they said, This fellow doth not cast out devils, but by Beelzebub the prince of devils. And Jesus knew their thoughts, and said unto them, Every kingdom divided against itself is brought to desolation; and every city or house divided against itself shall not stand:…Wherefore I say unto you, All manner of sin and blasphemy shall be forgiven unto men: but the blasphemy against the Holy Ghost shall not be forgiven unto men. And whosoever speaketh a word against the Son of man, it shall be forgiven him: but whosoever speaketh against the Holy Ghost, it shall not be forgiven him, neither in this world, neither in the world to come."

For the entire passage, I would suggest reading Matthew 12:22-32, Mark 3:28-29, and Luke 12:10. I didn't include the entire passage because it is quite extensive. I included the main points that pertain to our purposes here. This passage is Jesus' description of what is commonly known as *"the unpardonable sin"*. I don't know all the ins and outs of it, but it seems that blasphemy against the Holy Spirit can negate someone's admittance to Heaven. I do not believe this pertains to things said out of ignorance, and I'm not even completely sure that a true Christian can commit this sin. What I do know is to attribute any gift of the Holy Spirit to the devil or a demon is, at the very least, flirting with the unpardonable sin. We should always consult God first and wait for His reply before taking any action if we have any doubt about anything being from God or Satan.

The gift of healing, just like any gift of the Holy Spirit, cannot be attained by any other means than by that of the Holy Spirit Himself. Satan does attack this gift, as well as others, and sets up forgeries in various places and times. We can pick out the counterfeits if we use wisdom by going directly to God if we have any doubts. There is nothing wrong with at least accepting the possibility of an interpretation, especially one such as this, that falls right in line with the Bible's teaching and examples. We need to learn to get past our own skepticism, prejudices, and traditional teachings if they conflict with the Bible so we can embrace this for what it is. This is a very powerful and important gift of the Holy Spirit. It can be incredibly useful to accept and, if possible, put into practice to help get us through these last days.

MIRACLES

The word *"miracles"* comes from the Greek word *"dynamis"* meaning *"force"*. All throughout the Bible are examples of miracles being worked either directly by God, through an angel, or through a person. Examples of the Holy Spirit working a miracle from God through a person would include Moses parting the Red Sea, David being able to defeat Goliath, and Jesus walking on water. Of course, there are many more examples found throughout the Bible of miracles, but I think the main thing to understand here is that God makes this power available to us as He sees fit. Remember the words of Jesus, recorded in the book of John 14:12, which reads…

"Verily, verily, I say unto you, He that believeth on me, the works that I do shall he do also; and greater works than these shall he do; because I go unto my Father."

If we are to believe Jesus was telling us the truth then we must believe that each one of us who accepts Him as our savior can have access to the things He did and more. This does not mean that we can learn these for ourselves and put them into practice according to our own will. This means that Jesus will give people certain gifts at certain times to fulfill His will on Earth. We all have the potential but it is ultimately up to God what He will use us for.

The power and gift of working miracles is not for our own glory or for our own purposes. It is not a gift we can learn on our own and utilize as we see fit. It is a gift that God gives through the Holy Spirit in accordance to His will and His timing. The gift of miracles, just like the rest of the gifts of the Holy Spirit, is not for us individually but is for the benefit of the entire Church.

PROPHECY

The word *"prophecy"* comes from the Greek word *"propheteia"* and means *"prediction (scriptural or other)"*. This is another controversial gift that has many people attacking through unbelief. The gift of prophecy does not only include predicting the future but can include a wide variety of predictions, such as predicting how to handle an issue, a teaching from the Bible someone can use in their lives, or how God feels about a certain thing.

This gift is absolutely not the same as fortune-telling or any such forms of witchcraft. Prophecy is a gift from the Holy Spirit that we cannot turn on or off at will. It is up to God to reveal things to us for His own purposes. Fortune-telling would be a type of deceptive shadow of prophecy from the enemy. This is when a person tries to take power into their own hands for earthly purposes that exclude God. When someone is involved in witchcraft, they are consulting with demons and fallen angels. When someone is involved in prophecy, they are consulting God Himself.

Many Christians teach that the gift of prophecy is being able to apply the Bible and God's teaching into their own lives and instruct others to do the same. I do believe that is a type of prophecy but it does not end there. Again, that would be something any one of us have access to at any given time. At any time I can pick up the Bible, look up a verse, read it, and gain insight from it. If there is something that I do not understand, I always have the option of asking a pastor or other spiritual leader who can guide me through it. While this is a great thing to do that we should all be doing in our daily lives, there is nothing that sets that apart as a gift that only comes from the Holy Spirit.

For example, when John wrote the book of Revelation, he was not given that information by his own accord. He was not actively seeking to learn what the last days would be like. He was praying and, by power of the Holy Spirit, had a conversation with Jesus, was caught up to Heaven, and was made aware of things God wanted the world to know. John did not receive the knowledge of the events recorded in Revelation by reading earlier scripture, interpreting it, and applying it to his life. He was given the entire book of Revelation by divine inspiration of God.

Prophecy can come by many different ways. It can be a voice, a feeling, a thought, or a simple revelation. Though it can be controversial throughout the Church, the gift of prophecy can also manifest as a dream or a vision. The importance of dreams and visions cannot be ignored. God has always talked to His people through dreams and visions. Today is no different. We can get our battle plans from our Commander, as well as other things, through properly interpreted dreams and visions. Sometimes God will use a dream or vision to give us insight on His Word or His feelings.

One of the strongest manifestations of the Holy Spirit I ever experienced came in the form of a vision. I didn't specifically ask for a vision prior to the experience, but I had made it known to God in the past that I would be open to receive anything He had for me. When the vision came upon me, I wasn't praying, fasting, or even expecting any kind of spiritual experience. God just decided He wanted me to see something, so He showed me.

I was lying in bed with the television on, just about to go to bed for the night, and I was immediately caught up to what looked like the inside of an auditorium. There was a group of about fifteen or twenty other people around me and we were all facing a brightly-lit stage. A person, be he a man or angel, I don't know, was speaking from behind a podium in the middle of the stage.

Through this whole experience, there were certain facts that were left out and not revealed to me. There are a couple of details from the experience that I was not made aware of. Without proper clarification, these missing details could make it more difficult to describe the events. To minimize confusion, a couple of substitutions must be made.

Concerning the person on stage behind the podium, his name was never revealed to me so, for our purposes here as well as maintaining clarity, I will refer to him as the

Preacher from here on out. He was preaching a message in the same fashion a pastor in a church would so calling him by the title of Preacher would be accurate. Also, I cannot remember the exact wording of everything the Preacher spoke so I will have to paraphrase.

The Preacher was telling us about God and Adam in the Garden of Eden. He was detailing a conversation that God had with Adam right after Adam sinned. The Preacher told us how God, with a broken heart, had explained to Adam what the consequences of sin would be. God, through unexplainable sorrow, was telling Adam that he would have to die.

The Preacher then told us that God was explaining to Adam the physical and spiritual consequences of sin in detail. God was telling Adam that his sin would not only result in his physical death, but would also result in his spiritual death. Then the Preacher said something truly profound. He said...

"Then God told Adam that He loved him so much, He would rather lie down and die with him than be eternally separated from him. God Himself would rather die than lose Adam forever."

At this point, the Preacher paused briefly as all of us in the audience waited expectantly for what he would say next. The Preacher then looked at us, smiled lovingly with a tears forming in his eyes, and said…

"And that is exactly what He did on the cross."

At that exact moment, all of us in the audience burst out in tears, began weeping with joy, praising with outstretched arms, and worshipping God with the most absolutely pure love I had ever experienced.

Never before that moment had I felt and understood the absolute depth of God's love, not only for Adam, but for every person on Earth. Of course, I had originally heard the story we are all familiar with from the book of Genesis many times before, but had never heard it from that perspective. Hearing that Heavenly teaching was completely, totally, and wholeheartedly incredible, yet still utterly indescribable. I will never be able to adequately explain what the whole experience did to and for me. It was then, in that Heavenly place, that I fully understood how much God truly loves me.

The weeping, praising, and worshipping went on for a short time before I felt myself start to get pulled back. I did not want to leave because I knew I would not be able to retain the complete overflow of emotion and love I was feeling. I knew I would be able to bring back the memory of what happened, but not the absolute fullness of emotion.

The sensation of being pulled back is a bit difficult to explain. I suppose I would describe it as feeling increasingly condensed or becoming more solid the further I was pulled. The thicker, or more solid, I felt, the more I lost of the ability to feel the fullness of emotion. When I was finally back, the first thing I realized was I felt as if I were a brick wall blocking the fullness of emotion. I felt like I was too solid for anything but a small percentage of that flowing love and emotion to get through.

I realized that, even in our deepest times of worship, even during those times we feel the love of God so powerfully that we feel like we can't handle anymore, the strongest and most fulfilling feelings we can experience on Earth in our physical bodies are nothing but a miniscule window, only letting in a minute percentage of what is waiting for us in Heaven. I don't know if it is our physicality, our sin, the fallen world, or all three that keeps out the vast majority of Heavenly emotion and love. Whatever the exact cause, when I returned from the experience, it just felt like I was too dense, thick, solid, squeezed, and condensed to be able to take in more than a very small amount. There is something about physical reality that shuts out a lot of Heavenly things, keeping them hidden and secret from us.

I think doubt and unbelief plays a large part in shutting out Heavenly things as well. All we have to do is read in the Bible about the Pharisees in Jesus' time and apply it to our modern day. There are many Christians who would hear or read a detailed account of a vision, such as what I have disclosed here, and automatically assume it was only a dream, imagination, hallucination, demonic deception, or flat-out lie. There was a time, early in my life, when I would have felt that same way.

Many years ago, my Christian life and walk with God were completely different than now. I used to have a very doubting heart and unbelieving spirit. I didn't believe in that type of power of the Holy Spirit or that it would ever manifest that way in our time. I didn't believe the gifts of the Holy Spirit ever went beyond Jesus' day and into our modern day. I didn't believe any claims of supernatural manifestations from God were real and assumed they were all fraudulent.

I didn't believe in prophets. I didn't believe in visions. I didn't believe dreams had any real meaning. I didn't believe a person could actually hear the literal voice of God. I didn't believe in much of anything beyond what I was taught I had to believe in order to have salvation.

It took God a long time through a lot of patience to get through to me about the true power of His living Holy Spirit. It wasn't until I was willing to accept His Spirit for who He is that God began manifesting Himself in various ways. Now that I have experienced the Holy Spirit in the ways the Bible describes, I look back on how I used to be and shudder at the type of Christian I was.

I was spiritually asleep. I may have even been close to being spiritually dead. However, now that I am awake, I want to help other Christians wake up as well. One way I am attempting to do this is by sharing my testimony, experiences, and teachings through the writing and distribution of this book.

If you don't know or have never felt the power of the Holy Spirit, I would highly suggest spending some one-on-one time with God to ask Him about it. You should not just take my word for it. You should discuss it with God yourself. I hope and pray my testimony is enough to bring you to the point to, at the very least, ask God about it openly. What I am talking about is known as the *"Baptism of the Holy Spirit"* and is described many places in the Bible. I can say from personal experience, now that I know the truth of the Holy Spirit and have felt His power, I will never turn back. Truthfully, looking back, I don't know how I ever got along without Him (I say "Him" because the Holy Spirit is one of the Persons of the Holy Trinity of God, just as is Jesus the Son and God the Father).

It is a deeply personal and intimate experience that every Christian who has a relationship with God through Jesus should know. Walking with God by being saved through Jesus is a wonderful thing but is incomplete without the Holy Spirit. Welcoming in that last Third of the Trinity of God, the Holy Spirit, completes the fullness of the relationship with God and adds an amazing experience.

The experience in no way is lifted above the relationship. The experiences that come through the power of the Holy Spirit enhance and strengthen the relationship with God. The relationship still comes first before the experience, though they both complement each other. For me, the added experience has become one with the existing relationship. I wouldn't trade it for anything.

I have only had a handful of visions in my life and the one I shared here was undoubtedly the most profound and indescribable of all thus far. I can recall the events, sights, people, and words spoken but it pretty much stops there. I know *of* the feelings I felt but I am not able to fully retain the experience in my physical state of being. I am incredibly blessed that God allowed me to bring enough it back that I still get choked up when I think or talk about it.

To conclude my testimony of this Heavenly experience, I will say that there is no way I can put into words what hearing that message on the other side did for my understanding of God's love. I remember the teaching in principal and application into history. Even more than that, I have retained enough of the emotion to be able to say, truthfully and without speculation, that it was the most powerful sermon I have ever, or will ever hear in this life.

Getting back to our teaching on prophecy, the Bible is full of examples and instructions for receiving and interpreting dreams and visions. God can choose to make it subtle, as Job 33:14-15 explains and 1 Samuel 3:1-10 illustrates. Sometimes we choose to shut out God through doubt, unbelief, or our own inner voice. Instead of only seeking out God in all the outside aspects of our lives, we need to learn from Elijah in 1 Kings 19:11-13 and realize that sometimes God is merely a voice trying to speak to us softly. We need to learn to listen to Jesus who dwells in us.

The belief that there are no more prophets and God does not honor the gift of prophecy anymore holds no water. I believe this is yet another attack from the enemy in an attempt to cause the Church to fall into unbelief. It is absolutely true that the Bible tells us what is on the road ahead prophetically. Also, it tells us how to prepare for these events.

What the Bible does not tell us, however, is that the gift of prophecy is dead and that God is finished with prophets. If that were the case then I would say, with all the writings of Paul in the book of 1 Corinthians, the Bible could be considered quite misleading. Paul puts extensive importance on the gift of prophecy and gave many reasons why. In 1 Corinthians 14:24-25, Paul said…

"But if all prophesy, and there come in one that believeth not, or one unlearned, he is convinced of all, he is judged of all: And thus are the secrets of his heart made manifest; and so falling down on his face he will worship God, and report that God is in you of a truth."

As described here, the gift of prophecy is so strong that it can make an unbeliever fall on his face and worship God because the secrets of his heart are made known. This is what the gift of prophecy from the Holy Spirit can do. The gift of prophecy can give you direction through a person's heart, tell you the secrets that person is keeping, and be able to manifest those secrets to the person as proof that God is real and working through the members of the Church. This is comparable to when Jesus was talking with the Samaritan woman at the well and told her the secrets of her heart. She left that encounter knowing without a doubt that Jesus was the Son of God.

Prophecy is a gift, along with the others, that is under heavy spiritual attack. There have been many false prophets and failed prophecies throughout the years. Jesus warned us of this, though, and we know how to detect the frauds. All we have to do is test the prophet and prophecy against scripture. If it conflicts, then we keep the Bible and throw the prophecy, as well as the prophet, out.

A true prophet will be correct and accurate every single time he utters a prophecy. Anything less cannot be of God. We are told this in the Bible. Deuteronomy 18:20-22 tell us that a true prophet of God and his prophecies will come to pass as he said it would. Deuteronomy 13:1-3 tells us that if the prophecy comes to pass, yet the prophet gives credit to something else other than God, then we are not to follow that prophet or his prophecies. We have specific rules throughout the Bible instructing us exactly how to handle prophecy and prophets, correctly discern if they are of God or the devil, and properly utilize the methods on how to handle it in either case.

I believe that God gives us personal prophecies as well, such as what job to take, who to marry, or where to live. God is a deeply personal and loving God. He wants to speak with us, which is why He spent so much time in the Bible telling us how to approach Him.

Our God is not a phantom. He is there to listen, as well as speak, to us. Just because there are frauds out there does not mean we should not try and grab hold of the real thing. We must not allow Satan to take this gift away from us. It is too important to lose.

We need God's personal direction to get us through our lives on this planet. Again, God is a gentleman and He will not force us to accept Him. We can choose to shut our ears to His voice, literally and figuratively, if that's what we want to do.

Jesus said many times throughout the book of Revelation *"He that hath an ear, let him hear what the Spirit saith unto the churches"*. This is in regard to the letters to the seven churches but it also shows us another important point. The Holy Spirit was speaking to the churches. Jesus didn't say *"who has eyes to read, let him read the letters I told John to write"*. Jesus said that if we have an ear for it, if we are open to hearing Him, then the Holy Spirit will speak to us. We should all embrace prophecy for the wonderful gift of the Holy Spirit that it is.

DISCERNING OF SPIRITS

The word *"discerning"* comes from the Greek word *"diakrisis"* meaning *"judicial estimation"*. The word *"spirits"* as used here comes from the Greek word *"pneuma"* meaning *"a current of air, i.e. breath (blast) or a breeze; by analogy or figuratively a spirit, i.e. (human) the rational soul, (by implication) vital principal, mental disposition, etc., or (superhuman) an angel, daemon, or (divine) God, Christ's spirit, the Holy Spirit"*. So here we have a little of everything.

The gift of being able to discern spirits includes being able to tell if something is of God or Satan, what someone's intentions are, or if someone or something is in right standing with the will of God, as well as others. Discerning spirits is a powerful gift to have as there are many gray areas in life that need direct instruction from God to get through. This is not only being able to discern what the Holy Spirit is telling someone, but also being able to discern other spirits, whether human or angelic, and knowing what their true motivation is.

This is another incredibly important gift to understand and have as it will be crucial in keeping us out of deception. We are told to test the spirits and how to do so (1 John 4:1-4), which is something any of us has the ability to do at any given time. The gift of discerning spirits is set apart as a divine manifestation of the Holy Spirit within one's own spirit to know directly the motivations of other spirits.

This can be used to know the spirit behind a person's actions, the very spirit of the person, or even an angelic spirit. It can tell us if the source is something demonic or heavenly. This is our way to escape deception. The most evil spirit in the world can still lie and say it is coming out of love, but with this gift of direct inspiration of the Holy Spirit, we can see through the facade and expose the spirit for what it truly is.

TONGUES AND INTERPRETATION OF TONGUES

I am grouping these two gifts together because they go hand in hand as they pertain to the same phenomena. This is, at least in my experience, perhaps the most attacked out of all of the nine gifts of the Holy Spirit. I have heard people calling this gift everything from a misinterpretation to a lie from the devil.

Fortunately for those of us who accept it, this is one of those cases that the Bible does an incredibly good job of interpreting itself. Unfortunately for the entire Church, many Christians still have a difficult time acknowledging it for what it is. I was in this boat years and years ago. I never really understood what the gift of tongues was until I read Paul's words for myself and allowed myself to understand their meaning. This was definitely one of those situations where I had to cast aside my traditional teachings for biblical truth.

The word for *"tongues"*, as used in the passages we will be exploring, is from the Greek word *"glossa"* meaning *"of uncertain affinity; the tongue; by implication of a language (specifically one not acquired naturally)"*. This is a completely different word than the other Greek word for *"tongue"* which is *"heteroglossos"* meaning *"other-tongued, i.e. a foreigner"*. There is only one time in the book of 1 Corinthians that the Greek word *"heteroglossos"*, meaning a foreign language, is used for the English word *"tongues"*. 1 Corinthians 14:21 reads...

"In the law it is written, With men of other tongues and other lips will I speak unto this people; and yet for all that will they not hear me, saith the Lord."

This verse is debatable in the proper interpretation of the meaning of *"tongues"*. Some say it is spiritual and some say it is physical. Either way, we do not need this verse specifically to prove the legitimacy of the gift of tongues. There are many more that have very concrete and specific interpretations that leave very little room for error.

Every other time the word *"tongue"* or *"tongues"* is used in 1 Corinthians, it is from the Greek word *"glossa"*. This tells us that the gift of tongues is not merely being able to learn and speak in different languages. If this was the case, the word *"heteroglossos"* would be used, and you would have to explain a lot of conflicting scripture that would create.

The gift of tongues is the gift of being able to speak earthly and heavenly languages. Sometimes this gift will supernaturally manifest in the way of someone speaking a language they have no knowledge of to be able to witness or minister to a foreigner. Sometimes this gift will manifest in the way of someone speaking a heavenly language. Paul said in 1 Corinthians 13:1…

"Though I speak with the tongues of men and of angels, and have not charity, I am becoming as sounding brass, or a tinkling cymbal."

Paul is speaking of the importance of charity here but one thing is made clear. There exist tongues of men and of angels. The gift of tongues and the gift of the interpretation of tongues is the gift to speak in and interpret this angelic language.

I know this causes a lot of controversy in a lot of different ways. Some Christians will say it only means natural and earthly languages. Some will say it only means being able to speak natural and earthly languages supernaturally. Some will say it is only an angelic language. Some say it is a prayer language. Some say you must speak in supernatural tongues to be saved. Some throw the whole thing out and say speaking in tongues is of the devil.

What we need to do with each of these viewpoints is compare them with scripture, see which ones we can keep, and throw away the ones that conflict. Paul is very extensive in explaining all aspects of the gift of tongues. If we can set aside our preconceived notions and prejudices by letting the Bible speak for itself, then the information presented here should clear up a lot of confusion.

Some Christians say the gift of tongues means only natural and earthly languages that are learned naturally and not inspired supernaturally. To address this, the best place to go is the beginning, when the gift of tongues first manifested. Acts 2:4-6 reads...

"And they were all filled with the Holy Ghost, and began to speak with other tongues, as the Spirit gave them utterance. And there were dwelling at Jerusalem Jews, devout men, out of every nation under heaven. Now when this was noised abroad, the multitude came together, and were

confounded, because that every man heard them speak in his own language."

We can plainly see here that this was a supernatural event. The Holy Spirit came down and those who received it were able to speak a tongue that everyone else could understand in their own language. From this verse we can at least understand that the gift of tongues is a supernatural gift of the Holy Spirit that, at the very least, pertains to the languages of men.

Some Christians will accept that this happened back then and it was supernatural, but it is not in effect now, and even if it was, it certainly would not manifest in an angelic language that nobody can understand. To address this issue, we need to go no further than the book of 1 Corinthians. First, remember what Paul said in 1 Corinthians 13:1, that there is an angelic language. This angelic language is not naturally known by man and is not of the earthly languages. 1 Corinthians 14:2 states…

"For he that speaketh in an unknown tongue speaketh not unto men, but unto God: for no man understandeth him; howbeit in the spirit he speaketh mysteries."

Paul clearly explains what the unknown tongue is. It is a language that is not meant for men, but used to speak directly to God, and comes from the Holy Spirit. It plainly says that no man can understand this language.

This would exclude all earthly languages because for all earthly languages there is a man that can speak it. The idea that this is speaking of an earthly language just does not fit and one would have to twist scripture to attempt to force it in. In 1 Corinthians 14:23, Paul says…

"If therefore the whole church be come together into one place, and all speak with tongues, and there come in those that are unlearned, or unbeliever, will they not say that ye are mad?"

If the gift of tongues was only a supernatural ability to speak an earthly language, why would Paul be concerned of unbelievers thinking those who spoke in tongues were mad? If that is what the entire gift was, the unbeliever would just hear what is being said in his own language and would not think the church was crazy but would probably just think that they know how to speak other languages. Why would they think the members of the church were mad?

On the other hand, if a person is an unbeliever and knows nothing of the gift of tongues and he goes into a church where everyone seems to be babbling incoherently, then I could see that person thinking the members of the church are crazy. We can think of scenarios like that to help understand what God is trying to teach us. We have to use common sense and allow the Bible to interpret itself for us.

For the benefit of the curious unbeliever walking into a church, so as to not think the congregation is completely crazy and thereby turning them off to God, Paul laid out some very precise rules and instruction on how to handle the gift of tongues within a church. 1 Corinthians 14:27-28 reads…

"If any man speak in an unknown tongue, let it be by two, or at the most by three, and that by course; and let one interpret. But if there be no interpreter, let him keep silence in the church; and let him speak to himself, and to God."

It doesn't make sense to have an interpreter of tongues if the gift of tongues is only speaking in a language that everyone can understand.

Again, we must let the Bible interpret itself and use common sense. To keep the standpoint that this is only speaking of earthly languages, even saying it is supernaturally inspired, is to twist the Word of God to fit your own beliefs. We must not fit the Bible around our beliefs. We must fit our beliefs around the Bible.

There is also the viewpoint that the gift of supernatural tongues was present in Paul and the other apostles, but was not present in anyone else, and it died off with the apostles. If that were the case, it would have been pointless for Paul to give clear direction on how the gift of tongues and interpretation of tongues should be handled within a church. We would not need that information, if that were the case, meaning there are parts of the Bible that are meaningless to us and not applicable in our lives. Would you be so quick to say there are parts of the Bible that are useless and meaningless? I know I wouldn't and I would not expect any member of the Church to take such a stance just to try and prove themselves right.

There are Christians who accept the gift of tongues for what it is but say that you must speak in tongues to be truly saved. This is absolutely not the case and Jesus never claimed the gift of tongues as a prerequisite for salvation. Paul said in 1 Corinthians 12:29-30…

"Are all apostles? are all prophets? are all teachers? are all workers of miracles? Have all the gifts of healing? do all speak with tongues? do all interpret?"

1 Corinthians 14:4 states…

"He that speaketh in an unknown tongue edifieth himself; but he that prophesieth edifieth the church."

Paul is making a clear distinction here. Some Christians have certain gifts that others don't. Some Christians speak in tongues and other Christians prophesy.

There are many gifts that God can give us but that doesn't mean we will all have every single one all of the time. Some Christians simply will not have the gift of tongues and that is okay. It has nothing to do with their salvation. Nowhere in the Bible does it say a person must speak in tongues to truly be saved.

John 3:16 clearly explains what it takes to be saved and tongues is nowhere to be found. To believe a person must speak in tongues to have salvation would be to believe that the apostles were not truly saved until they received the gift of tongues. That would mean that the thief on the cross next to Jesus was not truly saved because he did not speak in tongues making Jesus a liar. Again, we have to use common sense, look where the logic of doctrines lead, and properly discern the interpretations and true meanings of the Bible's teachings, regardless of what our traditional beliefs and preconceived notions might be.

There are also Christians, which now is appalling to me, who claim that speaking in tongues is of the devil. As I said before, I believe saying things like this is flirting with the unpardonable sin. Now, I don't necessarily believe if someone believes this out of ignorance they are going to Hell. I do believe, if it is even possible for a Christian, that to commit the unpardonable sin would take a great deal of conscious rebellion against God and a hardened heart that is full of hate.

Speaking in tongues and interpretation of tongues are two of the nine gifts of the Holy Spirit, pure and simple. They are something we can utilize if we want to and if God allows it but it is not something we have to take part in. Of course, if God is directing us then we should not fight it. Speaking in tongues is a gift that can also be incredibly edifying and can be used at any time in our personal lives.

Paul laid out some ground rules of how the gift of tongues should be utilized in a church and we should absolutely follow them. I have been to churches where the entire congregation would be shouting in tongues and it made even me uncomfortable. If it made me, an actively practicing Christian, uncomfortable, imagine what it would do to an unbeliever.

Paul's explanation of why not to do this can even be looked at as a prophetic message. Just look at what has happened as a result of churches not following Paul's instruction. I remember when I was a kid I would see television broadcasts of these churches that seemed to be completely insane and out of control. Because of this, it supported my family's belief that speaking in tongues was of the devil. I thought the same thing until I decided to test my traditional teaching against the Bible and read Paul's words for myself.

It is just as Paul said it would be and has even gone a step further. It is not only nonbelievers that think it's insane but it is believers as well. My family and I thought they were crazy and even possessed. Now there is a division in the Church concerning this issue.

The enemy is really good at keeping people riled up and focused on this issue instead of the really important ones. I have seen so much outrage from members of the Church concerning issues like speaking in tongues, the rapture, and other beliefs that have nothing to do with salvation or God's will for the Church. Why isn't there that kind of outrage against abortion, or false religions, or Christian-based hate crimes? I'm not saying we should be screaming, yelling, and throwing out hate at anyone, but if we put the energy we spend on fighting about difference of beliefs within the Church into spreading the Word of God, fixing this broken world, and destroying the works of Satan, then we would really be on the right track toward expanding God's kingdom and the Church.

If you have any other questions or concerns about the gift of tongues, I would suggest reading the entire book of 1 Corinthians with an open and unbiased mind. Ask God to show you the truth. Let Him interpret it for you. Once you can grasp what it really is, 1 Corinthians is an incredibly easy book to read and understand. However, if you go into it with a preconceived notion that is contrary to what Paul is talking about, you will have an extremely difficult time forcing your personal convictions and beliefs to fit.

People can believe different things than others, which is not wrong, as long as they do not conflict with the Bible. We need to allow people to have differences in beliefs under God. We are all human, we are all flawed, none of us will ever know everything, and any one of us could be mistaken. We should all be praying for each other at that point. Don't let this issue cause a division in the Church. Paul says in 1 Corinthians 14:38-40…

"But if any man be ignorant, let him be ignorant. Wherefore, brethren, covet to prophesy, and forbid not to speak with tongues. Let all things be done decently and in order."

CONCLUSION

We have to accept that we are in a war against Satan and his angels. We need all the weapons we can get. We have an infinitely powerful Commander in this war, Jesus Christ, and He has equipped us with all of the tools and weapons we need to defeat Satan and destroy all of his works. We even have a manual to teach us how all of these weapons and tools work.

We should be spending our time learning about the weapons we have at our disposal and the devices of the enemy so we can be better prepared. We need to learn to let God guide us through this time and throughout our entire lives so we can claim the victory with Him. We need to learn how to not let the enemy infiltrate the Church which is our base of operations.

We need to learn to work together as a single army. We all have different positions, different talents, and different jobs, but we are all working toward the same goal. We must embrace that and not let the enemy bring about division within the Church.

If we are divided against ourselves then we cannot stand. The enemy knows this and has already been putting it in practice. We must choose to fight against the enemy instead of fighting amongst ourselves. We need to embrace the gifts that the Holy Spirit brings to us and learn to put them into practice. We must not go into this war unarmed.

Most importantly, we need to learn to let Jesus Christ do His job as our Leader. We need to not get in His way. Embrace His leadership, follow His plan, accept His weapons of choice, trust His guidance, assist in His goals, give Him our lives, and let's fight beside Him to destroy the works of Satan.

Chapter 10

SPIRITUAL WARFARE

It is important to accurately know the facts about the war we are in. We must know what we are up against and how to fight the battles to claim victory of the war. A vital element of this is to know what the Bible teaches about spiritual battles and how to overcome them. God has given us many weapons to use in our individual battles, but they do us no good if we don't know who we are supposed to be fighting against.

The Bible tells us that people are not our enemy. Satan, his angels, and every evil spirit are our true enemy. We can look at other people, especially unbelievers, as prisoners of war. The enemy has deceived them into a prison of doubt, denial, fear, unbelief, pain, and personal pride. One way we can claim them back to our side is by individual and group prayer. We gain a greater chance at winning souls through intercession. The same approach can be taken with Christians who have fallen away from the faith.

We need to know what the Bible says about spiritual warfare. It is important to apply certain things in our daily lives to defend ourselves against the enemy. If we are caught in a spiritual battle, we not only need to know how to defend ourselves but we also need to know the proper offensive attacks against the enemy. The Bible makes it clear for us how to engage in any kind of spiritual warfare as well as how to claim victory.

KNOWING THE ENEMY

To know how to have victory in our spiritual battles, we need to know who we are fighting against. We need to know who the true enemy is. I will go into this further and more specifically in the following chapters, but for now we need a foundation to work from. Paul gives us a perfect basic layout of the true enemy we need to contend with. In Ephesians 6:12, Paul tells us…

"For we wrestle not against flesh and blood, but against principalities, against powers, against the rulers of the darkness of this world, against spiritual wickedness in high places."

We first are told that our battle is not against flesh and blood. People aren't the problem. The enemy has done a great job at causing division within the Church. We have Christian brothers and sisters focused on arguing about things like the timing of the rapture, the age of the Earth, and many other trivial issues of opinion. Paul is telling us that we should not be fighting against other people, especially other Christians. We should be unified, regardless of personal opinions, against all of the things Paul listed out for us. To gain a deeper understanding of what we are up against, we can look to the original Greek language used within the text.

The word *"principalities"* comes from the Greek word *"arche"* and means *"a commencement or chief"* such as *"magistrate, power, rule"*. The word *"powers"* comes from the word *"exousia"* meaning *"mastery, superhuman, influence"*. The word *"rulers"* comes from *"kosmokrator"* meaning *"a world-ruler, an epithet of Satan"*. The word *"darkness"* comes from *"skotos"* meaning *"shadiness i.e. obscurity"*. The word *"world"* comes from *"aion"* meaning *"age"*. The word *"wickedness"* comes from *"poneria"* meaning *"depravity, malice, plots, sins"*. Lastly, the word *"high"* comes from the Greek word *"epouranios"* meaning *"above the sky"* such as *"celestial, heaven, heavenly"*.

At first glance, that may seem like a lot to take in and study. It can all be summed up by realizing what the words all have in common. They are all spiritual, not physical, and they are all in reference to malevolence. In the way Paul used these descriptive titles, they are all satanic groups. They can all be looked at as different branches of a spiritual government controlled by Satan.

The principalities would be the highest rank, either including or directly under Satan himself. The powers would include demons, possessing spirits, the spirit of the Nephilim, and even the Nephilim themselves, be they ancient or modern-day. The rulers of the darkness of this world would be the spirits of deception that closely follow Satan's tactics in obfuscating truth, propagating lies, and making falsehoods attractive in our dispensation of time.

Lastly, the spiritual wickedness in high places would be the lies, sins, and false doctrines themselves that are spread by satanic forces and deprave people of a true relationship with God.

All of these things plot out the enemy's structure, purpose, and tactics that make up the government of Satan. The government's structure is purely spiritual and evil in origin. The purpose of this government is to bring about the complete destruction of all of humanity, physically and spiritually. The tactics used to achieve this goal are lies, deceit, doubt, unbelief, and various temptations to keep us living a life of sin. This is our enemy. The satanic government is an evil, spiritual empire put in place to destroy us with deceptive lies and temptations of sin.

Other people aren't the problem. With the right information and training, other people can become a part of the solution. One lie the enemy will use time and time again is that our war is against unbelievers or backslid Christians. The enemy knows if he can keep us divided, we will eventually fall into destruction. We cannot allow that to happen.

We must endure the enemy until the end. We must continue to fight against the devil and his devices until our

Great Commander returns. We must battle Satan and his angels until the glorious appearing of our Savior, the Lord of Lords and King of Kings, Jesus Christ.

WEAPONS AND ARMOR

Now that we know our true enemy, we need to understand the tools at our disposal. The enemy will bring about all sorts of different battles into our lives. The fortunate thing is that the enemy has no new tricks or devices. Satan might repackage his old tricks but at the core they are still the same tactics he used in the Garden of Eden. We know there is nothing that is truly new (Ecclesiastes 1:9). Time itself may be linear but the events in time are cyclical. In other words, history repeats itself.

Since Satan and his angels have nothing truly new to use against us, only new ways to present their old devices, their tactics are predictable. The Bible gives us many examples to go by. If we want to know what the enemy is going to do in our lives, we only need to look at the accounts of spiritual battles in the Bible.

Though we call them *"spiritual battles"*, that does not mean they will only be spiritual in effect. We call them *"spiritual battles"* because the battles are from a spiritual force working against us. Most times, they will manifest to us in physical ways. Paul wrote about his various battles in 2 Corinthians 11:24-28 which reads,

"Of the Jews five times received I forty stripes save one. Thrice was I beaten with rods, once I was stoned, thrice suffered shipwreck, a night and a day I have been in the deep; In journeyings often, in perils of waters, in perils of robbers, in perils by mine own countrymen, in perils by the heathen, in perils in the city, in perils in the wilderness, in perils in the sea, in perils among false brethren; In weariness and painfulness, in watchings often, in hunger and thirst, in fastings often, in cold and nakedness. Beside those things that are without, that which cometh upon me daily, the care of all the churches."

Spiritual battles almost always manifest in physical ways. In this passage, we are given a key to success no matter how bad any spiritual battle may get. After Paul listed out the various obstacles he had while trying to spread the gospel, he pointed out a solution. He made reference to *"the care of all the churches"*. All of the churches that are giving Paul care would be included in the Body of Christ. Paul is telling us here, as well as many other places, that fellowship among Christians and having an active Church-life is a great way to combat the enemy. One of the most effective weapons we have against Satan is each other. There truly is strength in numbers.

Paul spoke extensively about overcoming spiritual battles on a personal level as well. We read in Ephesians 6:13-18...

"Wherefore take unto you the whole armour of God, that ye may be able to withstand in the evil day, and having done all, to stand. Stand therefore, having your loins girt about with truth, and having on the breastplate of righteousness; And your feet shod with the preparation of the gospel of peace; Above all, taking the shield of faith, wherewith ye shall be able to quench all the fiery darts of the wicked. And take the helmet of salvation, and the sword of the Spirit, which is the word of God: Praying always with all prayer and supplication in the Spirit, and watching thereunto with all perseverance and supplication for all saints."

These are our daily defensive and offensive weapons. We have truth, righteousness, the gospel of peace, faith, salvation, the Word of God, and prayer. Those seven things that make up our armor will ensure a victory over any battle if we utilize them properly.

We must be rooted in truth. This comes from God Himself through His Word. This is how we know the tactics of the enemy and the tools at his disposal. This is how we know what to do when any problem arises. We can't fall into the enemy's lies.

We must be actively practicing in righteousness. This means a right-standing with God. Our hearts have to be right with God. We can't let ourselves get caught up in continuing to live carnal and sinful lives.

We must have the preparation of the gospel of peace. We must be ready to share the gospel at any given time. We must also use the gospel for our own edification and growth by keeping it prepared in our minds. We must always be ready to proclaim the gospel and the promises of God. We cannot fall into any doctrines of devils.

We must have faith in God. We may not always know what He is doing or why but we need to trust Him. We have to have faith that He will make good on His promises. We need to have faith that the Bible is completely accurate and that everything God has said through His Word is true. We must not allow ourselves to fall into spiritual or physical doubt that comes in the form of fiery darts from the enemy.

We have to know and have assurance in our salvation. We can't allow ourselves to find comfort in false teachings. We have to discover what true salvation is and allow God to lead us in it. We must allow ourselves to find true salvation through God's truth instead of the enemy's lies.

We have to know what's in our Bibles. We have to know and understand God's Word. This is our main offensive weapon. When Jesus was being tempted by Satan in the wilderness, He quoted scripture to fend him off. We know this was successful because every time Jesus quoted scripture, Satan had to leave for a while and come back again later. The Word of God is our main weapon against our enemy. We must not let the enemy keep us out of our Bibles.

Lastly, we need to know how to pray. We need to have an active prayer life for ourselves and our Christian brothers and sisters. We shouldn't only be asking God for things we need but we should also be giving Him praise and thanks for everything He has done for us. We must keep an open communication with our Great Commander. We must not let Satan intercept our prayers or interfere with our prayer life.

Those are the main weapons and armor God has given us against the enemy. If we can become informed and trained in those seven things, there is nothing the enemy can throw at us that we can't handle. We need to be united as a collective Church under Jesus Christ against the enemy. We must follow Paul's instruction. Ephesians 6:10-11 reads...

"Finally, my brethren, be strong in the Lord, and in the power of his might. Put on the whole armour of God, that ye may be able to stand against the wiles of the devil."

We have the power of God at our disposal; we just need to know how to use it. The power, strength, and might of God are in the form of His armor that He has provided for us. We will never be able to stand against our enemy without it.

We need to put on the whole armor of God daily and not just bits and pieces occasionally. We need to be prepared always, even when things are going good. We should not wait until we have a problem to utilize God's armor. We live in a battlefield with a constant war waging around us. We must always have on our armor. That is how we overcome any spiritual battle. The more practice and experience we can have in proper spiritual warfare, the stronger the entire Body of Christ will be.

To close out this section, though it is not mentioned specifically in Paul's list of the armor of God, we have another very powerful weapon at our disposal. This weapon is our tongue. Proverbs 18:21 states…

"Death and life are in the power of the tongue: and they that love it shall eat the fruit thereof."

We need to be aware of the things we say. We have the power to speak curses or blessings into our life even to the point of life and death. Though there are many alternate weapons described throughout the Bible, I want to focus on this one because of the importance of its power.

Most of us don't really pay much attention to the kinds of things we say and the words we use in day to day life. This is not only merely about being optimistic or pessimistic. We can look at it in another way.

The absolute pinnacle of Satan's power is causing death. God's ultimate power is life. Proverbs 18:21 is telling us that death, life, and everything between are in the power of the tongue. The tongue's power is its ability to speak for us. Depending on what we speak, we can bring death or life into our lives or the lives of the people we are involved with. This is why prayer, praise, and worship are such strong tools in our lives.

When we pray, we are speaking directly to God. When we praise, we are giving God the glory He deserves. When we worship, we are expressing how much we love God. When we put these three things together, we can really get a sense of how powerful the tongue truly is. These are three things we can use to speak blessings into our lives in accordance with the will of God.

We have to watch out so as to not speak curses in our lives. Many times, when people become angry, they will say things they really don't mean. The recipient of the things being said can be hurt, even utterly destroyed emotionally, sometimes for their entire lives. This also depends on who it is, the relationship they share, and the emotional fragility of the recipient. Regardless, the fact still remains, if those curses were never spoken, the recipient would not have been hurt in that way.

One lie from the enemy came to humanity in the form of an innocent sounding children's rhyme. It goes…

"Sticks and stones may break my bones but words will never hurt me."

Parents will teach this to their children as an attempt of making them emotionally stronger so verbal abuse will not hurt their feelings.

I remember saying this as a kid when I was bullied. While saying that rhyme may have given me the appearance of a child who didn't care about the words that were being spoken, it did not change how I felt on the inside. It still hurt and I didn't know how to deal with the aftermath.

Rhymes like that are just examples of the attitude many of us have toward verbal abuse in our culture. Instead of being taught the proper measures to be taken against a verbal abuser, we are basically taught to just ignore it and eventually it will go away. The problem is that it is not going away. Verbal abuse, as well as all abuse, is getting worse as time goes on. There are no benefits to allowing verbal abuse to carry on. All that is doing is allowing more curses to be spoken into our lives.

However, if we can learn to speak blessings against the curses, then we have learned a very powerful strategy in winning our personal battles. When someone speaks a curse of any form against us, we should either speak a blessing toward them personally and immediately, or later when we are away from that person. It is a difficult thing to put into practice but is incredibly powerful when we do.

I know that might sound foolish at first, but there is real validity there. When I first heard of this, I didn't really believe it either but I can say that it truly does work. Jesus said in Luke 6:27-28...

"But I say unto you which hear, Love your enemies, do good to them which hate you, Bless them that curse you, and pray for them which despitefully use you."

We have to consider the origin of the reason why a person would speak curses against us. They are being manipulated by the enemy. These people are just carriers of Satan's curses against us.

They may have been abused in their past or just be an angry person but the root cause will always lead back to Satan. This is why we have to look at people who curse others as cursed themselves. They are prisoners of war and not our true enemies. They are being used by Satan.

Our true enemy is Satan, including every evil spirit under him. Satan is just trying to use other people as his weapons and carriers of his tactics. If those people really knew what was going on and truly understood how they were being used, they would never speak curses against anybody. This is why Jesus told us the right way to handle those who curse us.

Jesus instructed us how to treat our human enemies in the right way, regardless how they are treating us. We must pray for them and speak blessings into their lives as well as our own. This will also bring forgiveness into our hearts and cast out hate, anger, pain, sorrow, and resentment. As the book of Proverbs discloses to us, death and life truly are in the power of the tongue.

CONCLUSION

There are three main things we need to be aware of to be able to claim victory of the war. First, we need to acknowledge and understand the war we are living in. Second, we need to know who our enemy is and his tactics so we know who our true battle is against. Third, we need to have a deep understanding of the tools, weapons, and armor we are to use to fight against the enemy effectively. Once we understand the war, our enemy, and our weapons, we will know our advantages, the enemy's weaknesses, and everything we need to do in order to claim victory in the war.

We need to recognize the Lordship and leadership of our Savior. Jesus Christ, our Great Commander, will absolutely lead us in our collective and personal battles if we allow Him. He made that clear in His sermon on the mount. In Matthew 7:7-8, Jesus tells us…

"Ask, and it shall be given you; seek, and ye shall find; knock, and it shall be opened unto you: For every one that asketh receiveth; and he that seeketh findeth; and to him that knocketh it shall be opened."

Jesus is our supplier of all the things we need to make it through this life. He wants to help us be victorious over our enemy. All we have to do is ask God and He will always come through for us. It may not always be in the way we expect but it will always be for our greater good.

We do not need to completely understand God's ways to claim victory in the war. We do not need immediate full disclosure to fight and win our personal and collective spiritual battles. We only need to trust that He knows what He is doing and follow His instruction. We all need personal discipline to follow God's lead effectively. We need to cast aside the things the enemy will throw at us, such as pride, doubt, fear, and unbelief as well as many others. All we have to do to be successful is follow the commands of our Great Commander.

Jesus has already won the war. The war over Satan was won on the cross. Satan is upset about it and is trying to extend and continue the war. We know from the Word of God that all of Satan's efforts are done in vain to those who dedicate their lives to Jesus Christ. If we stay and fight with Jesus and learn His instruction, Satan can never claim victory over us or bring about our destruction.

All we have to do now is endure until the end. We have to overcome. We have to dig in our heels and remain with God's leadership until the return of our Savior. When Jesus Christ returns to this Earth at His appointed time, we can all claim the victory over Satan together. We should all be praying faithfully and waiting expectantly for that great day!

PART 3

PROPHETIC BATTLE PLANS AND SPIRITUAL REALITY

Chapter 11

INTERPRETING PROPHECY

I must say that I do not know all of what our future holds. I know and believe what is written in the Bible concerning the future. I also know that much of that biblical information is open to personal interpretation. It is wise for us to accept that nobody knows exactly what these last days are going to be like, but everybody has different ideas about it. We have to accept that, while many might be wrong, there are equally as many that might be right. If we can get past our own traditional beliefs and realize that they are only beliefs and not proven facts, then we can begin to accept other's beliefs as equal to our own. That is, of course, as long as they line up with scripture.

The third part of this book includes some of my personal beliefs of possible future events. I say "possible" because I realize that any one of these could turn out to be inaccurate. I believe we will gain more understanding of scripture and prophecy as time goes on. Once a prophecy is fulfilled and we can see how it is all playing out, then we will know for sure what the correct interpretation is. Until then, it is all speculative. I accept that some of my beliefs about the future may prove all or partially wrong. We should be prepared for all outcomes. We must get past our own prejudices and at least accept the possibility of a different viewpoint as long as it lines up with the Bible.

The problem is there are so many ideas about the future and so many different interpretations of scripture. I believe it is increasingly important for us to consider as many as we can and come to personal conclusions for each and every one. That way, when it turns out that one of those theories is coming into our reality, we can be prepared and know what to do.

THE RAPTURE EXAMPLE

What I am talking about and leading into can be illustrated with the various rapture theories. There are many different beliefs, viewpoints, and information concerning the rapture of the Church. Many views have solid biblical verses to back them up.

One disturbing fact is that sometimes people with one view about the rapture will call the other views heresy and treat such beliefs as damnable sins. I have even heard people say outright that other people are going to Hell if they have a different viewpoint. I must say that this is just downright wrong behavior against our Christian brothers and sisters. Heresy in the Church would be to deny Jesus as our Savior, His birth from a virgin, or His resurrection. Heresy is to attack the very foundations of the Bible and our faith. Heresy is not merely having a different belief on a biblical issue that no one can scripturally prove one way or another. Also, to be a Christian, have a different view, and to be able to back it up with scripture will absolutely not send you to Hell. For someone to say something like that to another person is to take the place of God as Judge over a person's soul. We have never and will never be given the authority to decide where someone will spend eternity. James 4:11-12 reads…

"Speak not evil of one another, brethren. He that speaketh evil of his brother, and judgeth his brother, speaketh evil of the law, and judgeth the law: but if thou judge the law, thou art not a doer of the law, but a judge. There is one lawgiver, who is able to save and to destroy: who art thou that judgest another?"

If someone shares a belief with you, and you believe it is wrong, be respectful and show them in the Bible what has led you to that thought. God has the ultimate authority over us and only He can say who is truly right and wrong because He is the only one who knows the absolute truth of everything.

We don't have to all believe the same things on issues that aren't made absolutely clear in the Bible. With the issue of the rapture, Paul even called the whole thing a *"mystery"* in 1 Corinthians 15:51. Jesus Himself did not even know the day of His return (Matthew 24:36, Mark 13:32). With so much unknown about the time of the end, how can we expect to have all the answers? With things like this, it is important for us to have an open mind and consider all opinions.

262

Concerning the rapture, there are four major views. These views, in their basic form and with the most common supporting biblical evidence, are…

1. **Pre-tribulation Rapture** – This view states that the rapture could come at any time before the tribulation begins. In this view, there are no more signs or prophecies that have to be fulfilled in order for the rapture of the Church to take place. It could happen seconds from now or could be decades away. The main verses used to support this belief are Jeremiah 30:7-11, 1 Thessalonians 4:13-18 and 5:2, Matthew 24:41, Luke 17:36, 1 Corinthians 15:51-53, Mark 13:33, Revelation 3:10, and Revelation 4:2.

2. **Mid-tribulation Rapture** – This view states that the rapture will occur in the middle of the tribulation period, three and a half years after the seven year tribulation begins. It states that the trumpet in 1 Corinthians 15:52 is the same as the trumpet in Revelation 11:15. The Revelation 11:15 trumpet is the last of the seven trumpets and sounds midway through the tribulation. This is said to be the same as the last trumpet in 1 Corinthians 15:52.

Verses to support this theory are Matthew 24:9, Matthew 24:41, Luke 17:36, 1 Corinthians 15:51-53, 1 Thessalonians 4:13-18, and Revelation 11:15.

3. **Post-tribulation Rapture** – This view states that the rapture will occur at the very end of the tribulation. It states we will all have to endure the tribulation but God will gather together everyone who has accepted and followed Him at the very end of the seven years. It also states that the raising of the dead in 1 Corinthians 15:52 is the same as the resurrection of Revelation 20:5. The belief is that since it is called the *first* resurrection in Revelation 20:5, there could not have been a resurrection, or a raising of the dead, before the Revelation 20:5 occurrence. Verses to support this view are Matthew 24:31, Matthew 24:41, Mark 13:13, Luke 17:36, John 6:39, Acts 14:22, 1 Corinthians 15:51-53, 1 Thessalonians 4:13-18, 2 Thessalonians 2:1-3, and Revelation 20:4-6.

4. **No Rapture** – This theory states that there will be no rapture of the Church. It states that we will all go through the tribulation together but there will never

264

be a time when God takes the Church out of the world. According to this theory there will never be a time when all of the Christians will miraculously disappear out of the earth and there is no escape from the tribulation for anyone. The main supporting argument for this belief is that the word *"rapture"* is not in the Bible. Another supporting argument is the belief that all prophecy in the Bible has already been fulfilled. It is also believed that the rapture and the second coming of Jesus are the same event. There are no stand-alone verses not already cited to support this theory. The verses used to support this theory are just different interpretations of the Bible verses already mentioned.

As we can see, there are many verses found in the Bible to support each of these main theories concerning the rapture. Each viewpoint has people who find problems with each of the other viewpoints. Each viewpoint has a collection of Bible verses to support their claims. Each viewpoint uses a lot of the same Bible verses with different interpretations and understandings.

This is just a brief overview of the various rapture beliefs. I went through a period of months nearly obsessing over this topic when the other beliefs were first brought to my attention years ago. I was raised to believe in a pre-tribulation rapture. When I first heard some of the arguments concerning the other beliefs, I did not know what to think or believe. This sent me on a quest for truth and to a personal discovery. When I began this journey, I had no idea when the rapture is going to happen, if at all. After years of intense study, prayer, research, spiritual signs, and God speaking to my heart, I have no idea when the rapture is going to happen, if at all. This may seem like a lot of time and work with nothing to show for it, but nothing could be further from the truth.

Throughout my years of study, there was a time I accepted each belief as truth. I began with the pre-tribulation belief, then moved on to believing there would be no rapture, then found more information to lead me to believe in a mid-tribulation rapture, then after more study I accepted the post-tribulation rapture, and now finally I am back to believing in the pre-tribulation rapture. It has been a long and strenuous journey, but I gained something incredibly valuable from the experience. I realized that nobody has the full answer. Nobody knows for absolute sure if or when the rapture will take place. All beliefs have valid biblical evidence to support them. So what are we to do? How do we know what to believe? Which belief is right?

The answer, like my grandmother's answer to me years ago, is a simple "I don't know". I wish I did know but I must be honest. I cannot say for sure either way. I would be doing a disservice to everyone reading if I tried to sway you one way or another on this. With the rapture theory, all I can do is tell you what led me back to a pre-tribulation rapture belief and encourage you to do your own research on the topic if it is an important issue for you. Come to your own conclusions, but remember to always compare with scripture and hold the Bible above your own beliefs.

What led me back to a pre-tribulation belief is when I looked at the spiritual benefits of each one and the fruits of the people supporting each belief. I am not saying all, but I have found the majority of arguments for the other beliefs to have a spirit of anger, and even sometimes hate. Now, I have heard this from the pre-tribulation side as well, which is what I was discussing earlier. Either way it is wrong, but I have experienced it most from people of the other views. I have seen a lot of pride and ego driven

267

arguments that were insulting to others of different beliefs. As I have said, this does not come from everyone, but it seems to be more from the other views. Matthew 7:16-20 tells us we will know people by their fruits. When I see people reacting with hate and anger, I tend to stop listening, because this shows their fruits are not of God. I am drawn more to people who react out of love and honor backed with scripture. This shows their fruits to be plentiful and of God. This was the first thing that led me back to a pre-tribulation rapture belief.

The second and most prominent thing that led me back, beyond all of the scriptural evidence, was when I looked at the spiritual benefits. The only view that has any kind of spiritual benefit attached to it is the pre-tribulation view. With all the other views, there is still something that needs to happen before the rapture can take place, if it will even happen at all. With that, it is easy to get caught up in certain sinful behaviors and just assume there will be time to repent and ask forgiveness. There is not that sense of urgency or fear that Jesus could snatch you into Heaven at any time.

With the pre-tribulation rapture belief, there is a sense of urgency and respectful fear to keep us on the right path. There is urgency to get right with God as soon as possible and get as close to Him as we can as soon as we can because He could come get us at any time. It keeps us away from certain things for fear of being caught up into Heaven while being involved in a sinful act. It is the only belief that can really improve a person spiritually and bring them closer to God in a biblical way. To me, it is the only belief that has God's fingerprints all over it. The only downside I really see is that some Christians will use their pre-tribulation rapture belief as an excuse to not learn Bible prophecy. Sometimes they claim that, since we are not going to be here, we do not need to study what God says about the future. I believe this to be a grave mistake because, even with a pre-tribulation rapture, we do not know for sure which prophecies will come before the rapture.

Taking that into consideration, I still compare all fruits and benefits to make a decision. Considering all the spiritual benefits of believing in a pre-tribulation rapture and all of the spiritual consequences that can come out of believing any of the other three, I must go by the spiritual fruit and accept the only one that can help me spiritually and bring me closer to God. For me personally, I must put my belief in a pre-tribulation rapture.

This is not to say that I do not accept the possibility of the other beliefs. It is very important that we keep an open mind and consider the possibility of other viewpoints. I know that I could be wrong. I am mentally and spiritually prepared for it. If the tribulation begins and we are all still here, we need to be prepared. If we aren't, we could be putting our souls in jeopardy.

What if the mark of the beast system is instilled on the people of the earth and we are still here? Will we just believe that since the rapture hasn't happened yet, it could not be the real mark of the beast? Will we hold onto that belief so tightly that we will blindly accept the mark, not realizing what we are doing, and lose our souls over it? It is so important that we keep an open mind and be prepared for any and all outcomes so when something happens, we will know what to do.

We don't know exactly what the world is going to be like leading up to the tribulation. All we know is that things will be rough around that time. We just do not know to what exact capacity. The Bible tells us there will be many life and death choices to be made during that time. Given how close we are to the end, it is increasingly possible that you will be faced with a choice, to deny Jesus or lose your life. Are you prepared for the possibility of dying for you faith? Grim though it might be, these are things each and every one of us needs to be thinking about, for the time is coming when this could all take place.

CONCLUSION

We must hear out every theory and consider them against scripture so that, when one of those theories proves to be accurate, we can be prepared. For the sake of our lives and souls, we must be willing to consider all possibilities that line up with the Word of God. We do not want to be deceived. Time is running out. We must learn to have an open mind. We absolutely must accept the Bible over our traditional teaching and upbringing. The time is now to learn as much as we can, because when the beginning of the end comes, it will be too late.

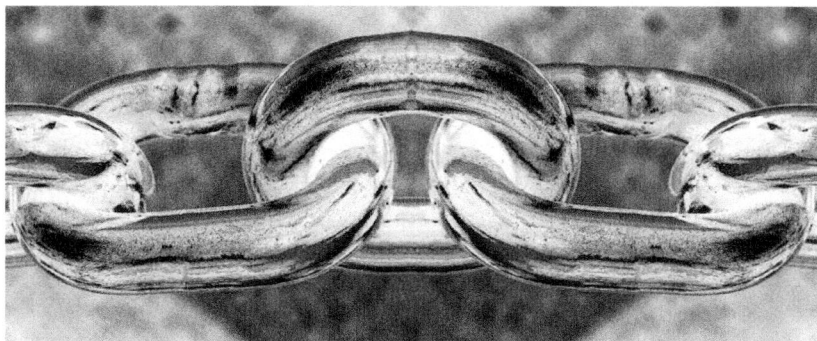

Chapter 12

THE NEPHILIM

These last few chapters are what the rest of the book has been preparing you for. Now you have a solid foundation to build on. Given everything said thus far, we can begin to get into the various beliefs concerning the end times, the Nephilim, and supposed alien life-form activity.

When we get into such things as aliens and UFOs, there is an almost involuntary sense of skepticism that immediately hits most people, especially us Christians. I experienced the same thing when I first began to study this. I was brought up with the traditional Christian belief that there is no physical life on other planets and any such evidence saying otherwise is a lie from Satan. I was taught that aliens do not exist and God did not create intelligent life elsewhere in the universe. I was also taught that the UFOs seen frequently in the sky were just demonic projections and alien entities were just spiritual demons taking form to lie, confuse, and mislead people. I still believe some of these things, in part, only now with a deeper understanding from the Bible.

This is another one of those instances where I circled around many different beliefs only to end up back where I started with much more information, evidence, and solid beliefs. God has led me through many fascinating conclusions and possibilities for the future. On many levels, I hope I am wrong in my conclusions and beliefs, but I am preparing for the possibility that this could all turn out to be true.

I am not expecting you to believe everything that is going to be presented in this chapter. I know that most, if not all, will be incredibly difficult to accept and incredibly easy to dismiss. I encourage you to give all of this a chance and test it against scripture. Have an open mind and do your own research into the topic as God leads you. It is important to at least file all of this into your mind and remember it in case these events begin to take place.

SONS OF GOD

I have heard the term *"sons of God"* cause much controversy within the Church. I have heard just about every definition imaginable for this term. I have heard *"sons of God"* called sinful men, descendants of Cain, demons, and even aliens from another planet. This is why I say it is best to compare scripture with scripture.

To understand this viewpoint to the fullest, we must start at the beginning. For that, we go to the Bible. Genesis 6:1-2 reads…

"And it came to pass, when men began to multiply on the face of the earth, and daughters were born unto them, That the sons of God saw the daughters of men that they were fair; and they took them wives of all which they chose."

This verse does not directly tell us who the *"sons of God"* are. To define the *"sons of God"*, we must compare scripture with scripture. The term *"sons of God"* is defined for us twice in the book of Job. First we read in Job 1:6…

"Now there was a day when the sons of God came to present themselves before the Lord, and Satan came also among them."

Second we read in Job 38:4-7…

"Where wast thou when I laid the foundations of the earth? declare, if thou hast understanding. Who hath laid the measurements thereof, if thou knowest? Or who hath stretched the line upon it? Whereupon are the foundations thereof fastened? or who laid the corner stone thereof; When the morning stars sang together, and all the sons of God shouted for joy?"

This is a great example of how we can allow the Bible to define itself for us. Comparing scripture with scripture gives us a clear understanding of who these *"sons of God"* are. They are angels. We know two main things to support this. First is they presented themselves before the Lord. Second is they were present at the creation of the world. This could only mean angels. It doesn't specify their standing with God, whether good or bad, only what they are.

THE SETHITE THEORY

There is a misinterpretation of scripture that has been floating around the Church, even to the point that it is being taught in seminaries, that has caused quite a bit of confusion. It is called *"The Sethite Theory"* and I think it bears mentioning. I wasn't originally planning on writing about this theory but God has laid it on my heart to defend His Word and clear up confusion if at all possible.

I remember when I was first taught this theory. It was before I knew anything about the Nephilim or the pre-flood world. It was before I had any real scriptural backing of my own to base my beliefs on. I had a limited understanding of fallen angels and what actually caused the flood. I was under the impression that angels were nothing but ethereal beings with no physicality whatsoever. I could not understand how an ethereal being could impregnate a physical woman so I began asking around to find the truth. The problem was I was relying on other people for my answer instead of bringing it up directly with God. When you leave God out of the interpretation process, you get misinterpretations such as what was given to me in the form of *"The Sethite Theory"*.

There are many variations but the theory basically states that the *"sons of God"* mentioned in Genesis 6:2 were not angels but were the male descendants of Seth. The *"daughters of men"* mentioned in the same verse were the ungodly female descendants of Cain. The theory states that descendants of Seth mated with the descendants of Cain and produced the *"giants"*. There is disagreement as to what *"giant"* means within people who subscribe to this theory. Some believe it means actual giants while others believe it means just mighty human warriors. Some even believe it means evil offspring connected to the term *"seed of Satan"*, referenced from Genesis 3:15. The truth is, as we will discuss later, that it's a bit of all three.

The problem with this theory is it is completely unbiblical. I do not want to trample all over someone else's beliefs but we have to learn to take the Bible for what it is. We must not allow ourselves to lose the ability to discern the truth from God through His Word or it will be that much easier for the enemy to deceive us.

To make the Sethite theory fit, one would have to completely twist the scriptures, even in the original Hebrew, that define angels (Job 38:4-7), giants (Genesis 6:2-4), and man (Genesis 6:1-7). The Sethite theory just does not add up when it is compared to the rest of the Bible without completely rewriting the scriptures themselves. This is dangerous because it keeps the believer away from the truth. It can make a believer look for the wrong thing in people by trying to find out who is a descendant of the mating between Cain and Seth's line instead of looking at their heart and discerning their spirit. It can even lead to the believer lifting the Sethite theory over the validity of the Bible itself.

GIANTS

When we look to the Genesis 6 account, we find that it was angels who saw the daughters of men and took them for wives. Shortly after in Genesis 6:4 we read…

"There were giants in the earth in those days; and also after that, when the sons of God came in unto the daughters of men, and they bare children to them, the same became mighty men which were of old, men of renown."

The word *"giants"* is translated from the Hebrew word *"nepil"*, meaning *"bully"* or *"tyrant"*, which comes from the word *"napal"*, meaning *"to fall"*. Isaiah 14:12 uses the same word *"napal"* for our English word *"fallen"* to describe Lucifer.

A common word used today for these fallen tyrants, or giants, is *"Nephilim"*. There have been some arguments and word studies concerning this term and, though I will refer to the giants as Nephilim, just keep in mind that according to the Strong's Exhaustive Concordance, the actual Hebrew word is *"nepil"* which comes from the word *"napal"*. Admitting and acknowledging that fact, referring to them as the Nephilim should be no problem and should not be a source of confusion. *"Nephilim"* is just the plural term, just like *"cherubim"* is the plural form of *"cherub"*. The NIV (New International Version) Bible refers to these beings as *"Nephilim"*, whereas the KJV (King James Version) Bible refers to them as *"giants"*. Though I am quoting from the KJV, it should not be a problem to refer to these beings by using the word *"Nephilim"*. In our modern vernacular, the word *"Nephilim"* is the most common and recognizable word referring to the giant offspring of the fallen angels and human women. Thus, to limit confusion, instead of merely referring to them with the broad term *"giants"*, I will refer to them as *"Nephilim"*.

An interesting fact to know is the definition of the Hebrew word *"napal"* which is *"to fall"* and can also mean *"cast down, die, fall, fallen, inferior, be lost, perish, rot, throw down"* among other things. The Nephilim were fallen, inferior, and lost beings that perished with no hope of salvation. They were not fallen in the sense that the angels who created them were fallen. The angels once had a high estate in Heaven, disobeyed God, and then became fallen. The Nephilim, on the other hand, were fallen right from the start. They were always known as the Nephilim, even from the time they were first born. They were not men that were first created with a hope at redemption. They were born fallen. They were made to perish. In a spiritual sense, they were dead upon creation.

While this may seem harsh at first glance, we need to be aware of what actually happened and what we are dealing with here. When God created Adam, the first man, He breathed into him the breath of life and Adam became a living soul (Genesis 2:7). Since then, every descendant of Adam has had this spiritual component to their physiology, called a soul, passed on to them. Clearly, this did not happen with the Nephilim.

The Nephilim were something that was never supposed to be created. Given the Hebrew definition of their name, we can see that God did not bless these creatures with the breath of life or a living soul. They were in no sense children of God. They were children of the fallen angels. This begs the question, if the Nephilim did not have the breath of life or a living soul, what did they have?

To answer this question based solely on the Bible, the best we can really do is make informed speculations while admitting it is not completely and biblically provable. We can look at the fact that when a man and a woman make a baby, God blesses that baby with life and a soul. This is either passed down from Adam or is directly done by God every time a baby is born. I believe, given other biblical examples of things passed down from Adam (sin, genetics, all aspects of human biology, etc.), that the breath of life and the human soul are passed down from the mother and father coming together as one.

In either case, something quite different would happen with an angel and a human offspring. Based on the Hebrew definition, the angel/human hybrid, known as the Nephilim, would not have the breath of life or a living soul as humans do. The Nephilim soul would not be created by God. It would be created by the soul and breath of life of a human combining with whatever an angel has.

This may have been accidental or it may have been done on purpose. The fallen angels may have wanted to create something in their own image. For everything God has, Satan has an evil duplicate or shadow. The fallen angels may have been jealous of God's creation of man and may have decided to create something of their own. This is the belief I tend to lean toward.

The main problem would have been the spiritual part of the angel mixing with the soul of a human. The result would be some sort of abomination that would be halfway between human and angel. It would be enough to give the Nephilim physical life but not enough to carry them on into eternity with God in Heaven. Because of this, the Nephilim would have not had the ability to be a child of God and would have only known rebellion against God. This theory lines up with scripture when you compare it with how the Nephilim are described in the Bible.

There is one more speculation that is interesting to think about. If the Nephilim soul did not have the ability to have eternal life and was dead upon creation, what would

283

happen to the souls when the Nephilim died? It is possible that what we know today as "demons" are actually the disembodied spirits of the dead Nephilim. If the souls and spirits of the Nephilim were not created by God and could not achieve eternal life, there would be nowhere else to go when it died. According to scripture, the souls and spirits of dead Nephilim would not initially go to Hell upon death before the resurrection and judgment. Speaking of unsaved people at the judgment, Jesus states in Matthew 25:41...

"Then shall he say also unto them on the left hand, Depart from me, ye cursed, into everlasting fire, prepared for the devil and his angels:"

Though unsaved humans take part as well, Hell was originally created for the devil and his angels. This would suggest that the dead Nephilim would be cursed to remain on the Earth until the judgment. They would be what we refer to today as "demons". Since angels do not die, however, the fallen angels would continue to exist with Satan who reigns as the prince of the power of the air until the judgment (as we read Ephesians 2:2). This shows that demons and fallen angels are different altogether.

This is just speculation, but look at the nature of demons compared to fallen angels. It is well documented in the Bible that demons (or devils, unclean spirits, etc.) like to possess people and take control of their physical bodies if they can. Fallen angels, on the other hand, have a type of physical body that is far superior to our human bodies, as we will discover a little later in this chapter. This would seem to mean that fallen angels would have no immediate need for a physical human body. Of course, there are certain exceptions to this made in special circumstances, such as Satan possessing the body of Judas, but we do not see this as typically as we do with demons. If demons are the disembodied spirits of the Nephilim, it would explain why they would want to possess humans in the first place.

Also, before the account of the flood in Genesis, there is no mention of devils or evil spirits of any kind. There is only mention of fallen angels, Heavenly angels, and man. The Bible is not directly clear about what exactly evil spirits are and where they come from but, one thing that is clear, there are different Hebrew words used to differentiate evil spirits from fallen angels. If demons and fallen angels are different, as the Hebrew language seems to indicate, there would be nothing else for demons to actually be other than spirits of dead Nephilim. Again, this is just speculation but with as strictly descriptive and disciplined of a language as Hebrew is, I believe the same word would have been used to describe both if evil spirits were actually fallen angels. Though, as I said before, this is only a theory.

FALLEN ANGELS AND FLESH BODIES

So now we know that when the fallen angels married human women, the Nephilim were born. From the descriptions given to us in the Bible, such as in Genesis and the story of Goliath among others, we learn that these Nephilim were giants, exceedingly strong, and barbaric. The fallen angels who committed this act that led to the creation of the Nephilim were in direct violation of God's law. We read about it in the Genesis 6 account, but there is also a familiar verse in the New Testament that may help shed more light to how unacceptable this was to God. Speaking of people at the resurrection, Jesus says in Matthew 22:30…

"For in the resurrection they neither marry, nor are given in marriage, but are as the angels of God in heaven."

There is a common misconception regarding this verse. Usually when this verse is quoted or explained, the last part saying *"…of God in heaven"* is left out. This verse is sometimes used to say that all angels in existence have never and will never take part in marriage. Such a statement is a mistake and a misinterpretation. This verse is explaining an attribute of only *"the angels of God in heaven"* and not every angel. The angels that took part in the unholy union with human women are not angels of God nor reside in Heaven anymore. The angels that are in Heaven have never committed this terrible sin. In ages past, when certain angels decided to marry women and have children, they fell from Heaven and thus became what we refer to as "fallen angels". We can read more about this in Jude 1:6-8. It reads...

"And the angels which kept not their first estate, but left their own habitation, he hath reserved in everlasting chains under darkness unto the judgment of the great day. Even as Sodom and Gomorrha, and the cities about them in like manner, giving themselves over to fornication, and going after strange flesh, are set forth for an example, suffering the vengeance of eternal fire. Likewise also these filthy dreamers defile the flesh, despise dominion, and speak evil of dignities."

There are a lot of interesting things in this passage. At first read, we learn about the fallen angels and how their sin of mating with humans, or *"going after strange flesh"* compared with Sodom and Gomorrha, resulted in God locking them in chains until the judgment when they will suffer the *"vengeance of eternal fire"*. The base understanding of this passage gives us some interesting descriptions, but when we look at the Greek words used, we gain a much deeper insight to what is being said.

We can start at the beginning with the words *"first estate"*. The word *"first"* comes from the Greek word *"arche"* meaning a high rank, such as to be first in position of political power. The word *"estate"* comes from the Greek word *"peri"* which can basically mean a locality. From this we learn that the angels did not keep their highest ranking location. The highest ranking location an angel can have, or exist in, is Heaven. The angels left Heaven.

Now, let's look at the next part of the verse, *"...but left their own habitation..."*. The word *"habitation"* comes from the Greek word *"oiketerion"* and means a residence, such as a family household. This is saying that certain angels left their heavenly family (God and the other angels) in Heaven which was their home. These angels forsook God and the other heavenly hosts by leaving Heaven and coming to Earth. Their actions on Earth led to them now being bound in chains and waiting for their judgment of everlasting fire. Also, if we look at 2 Corinthians 5:2, Paul is talking about being *"...clothed upon with our house which is from heaven"*. When you read the entire chapter, it is clear the *"house"* is another word for a body. It is possible that the fallen angels not only forsook God and Heaven, but also forsook their heavenly spiritual bodies for a type of physical body they could use to operate within our physical dimension.

We can see here what actions led to the angels' judgment. This passage compares what they did to the sins of Sodom and Gomorrha. It says they were *"...giving themselves over to fornication, and going after strange flesh..."*. The word *"strange"* comes from the Greek word *"heteros"* meaning *"another, the other, or different"*. This is saying that the fallen angels were fornicating with flesh that was different than their own, meaning humans. There are a lot of theories of how this could be possible but apparently the fallen angels have some sort of physical bodies at their disposal. There are places in the Bible that mention angels with the appearance of men and even having physical attributes. Jacob wrestled with an angel in Genesis 32:24, which I believe was the pre-incarnate Jesus, and even Jesus Himself had a type of physical body after

He was resurrected. So it seems that, at least in some way and some form, some angels can have a type of physical body. It seems that even the fallen angels had this type of physical body and were able to mate with human women.

This can make sense when we think of what we are. We humans are really spiritual beings, soul and spirit, that has been put into a physical body so we can operate within physical reality. Our physical bodies are a type of vehicle for our souls and spirits to exist as intended within this dimension. It would make sense that if another type of spiritual being, like an angel, wanted to operate in our physical dimension, he would need a type of physical body too. This body would be different than ours, as we were created lower than the angels (Hebrews 2:7). The angel's body would be more powerful and able to do things that the human body cannot. The "flesh" of the angel's body would be different than human flesh. I really do not know if "flesh" would even be an appropriate word to describe an angel's body because it is clearly different than the flesh of a human. However, for lack of better word, I will just refer to it as a type of angelic flesh, different than human flesh.

GENERATIONS AND BLOODLINES

Going back to where we left off in Genesis, we read in Genesis 6:9…

"These are the generations of Noah: Noah was a just man and perfect in his generations, and Noah walked with God."

What is interesting here is there are two different Hebrew words used for our English word *"generations"*. The first time it is used in this verse is the Hebrew word *"toleda"* meaning family descent. The second time the Hebrew word *"dor"* is used, meaning a revolution of time, or an age. The word *"perfect"* comes from the Hebrew word *"tamim"* and means without blemish, complete, and undefiled. Going back to the Jude passage, the word for *"defiled"* also means corrupt, as in corrupted flesh.

So first Genesis 6:9 makes mention of Noah's descendants, and next it says he was a just man, then that he was uncorrupted in all his revolution of time. If only Noah was perfect, then by deduction the rest of the world was blemished, or defiled, or corrupted. In Jude, we learned that the fallen angels corrupted the human flesh by mating with them. It seems Genesis 6:9 is telling us that back in that time Noah and his descendants were the only people in the world that was completely uncorrupted.

The rest of the world was corrupted by mating with the fallen angels and the Nephilim. Noah's entire bloodline, all the way beginning with Adam, was completely pure and perfect; meaning no one in the bloodline from Adam to Noah had ever mated with a fallen angel or a Nephilim. Noah's perfectly human bloodline was the same bloodline that Jesus Christ would be born through. That is why God only saved Noah and his family from the flood. Satan's plan was to corrupt the bloodline that the Savior would be born through.

Jesus Himself was without blemish so he had to have been born through a perfectly human bloodline. Satan decided to try to corrupt the entire world and knew if he could do that then the Savior could not be born. Satan was nearly successful until God stepped in, preserved the last uncorrupted bloodline by means of the worldwide flood, and destroyed all corruption Satan had wrought upon the earth.

THE SECOND INFLUX

This was not the last time Satan tried to corrupt the bloodline of the future Messiah. There are many accounts of giants after the flood as well. One such account can be found in Numbers 13:33, which reads...

"And there we saw the giants, the sons of Anak, which come of the giants: and we were in our own sight as grasshoppers, and so we were in their sight."

Another example can be found in Amos 2:9, which reads...

"Yet destroyed I the Amorite before them, whose height was like the height of the cedars, and he was strong as the oaks; yet I destroyed his fruit from above, and his roots from beneath."

These verses, as well as many other passages in the Bible (including the story of David and Goliath), tell us that giants were once again born on the earth after the flood. There are two main theories that attempt to explain how the second influx of the Nephilim came about.

The first theory states that the fallen angels mated with human women again, after the flood, and brought about the second influx of Nephilim. This is possible since this is how it happened the first time. Unfortunately, the Bible isn't specific as to tell us if this is the origin of the second influx of the Nephilim or if it was something else.

The second theory states that it was not fallen angels who brought about the second influx of the Nephilim, but may have had something to do with corrupted genes surviving on the ark. We know two things about the pre-flood world in connection to the second influx of Nephilim. First, Noah was pure in all his generations (Genesis 6:9). Second, all of the rest of humanity was corrupted (Genesis 6:12). This would mean that Noah and his three sons would have been pure but, being that all other flesh was corrupted, the wives of Noah's sons would not have been. One or more of the wives could have carried the Nephilim gene.

At first this may not seem to make sense. It certainly did not make sense to me the first time I heard it. It may seem impossible to believe that God would have destroyed the whole world just to allow the Nephilim gene to be preserved in the ark. The problem is, either way we look at it, the Nephilim did manage to return. Whichever way you look at it, if God's purpose for flooding the Earth was only to destroy the Nephilim and prevent them from ever returning, He did not fulfill His task.

God does not make mistakes. Given this, if we are to believe the Bible, we must cast aside our preconceived notions and let the Bible define the reason of the flood for us. Since there was a second influx of the Nephilim on the Earth, the purpose of the flood must not have been to utterly destroy the Nephilim forever. I think it is entirely more likely that the purpose of the flood was to preserve the bloodline of the Messiah along with removing wickedness from the earth. Before the flood, the entire world was corrupted except for Noah and his sons. If God had let it go any further, eventually the fallen angels would have succeeded in corrupting the bloodline of the Messiah, ensuring Jesus could not be born, thereby winning the war. To preserve the messianic bloodline, God sent the flood and destroyed the main source of the corruption.

God would only need one of Noah's sons to produce a clean bloodline. This means that God would have only needed one bloodline of the many descendants of Noah to be free of the Nephilim gene. It is possible that Ham, Noah's son, had a wife that carried this Nephilim gene. It is possible that the Nephilim gene presented itself in Canaan, Ham's son. This could help to explain why Noah cursed Canaan instead of Ham in Genesis 9:25-27. Furthermore, when we read Canaan's genealogy, we read that Canaan begat the Amorite (Genesis 10:15). Again, in Amos 2:9, we read…

"Yet destroyed I the Amorite before them, whose height was like the height of the cedars, and he was strong as the oaks; yet I destroyed his fruit from above, and his roots from beneath."

We also see ties to Ham's son Canaan in Numbers 13:28-29 which reads…

"Nevertheless the people be strong that dwell in the land, and the cities are walled, and very great: and moreover we saw the children of Anak there. The Amalekites dwell in the land of the south: and the Hittites, and the Jebusites, and the Amorites, dwell in the mountains: and the Canaanites dwell by the sea, and by the coast of Jordan."

Then again, Numbers 13:33 reads…

"And there we saw the giants, the sons of Anak, which come of the giants: and we were in our own sight as grasshoppers, and so we were in their sight."

Given these two passages, we can see that the second influx of the Nephilim most likely came from the descendants of Ham through Canaan.

To support this further, Numbers 13:33 says the giants they saw were *"of"* the giants. It does not say they were of the fallen angels. This seems to state that the second influx of giants came from the first influx of giants and not from fallen angels mating with humans a second time. The only way this could be possible is if Ham's wife carried the Nephilim gene and it passed on to Canaan and his descendants.

Those are the two theories concerning the origin of the second influx of the Nephilim. Both theories are highly speculative since the Bible doesn't state clearly how the giants were able to return after the flood, but there is enough evidence found throughout scripture to form a reasonable hypothesis around either belief. I believe both have equal footing as valid possibilities but it seems the Nephilim gene theory has more evidence supporting it. This is one of those things that we must research ourselves to come to our own conclusions about which theory we want to believe in and support.

In either case, it seems possible that Satan and his minions were trying to corrupt the messianic bloodline again through the second influx of the Nephilim. I believe this is why, at least in part, God gave such strict rules regarding Jewish people not marrying outside of their own people (Deuteronomy 7:1-6). The surrounding lands had Nephilim and God did not want the messianic bloodline to become polluted with the fallen angels' original corruption. The Nephilim were not human and had nothing good in them. They served false gods (which could have been the fallen angels themselves) and even fought against the one true living God (1 Samuel 17:23-58).

It is clear that, since they did not have a human soul with the possibility of redemption, the Nephilim were soulless abominations to God that needed to be destroyed. This is further proven when we read the account of Jericho. In Joshua 6:21 we read...

"And they utterly destroyed all that was in that city, both man and woman, young and old, and ox, and sheep, and ass, with the edge of the sword."

The only people saved from Joshua and his army was Rahab and her family. She showed faith earlier by contributing to Joshua's success with the destruction of

Jericho. I believe this city was full of Nephilim and that's why everyone, even the young, had to be killed. The faith Rahab showed and her actions would have never taken place if she was of the Nephilim. I believe this is how Joshua and his army knew her whole family was worthy of being saved. Rahab's bloodline must not have been corrupted by the Nephilim. If it were, she would have never helped Joshua against Jericho.

Another interesting thing to look at is the fact that God commanded Joshua and his army to destroy all the animals as well. We read in Genesis 6:12-13 that all flesh was corrupted. The only thing that could cause this type of corruption was the fallen angels. Being that it says *"all flesh"*, this would have to include the animals as well as human beings. It is possible that the fallen angels did something to the animals that corrupted their bloodline as well.

I am not suggesting that bestiality took place. I find it more likely that some sort of gene manipulation and DNA tampering occurred. We have no idea of the technologies the fallen angels had at their disposal (for more information, refer to the chapter entitled *"The Ezekiel Prophecies"*). With all of the ancient legends and myths of human/animal hybrids throughout the world, such as in Greek mythology, I believe it is at least possible something could have happened to create other abominations. The fallen angels may not have stopped with the Nephilim. They may have tried their hand at creating other hybrids.

It should not be too difficult to accept the possibility because there are scientists throughout the world doing the same thing today. As it says in Ecclesiastes 1:9-10...

"The thing that hath been, it is that which shall be; and that which is done is that which shall be done: and there is no new thing under the sun. Is there any thing whereof it may be said, See, this is new? it hath been already of old time, which was before us."

If it is happening now, we can be assured it happened somewhere in our past. All we have to do is look to our past to decipher our future and look to our present to interpret the past. There are many cases of different types of human/animal hybridization programs implemented throughout the world. In Britain alone, there are 150 cases of human/animal hybrid embryos being created in laboratories.[1] There have been various unnatural animal hybrids created as well, such as the liger (half lion, half tiger) which is a giant on its own as the world's largest cat.[2]

If it is happening now and if we are to believe the words of the Bible, we know without a doubt that it happened in our past. The best time for this that fits with scripture is when the fallen angels and Nephilim were present on the Earth. I believe this is why Joshua was commanded to destroy all the animals as well as the people of the city. God wasn't being cruel or unjust in any way. The Nephilim and the animal hybrids were not created by God. They were all abominations and were never meant to be created in the first place.

FUTURE PROPHECIES

We know there was an original influx of Nephilim before the worldwide flood destroyed them all. We know there was a second influx sometime after the flood. Is it possible there will be a third influx of Nephilim and, if so, could we possibly be seeing it within our lifetime?

In Luke 17:26-30, Jesus said the last days would be as the days of Noah and Lot, and then He lists some examples. The main point Jesus is making here is that the world will not see His return coming until it happens. The people of the world will not be expecting it. For those not remaining watchful and not spiritually prepared for it, by the time He does return, it will be too late. Their fate will be sealed. While this is a very clear and direct teaching, I believe it is possible there is a hidden truth, or a hint, found within this passage concerning end time prophecy.

Of all of God's unexpected judgments Jesus could choose from, He used the days of Noah and Lot as His examples. We know that Noah's days were unique because of the presence of the Nephilim. We read in 2 Peter 2:4-7...

"For if God spared not the angels that sinned, but cast them down to hell, and delivered them into chains of darkness, to be reserved unto judgment; And spared not the old world, but saved Noah the eighth person, a preacher of righteousness, bringing in the flood upon the world of the ungodly; And turning the cities of Sodom and Gomorrha into ashes condemned them with an overthrow, making them an ensample unto those that after should live ungodly; And delivered just Lot, vexed with the filthy conversation of the wicked:"

We see much similarity when we pair this passage with the Jude 1:6-8 passage described earlier. Here is talking about Noah and Lot. This passage, like Jude 1:6-8, begins with talking about the angels that sinned. It even calls them examples. I believe it is possible that Jesus used the days of Noah and Lot to describe the end days because of the Nephilim and these two passages can be used to back it up. Also consider that in the account of Lot, whether they knew it or not, the people of Sodom were trying to have sexual relations with angels. They may have seen the angels that were sent for Lot as mere mortal men, but scripture isn't completely clear. Either way we look at it, the fact is they were angels and the people of Sodom were trying to have sexual relations with them.

This is why it is so important to compare scripture with scripture. I believe in the possibility that during the last days, which I believe we are right on the edge of, the fallen angels will yet again attempt this unholy union with human women and produce Nephilim, more than likely through genetic manipulations rather than sexual relations. I don't believe Satan will use the exact same tactics as before. He has tried this before and has failed. I believe Satan has had thousands of years to think and plan this all out. I believe this time around it will be an even more deceptive attempt. There is a verse, Daniel 2:43, which can be used to explore this further. It says...

"And whereas thou sawest iron mixed with miry clay, they shall mingle themselves with the seed of men: but they shall not cleave one to another, even as iron is not mixed with clay."

This is explaining the vision of the statue where each descending part represented a future empire. The last one, described here, is the feet made of iron mixed with clay. The interesting thing is the line *"they shall mingle themselves with the seed of men"*. While it does not directly define who the *"they"* are here, it is not difficult to figure out. The way this sentence is formed grammatically, the *"they"* would be a different group than the *"seed of men"*. All of humanity would be the *"seed of men"* as we all have been created from the seed of our biological father in one way or another. The only other group that are not human that have been known to *"mingle themselves with the seed of men"* are the fallen angels and/or the Nephilim. I believe it is possible this is saying the fallen angels, or possibly the Nephilim, are going to somehow mix with human women again in the last empire during the end times.

When we bring this into our day and try to look at it from the present day perspective, there really is only one event that may fit in with this, and that would be the alien abduction phenomenon. I know that might be easy to scoff at and dismiss at first but, before you make a final decision, I would greatly encourage you to look at the evidence and do your own research first. After all, Proverbs 18:13 tells us...

"He that answereth a matter before he heareth it, it is folly and shame unto him."

We should at least consider the evidence against scripture, and if it lines up but is still too much to believe, file it away in your mind and remember it, so if it does happen, you will be prepared.

There are a lot of variations, and if it interests you I would greatly encourage you to check out the large amount of information out there concerning this topic, but the basic Alien/Nephilim/Last Days theory is pretty simple. It states that all these alien abductions and activity people have been reporting are not actually caused by aliens from another planet, but by fallen angels from another dimension, which have a type of physical body and technology that surpasses what we know today. The fallen angels lie and say they are aliens from another planet to deceive people and change their worldview. These fallen angels posing as aliens have told various abductees that they created all humanity and religions, there is no God or Jesus, and that they have come to usher in a new enlightened age of peace for humanity. People have also claimed that they are trying to breed with humans by various methods of cloning and gene manipulation to create a type of super race to further their agenda.

It is believed by those who subscribe to this theory that these hybrids are modern day Nephilim. With all the ancient accounts of breeding between human and "gods", various cultures having seemingly unknowable knowledge of star systems in outer space, and reports all throughout history of these strange visitors claiming to be from another planet, I do not think this theory is too far-fetched. In fact, I believe if Satan wanted to deceive the whole world into worshipping him and his minions, and if he has the capability to do so, this would be the way to go about it. Just imagine how the world would change if alien spacecraft came down and made contact. When the world is looking at so-called reality right in their faces, who would deny anything the alien beings had to say? Crazy as it may seem, if something like that were to actually happen, it would not be long before the entire world would be handed over to Satan and the fallen angels.

CONCLUSION

We know Satan is the prince of the power of the air (Ephesians 2:2). We know he will come with signs and lying wonders, and to those who will believe him, God will send a strong delusion (2 Thessalonians 2:7-11). We know that men's hearts will fail them because of what they will see in the sky (Luke 21:26) and that, if it is possible, even the very elect could be deceived (Matthew 24:22-24). Can we really put anything past Satan, his angels, and their combined evil? Are there any lengths they would not go to in order to deceive mankind? Do we know the limit of their power?

The good thing through all this is regardless of what does end up taking place, we serve a God far more powerful than anything else out there. We are not given a spirit of fear, but of power, love, and a sound mind (2 Timothy 1:7). We may not know every detail of the truth that awaits us in the future, but God does, and as long as we are in good standing with Him through Jesus, we have nothing to fear. We are saved and Satan holds no power over us. We have comfort in the fact that, no matter what happens, we are safe. Even when we die, we are safe. God has us and nothing can take us out of His hands (John

10:27-30 and Romans 8:37-39). We never have to be afraid.

Since none of us know the full future, it is important for us to keep an open mind on theories like this. I have been studying Bible prophecy for years and I still don't know for absolute sure what will happen. I have my beliefs, and I find as I continue to learn, different things happen. Sometimes my beliefs will be validated and other times I have to change my beliefs. The important thing is to compare any theory with scripture before subscribing to it. There are a lot of unbiblical theories about the Bible out there and it can be easy to be deceived, or at least distracted for a while, if we accept something without checking God's Word first.

If there is a contradiction between a theory and scripture, you have to throw the theory out and find a new one, unless you are willing to forsake truth for an interesting story. Be smart, have a strong foundation in the Bible, and know God the best you can. If you will draw near to Him first, He will draw near to you (James 4:8). In any pursuit of truth, do your own research, test what you are learning and being told against the Bible, and most importantly, follow God's direction. He has a path for you, and His path will always lead to the truth.

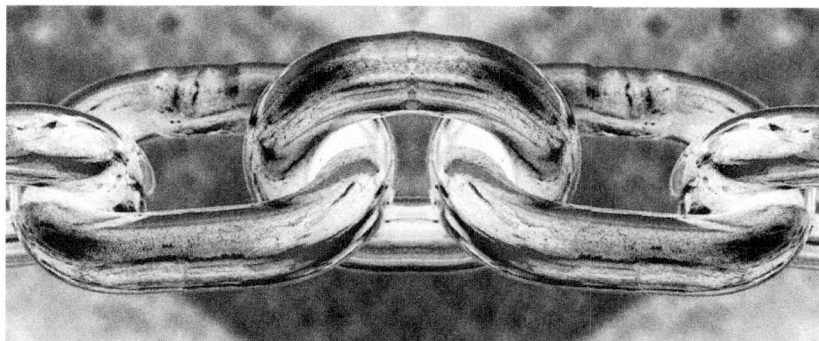

Chapter 13

THE EZEKIEL PROPHECIES

As far back as I can remember in my Christian life, I have always been fascinated with Bible prophecy. I loved the idea of knowing what is going to happen before it actually does. I loved learning about God and His truth. Also, I always loved a good mystery.

Bible prophecy can be very mysterious in the fact that there are many different interpretations to certain passages. When I was growing up, the only book of prophecy in the Bible I was aware of was the book of Revelation. As I grew older and began studying other prophecies found in the books of Daniel, Isaiah, and Psalms (as well as many others), I realized how fascinating the prophecies truly were. When I thought I had a fair grasp on what most Bible prophecy was saying, I began studying the book of Ezekiel, and it completely redefined my view of Bible prophecy as a whole.

The book of Ezekiel is one of the most fascinating books of the Old Testament due to its overwhelmingly specific and accurate prophecies. It was written roughly 2600 years ago and is still relevant today. Right now we are in a dispensation of time between two chapters of Ezekiel's prophecies concerning the last days. It is apparent that, upon studying this fascinating text, we do not have much time before the return of our Lord Jesus Christ.

EZEKIEL - CHAPTER 1

In the first run of Disclosure, I put forth an idea of what the first chapter of Ezekiel could be talking about. Of course, there are many interpretations of Ezekiel's vision out there, so I decided to pick the one that fit most close to the scope of my book and the themes later conveyed. I will first present what I originally wrote, then afterwards, will put forth a couple more ideas that should be considered.

312

The first chapter of the book of Ezekiel opens with a very strange and dramatic vision. Ezekiel gives the firsthand account of his vision as descriptively as he could by using words and terms he would have been familiar with in his own time. Given that fact, it is important to understand the original Hebrew words used to explain this vision so we may gain a deeper understanding of what Ezekiel actually saw. He wrote in Ezekiel 1:4...

"And I looked, and, behold, a whirlwind came out of the north, a great cloud, and a fire infolding itself, and a brightness was about it, and out of the midst thereof as the colour of amber, out of the midst of the fire."

There is a lot here so I will just get right into the Hebrew words and follow with a short explanation. The word *"whirlwind"* used here is actually translated from two Hebrew words. The first word, *"ruah"* can mean a *"violent exhalation or blast"*. The second word, *"seara"* can mean *"hurricane"*. The word *"north"* comes from the Hebrew word *"sapon"* which can mean *"hidden"*. The word *"sapon"* is from the primitive root *"sapan"* which can mean *"to protect"*, as in *"to hide by covering over"*. The word *"great"* comes from the word *"gadol"* which can mean *"older"* or *"eldest"*. The word *"cloud"* comes from *"anan"* and can mean *"as covering the sky"*. The word *"infolding"* comes from *"laqah"* and can mean *"carry away, fetch, bring, send for, or take away"*. The word *"colour"* comes from *"ayin"* and can mean *"outward appearance"*. Lastly, the word *"amber"* comes from the Hebrew word *"hasmal"* and can mean *"bronze"* or *"polished metal"*. So what we have here is Ezekiel trying to describe something extraordinary using ordinary words found within the vernacular of the time. Given the deeper meanings of these Hebrew words, this verse could be put together as saying something along the lines of...

"I saw something come out from the protective covering it was hiding in with a blast comparable to the power and violence of a hurricane. It was the oldest of its kind and it was covering the sky. It was moving by means of a fire. It produced its own light as the whole area of the sky around it was bright. The object was in the center of the light and fire. The object had an outward appearance of polished metal such as bronze."

Of course, this is highly speculative and is just one possible interpretation of many based on the Hebrew words used within this verse. Nevertheless, it is incredibly interesting how Ezekiel described what he saw and the words he decided to use. Continuing on to the next verse, Ezekiel 1:5 says...

"Also out of the midst thereof came the likeness of four living creatures. And this was their appearance; they had the likeness of a man."

The English word *"likeness"* comes from the Hebrew word *"demut"* and can mean *"resemblance"* such as a *"model"* or *"shape"*. The *"four living creatures"* are widely accepted as the same *"four beasts"* in Revelation 4:6-9 which are angels of Heaven. The word *"appearance"* comes from the word *"mareh"* and can mean *"form"* or *"pattern"*. This verse seems to be saying something like...

"After the first object, next out of the light came four other objects that were made to look like, or modeled after, the four living creatures. The formation pattern these objects were taking in the sky resembled the shape of a man (probably meaning the first one Ezekiel saw was in front or on top, the next two were behind or underneath, and the last two were behind or underneath that, such as a head, two arms, and two legs)."

Again, this is speculative. These are only my words and not meant as a redefinition of the Bible, only as a possible interpretation. Looking at these two verses, it is clear that Ezekiel saw something in the sky, some kind of large and brilliant object followed by four others, all metallic, and all keeping an aerial formation.

We find more descriptions as we continue reading the chapter. Each of the four objects has a type of *"feet"* that are straight and looking like brass, like the metal of the first object (Ezekiel 1:7). The objects were vehicles that could travel at light-speed (Ezekiel 1:14) and they were circular in shape (Ezekiel 1:16) with a ring of *"eyes"* (or what sounds like windows or portholes) around them (Ezekiel 1:18). We also find out that the four living creatures are actually piloting these heavenly vehicles, as it says *"...they went every one straight forward: whither the spirit was to go, they went..."* (Ezekiel 1:12) and *"...for the spirit of the living creatures was in the wheels..."* (Ezekiel 1:20). We also see these vehicles have some sort of translucent covering over them, what is referred to as a firmament, that possibly seems like a force field of some kind (Ezekiel 1:22) The last thing we discover in this chapter is that these vehicles were used in some way to bring down the very throne of God Himself from Heaven to Earth (Ezekiel 1:25-28).

I won't pretend that I understand everything contained within this chapter because I certainly do not. It could even be that the *"likeness"* of the living creatures was the living creatures themselves and not separate vehicles. The four living creatures could have been all inside the first vehicle mentioned. The four living creatures may have been piloting the same large vehicle instead of each having their own.

There are many possible interpretations of this passage. While I do not know the exact interpretation, I do believe what Ezekiel saw here was very real and very powerful. I believe that since no one can say for absolute sure what is happening here, it is justified to have thoughts, opinions, and theories about it as long as they do not oppose other biblical scripture. I have come up with some of my own theories, but before I share them here, I would again greatly encourage you to do your own research into any topics that God leads you in.

The fact is that we really do not know how angels actually get from Heaven to Earth. We know that they do not always just flash and appear suddenly in our world because of what Jacob saw in Genesis 28:12. Here, we read of a ladder from Heaven to Earth that had angels ascending and descending on it. God showed Jacob this vision and it holds meaning still today. Based on this account, we know that the angels at least have the option of a ladder of some sort to travel between Heaven and Earth.

We also know that angels are outside of our dimension and they do, at least sometimes, need a type of body to operate in this dimension as we do (refer to the chapter entitled *"The Nephilim"*). Is it then plausible to entertain the idea that perhaps, once in their physical angelic bodies, they could use a vehicle to travel between dimensions? I don't believe this is too far-fetched given the mysterious nature of Heaven.

The idea of angels using vehicles for various purposes is not unbiblical. There are descriptions of heavenly chariots of fire throughout the Bible (2 Kings 2:11, 2 Kings 6:17). I can only imagine that whatever type of technology exists in Heaven would far surpass the technology we will ever have on Earth before the return of Jesus. The question comes up, why would God need vehicles for transportation of His angels or anything else?

I think the answer is plain and simple; because He wants them. It is the same as why God has a throne to sit on. Does He need a throne because His legs get tired? Of course not! He has a throne because He wants a throne. I believe it is a way of expressing His power and position in Heaven and over all creation. I believe these vehicles could be an expression of his vast intellect of mechanical creation. We know God created all of the spiritual and biological creatures. We know God created various nonliving things that serve to provide a function, such as His throne for sitting and a ladder for the angels to climb. If He has the Heavenly technology to create a ladder or a throne, is it then impossible that He would create a mechanical vehicle for His angels with that same Heavenly technology? I don't see why not.

Another point to consider is if the angels of Heaven have access and knowledge of these vehicles, would the fallen angels have access to them as well or at least have the knowledge to build their own? If a fallen angel were to build a vehicle, would it not be modeled after the most powerful vehicles in existence, the vehicles of Heaven? If the fallen angels could somehow build these vehicles, whether in this dimension or the next, would they be subject to imperfections? Could they sometimes malfunction or even crash on Earth?

We know nothing of what technology in the dimension of the fallen angels is like. We know nothing of the limits to their understanding of technology. We know nothing of what they are capable of or the materials they could have at their disposal.

Could it be possible that all of these UFOs being seen around the world are not from other planets, but from another dimension? Could it be that all these alien abductions are not perpetrated by actual beings from other planets, but by fallen angels from the next dimension? Could it at all be possible that Satan and his fallen angels are masquerading as alien beings piloting UFOs to deceive all of us human beings into thinking we were not created by God? If Satan had the power and the ability to destroy everyone's faith in God and make them believe a lie that would ultimately lead to their eternal destruction, don't you think he would do it?

Another way to look at this entire vision of Ezekiel is basically to take it for exactly as it says. While that might seem deceptively simple, I assure you, it is not. In my continued research after the writing of the first run of *Disclosure*, it was brought to my attention that much of the iconography of Ezekiel's day shows various aspects of the same things he saw. It would seem there were others who witnessed similar things and attempted to depict them visually. We have access to this iconography today and can compare them to the descriptions Ezekiel gave us. For more information on this, Dr. Michael Heiser has a very information presentation about Ezekiel's vision that can be found on YouTube.

EZEKIEL – CHAPTER 37

This chapter contains Ezekiel's vision of the dry bones. The amazing thing about this chapter is that it predicts, among other things, the regathering of the Jews to their native land of Israel that happened in 1948.[1] This chapter is a good source of foundation for prophecy as we can see how it has been fulfilled exactly how the Bible said it would be.

The chapter opens up with a vision from God to Ezekiel of a valley full of dry bones. God tells Ezekiel to prophesy to bring life back to the bones. All of a sudden, the dry bones start coming together and skin starts growing over them. They form into living people making up a great army. God tells Ezekiel that the bones are the people of

Israel who have been taken from their land (this happened in 70 A.D. which would have been roughly 500 years after this prophecy was written).[2] Then God goes on to say that He will regather the Jews from the nations and bring them back to their homeland.

What makes this prophecy so amazing and important is how incredibly specific it is and how it lines up with other Bible prophecies concerning the regathering of the Jewish people to their native Israel (see Isaiah 11:11, Jeremiah 29:14, Jeremiah 30:3). This passage is also amazing because of how it interprets itself. We don't have to guess what the dry bones represent. God tells us in Ezekiel 37:11…

"Then he said unto me, Son of man, these bones are the whole house of Israel: behold, they say, Our bones are dried, and our hope is lost: we are cut off for our parts."

The dry bones are a picture of the Jews as they were scattered among the nations after 70 A.D. and the coming together of the bones shows the actual Jewish people coming back together.

A very interesting interpretation includes the fact that just before the modern state of Israel was established, the Jews went through the most horrific persecution in history, the Holocaust. The dry bones are a symbol of the Jews during the Holocaust, and if you have ever seen any of the pictures taken of the Jews during this persecution, dry bones would be a very accurate way to describe them. They were terribly malnourished and because of their extreme dehydration and starvation, many were dangerously underweight, even to the point of death.[3] The interpretation goes that the coming together of the dry bones with life breathed into them is showing the Jews coming out of the Holocaust. Next God says he will regather His people from the heathen and make them one nation, which is symbolizing the Jews returning to their homeland and the modern state of Israel being established.

Even Israeli Prime Minister Benjamin Netanyahu recognized this interpretation while he was addressing the people of Poland at the 65th anniversary of the liberation at Auschwitz. He claimed the prophecies of Ezekiel 37 have been fulfilled.[4] If that is true, and I believe it is, then that would put us right on the cusp of the fulfillment of the next prophecy in the book of Ezekiel.

EZEKIEL – CHAPTER 38 AND 39

The prophecy talked about in these two chapters describes a horrific war between Israel and the surrounding nations. It gives us all the facts, in very clear and specific detail, of what will transpire during this war. This prophecy is commonly referred to as *"The War of Gog of Magog"* or *"The Ezekiel 38 war"*.

Chapter 38 begins with God describing Gog of Magog and all the nations who will take part in this war against Israel. The way to discover what these nations are today is to look at what area is being described from the time of Ezekiel. For example, we know the land of Persia from Ezekiel's time is now called Iran.[5] We can use this method to discover what the rest of the nations are. Listing them in order of mention, first we have Magog.

There are a few different places that Magog is thought to represent. Some say it is Armenia [6], others say it is in what the Greeks called Scythia, or Russia today [7], and others recognize it as Turkey.[8] To be safe, I keep my eye on current events of all of Israel's surrounding nations. However, I believe Magog is more than likely either Russia or Turkey but I lean more toward Russia.

I lean toward Russia because Turkey is already mentioned by different names in this prophecy. I don't think it would make much sense to mention Turkey twice in two different ways. It would be like saying *"the United States, Canada, Mexico, and North America"*. All you would have to say is *"North America"*.

Next in the list of nations are Meshech and Tubal which are widely accepted as being in Turkey.[9] If Meshech and Tubal are places in Turkey, then when we look at how the passage is worded, we can see how Magog would probably be Russia. Ezekiel 38:2-3 reads…

"Son of man, set thy face against Gog, the land of Magog, the chief prince of Meshech and Tubal, and prophesy against him, And say, Thus saith the Lord God; Behold, I am against thee, O Gog, the chief prince of Meshech and Tubal:"

If Gog is the ruler (or *"chief prince"*) of Meshech and Tubal, and Magog is the land, then that would logically put Meshech and Tubal outside the land of Magog. Otherwise this verse could seem repetitive. If Meshech and Tubal are in what is now known as Turkey, then it would make sense that the land of Magog in Ezekiel's time would be our present-day Russia since Turkey is already mentioned.

325

Another interesting fact to mention, today Russia supplies various weapons to Iran.[10] This certainly would fit into the Ezekiel 38-39 war.

Next we have Persia which is now known as Iran, since 1935.[11] Then Ethiopia and Libya are listed. Ezekiel 38:4-5 says that present day Iran will be involved somehow, which is interesting given all of the media coverage nowadays concerning the tension between Iran and Israel. So far we see in this passage that Russia, Turkey, Iran, Ethiopia, and Libya will be involved against Israel somehow. It is interesting to note that Biblical Ethiopia may not be the same as present-day Ethiopia. Biblical Ethiopia would have been in the past what is now Northern Sudan.[12]

Next, in Ezekiel 38:6, we have Gomer and Togarmah listed as nations that will also have part in this coalition of nations against Israel. Gomer and Togarmah are also present-day Turkey and possibly Armenia. We have all of these nations coming against Israel in this passage. The interesting fact is that all of these nations in our time are primarily Islamic. It is no secret that radical Islamic Muslims are no friend to the Jewish people or to the state of Israel.

Another interesting thing to point out is that this passage says these nations will come against a *"land of unwalled villages"* (Ezekiel 38:11), a term used to reference modern-day Israel. What is interesting about this is that in Ezekiel's time, there would have been walls around all the villages to prevent attacks from other people and nations. Nowadays we use other forms of security to ensure the safety of our cities, towns, and villages. The way we accomplish security now would have been unheard of at the time Ezekiel was giving this prophecy.

Next we have Sheba, Dedan, and Tarshish mentioned in the prophecy. Ezekiel 38:13 reads...

"Sheba, and Dedan, and the merchants of Tarshish, with all the young lions thereof, shall say unto thee, Art thou come to take a spoil? hast thou gathered thy company to take a prey? to carry away silver and gold, to take away cattle and goods, to take a great spoil?"

We are told here that the cause of the attempted invasion into Israel is for spoil, not necessarily for destruction. The nations mentioned above seemed to be involved in more of a protest against the war in some way (probably financial). Sheba and Dedan are recognized as Saudi Arabia while Tarshish is thought to be Western Europe. This is interesting because the official emblem of England is the lion, as our official emblem is the eagle (also see the biblical prophecy of Daniel chapter 7).[13] This type of alliance between Western Europe and Saudi Arabia has happened before, during the Gulf War.[14] Given the similarities of events, I believe this part of the Gulf War could have been a shadow of what is to come in the Ezekiel 38-39 war.

After the nations are listed, we get some more information about how the war will play out. We even learn that there will be a great shaking in Israel (Ezekiel 38:20). This could be due to an earthquake or even some type of explosion. There is also a part of a verse that states *"...every man's sword shall be against his brother..."* which may signify that the loose coalition of nations against Israel will also be fighting amongst themselves (Ezekiel 38:21). We also see that the army of Gog (be it Russia or Turkey) will be massively devastated in this war. Ezekiel 39:2 reads...

"And I will turn thee back, and leave but the sixth part of thee, and will cause thee to come up from the north parts, and will bring thee upon the mountains of Israel:"

The next interesting thing is what is said about the weapons of Israel and how they will be utilized. Ezekiel 39:9-10 reads...

"And they that dwell in the cities of Israel shall go forth, and shall set on fire and burn the weapons, both the shields and the bucklers, the bows and the arrows, and the handstaves, and the spears, and they shall burn them with fire seven years: So that they shall take no wood out of the field, neither cut down any out of the forests; for they shall burn the weapons with fire: and they shall spoil those that spoiled them, and rob those that robbed them, saith the Lord God."

There are a couple different possible interpretations for this passage. Some feel that the weapons being burned are those of the nations, that by this time Israel has won the war, they are destroying the weapons of their enemies, and this task will take seven years to complete. Some others believe Israel is burning the weapons for heat and energy which would fit if they are nuclear weapons of some kind. Others theorize that Israel has won the war and, because of pressure from other nations not involved in the war, or possibly even due to Jesus' return to Earth, they are burning their own weapons, which again will take seven years to complete, as a sign for future peace. Another main theory is that, since this is an ancient prophecy trying to describe events from our time, terms known to the people of Ezekiel's time were used. Such as, the phrase *"set on fire and burn the weapons"* and the term *"spear"* could translate today as the propelling fire under a missile. This could make sense as weapons like that aren't made of wood in the way bows and arrows were in Ezekiel's day and the passage makes mention of them not cutting down forests or taking out wood. It is also theorized that it is saying the war itself will last seven years, as the burning of weapons is a way of saying they will be firing weapons against their enemies for seven years.

Next we read of the aftermath of the war in the land of Israel. Ezekiel 39:11-16 speaks of there being made a valley of graves for the enemies of Israel called Hamongog. It says the cleanup of the bodies of the dead takes seven months to complete. It even says that Israel will have to employ people to come and bury the dead in a way that if a bone is found, someone must put a sign by it until the special employees can come and bury the bone. This is a very strange and descriptive account of future events. It seems there will be some type of radiation or other toxicity for there to be a need to hire specialists to bury the dead in this way. The people of Ezekiel's time did not have these types of weapons at their disposal. To Ezekiel, the visions must have seemed fantastic, but through faith in God he still prophesied about them. The sobering fact is that now we do have weapons that can cause the type of destruction and devastation Ezekiel talked about.

CONCLUSION

Although some of these prophecies may seem bleak, it is important to remember that God wins in the end. We should all have an understanding of prophecy to be able to prepare for what is to come. With the Ezekiel prophecies, there are some things that are definite, and there are some things that can be open to interpretation. This is why we must hear out all opinions and weigh them for ourselves with our own research.

Someday these truths will become self-evident. What I mean by that is, at some point, either during or after the prophecy is fulfilled, we will all know exactly how everything panned out, but by then it could be too late to do much about it. While I do not believe we can prevent Bible prophecy, I certainly believe we should prepare for it. It is increasingly important to be knowledgeable and informed of what God has revealed about the future.

Bible prophecy is a wonderful thing to those who can appreciate it for what it is. Bible prophecy is a source of information about God and the future. We can use Bible prophecy to prove the legitimacy of God and His Word. Perhaps most excitingly, we can look to even further prophecies concerning Jesus' return, a perfect world, and experiencing God face to face to strengthen our own hope and faith during these tumultuous times.

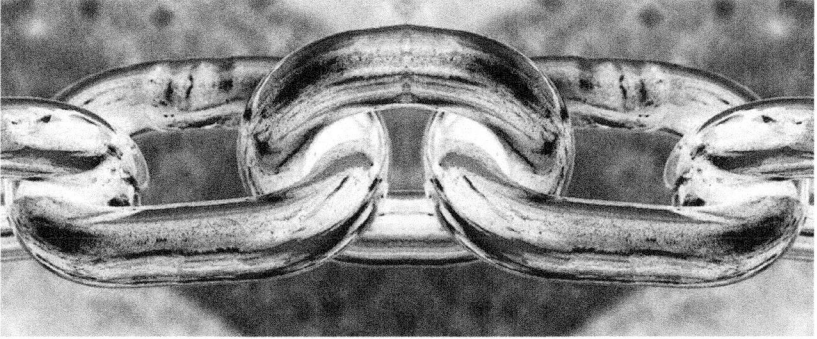

Chapter 14

SPIRIT OF ANTICHRIST

To properly fight the battles and claim victory of the war, we need to know our enemies and their battle plans. We need to know their tactics and characteristics so we can recognize our enemies when they show up. There is one in particular, an extremely powerful and vastly evil enemy, which we need to be aware of. This name of this enemy is either referring to Satan himself or a separate entity that would be in league and comparable to Satan in might and motive. The name of this dangerous enemy is *"the spirit of antichrist"*.

333

This antichrist spirit has been around since the fall of Satan as still rages strong today. It is a very cunning, deceptive, and convincing spirit that has led countless people astray in many different ways. John warned all believers against this spirit. 1 John 1:18 reads...

"Little children, it is the last time: and as ye have heard that antichrist shall come, even now are there many antichrists; whereby we know that it is the last time."

1 John 2:22 reads...

"Who is a liar but he that denieth that Jesus is the Christ? He is antichrist, that denieth the Father and the Son."

1 John 4:3 reads...

"And every spirit that confesseth not that Jesus Christ is come in the flesh is not of God: and this is that spirit of antichrist, whereof ye have heard that it should come; and even now already is it in the world."

2 John 1:7 reads...

"For many deceivers are entered into the world, who confess not that Jesus Christ is come in the flesh. This is a deceiver and an antichrist."

I decided to list all of these verses out like this for an important reason. These are the only four verses in the whole Bible that actually use the word *"antichrist"* in any form. Not even the book of Revelation or the book of Daniel actually uses the term *"antichrist"*. Through this realization, we are able to see the difference between the biblical *"spirit of antichrist"* and *"the antichrist"* traditionally taught.

The traditional Antichrist, or the beast of Revelation, is a person. The spirit of antichrist of 1 and 2 John is a force of deception, inspiration, and motivation from another dimension affecting our physical existence. Simply put, the spirit of antichrist is what drives the Antichrist. Knowing the difference of these two things is crucial in understanding much of end-time prophecy.

Though they are brief, these four verses from the first two epistles of John give us a wealth of information about the spirit of antichrist. The phrase *"last time"* used in 1 John 1:18 is referring the last days. The word for *"spirit"* used here is the same word used to describe the gift of discerning spirits in 1 Corinthians. The word *"antichrist"* comes from the Greek word *"antichristos"* meaning *"an opponent of the Messiah"*. The Greek word *"antichristos"* is made up of two words. The first is *"anti"* meaning *"opposite"* and the second is *"Christos"* meaning *"anointed, i.e. the Messiah"*.

This is telling us that there is something out there, be it a force or an actual intelligence, which is deceiving people into thinking Jesus Christ is not who the Bible says He is. That is where this spirit starts. When the spirit of antichrist attacks, it will first convince a person to deny God and Jesus. What comes after that can be any number of different things. There seems to be a common trend but that is not to say it is exact all of the time. Once the spirit of antichrist can convince a person to deny Jesus, that spirit is bound to that person, and what actions will present next are up to the spirit and the person.

What is so dangerous about this spirit is that, most times, the person does not realize they are under the control of a spirit. They believe they are acting in their own completely-free will. While the person still has a choice in what they do and because Jesus Christ can break any bond, the person afflicted with the spirit of antichrist still has a type of free will in the sense they are still responsible for their actions.

We are all held accountable for what we do and what we let in our lives. Once we allow a spirit like that to take dominion over us, it becomes increasingly more difficult over time to be rid of it and claim back our completely-free will. If a person decides to accept Jesus as his savior, regardless of what spirit is attached, he will still be able to make that choice. In that sense, the person still has free will. If a person decides not to accept Jesus and continues living his life how he wants, the door will be open for the spirit of antichrist to enter and that person will have a diminished ability to fight against it. Then, the spirit of antichrist will begin influencing his decisions without him knowing it. In that sense, the person has given up his free will.

It is important we realize what this spirit is and how to fight against it. For the vast majority of us, it is a spirit we will have to contend with at some point in our lives. This spirit can manifest as a doubt in our mind, a skeptical friend, a stranger threatening our lives because of our beliefs, or any number of other ways. No matter how it manifests, once we know how to combat it, we can be assured to always claim the victory. Once we can recognize something as the spirit of antichrist, we can deal with it the same way we deal with any evil spirit. We take authority with our faith by claiming the blood of Jesus because there is power over evil in His name (Revelation 12:11). Of course, before we can triumph over an enemy, we must battle that enemy. Before we can battle, we should learn our enemy's moves and tactics. We have now defined one of our enemies, the spirit of antichrist. Now let's look at how it has manifested throughout biblical history.

NIMROD

This is the first person mentioned in the Bible that seems to have the spirit of antichrist fully attached. There is not much said in the Bible about Nimrod directly but much can learned by looking at what he was involved in. The first description we are given of Nimrod is in Genesis 10:8-10, which reads...

"And Cush begat Nimrod: he began to be a mighty one in the earth. He was a mighty hunter before the Lord: wherefore it is said, Even as Nimrod the mighty hunter before the Lord. And the beginning of his kingdom was Babel, and Erech, and Accad, and Calneh, in the land of Shinar."

The first thing to mention here is that Nimrod was the king of Babel. This was where the people of Earth were all gathered together to attempt to create the first one-world government. As judgment for this sin, God scattered the people all over the world and gave everyone different languages. As it turns out, from the information in Genesis 10:8-10, Nimrod was the king of Babel, meaning he was more than likely the one who commissioned the building of the tower and the one-world government in the first place. When we compare this to the book of Revelation, we see this attempt of forming a one-world government as a tactic of the spirit of antichrist.

I believe this can be further confirmed by going back to look at what the city and tower of Babel was all about. Starting in Genesis 11:1, we read...

"And the whole earth was of one language, and of one speech."

I remember that I did not notice anything strange about this verse when I first read it as a child. When I began reading the Bible a bit deeper as a teenager, I thought it was strange that this verse seemed to repeat itself. I thought it was saying the same thing in two different ways. Now, since I began using a concordance to reveal the entire meaning of

Bible verses from the original languages, verses such as this one make much more sense.

The word *"language"* in the book of Genesis comes from the Hebrew word *"sepet"* meaning *"the lip (as a natural boundry); by implication language..."*. This is the same Hebrew word used anytime we see the English word *"language"* throughout the book of Genesis. There are two Hebrew words, however, used for the English word *"speech"* in chapter 11 of Genesis. The first one, found in Genesis 11:1, is *"dabar"* and can mean *"cause, commandment, counsel, evilfavourdness, iniquity, manner, message, oracle, power, purpose, task, thought, work"* as well as others that imply a type of belief system. This belief system, or religion, was probably set in place by Nimrod and had something to do with the purpose of building the tower. The other time the word *"speech"* is used, in Genesis 11:7, it is *"sepet"*, the same Hebrew word as is used for *"language"*.

To minimize confusion, let us look at the verses again, only this time with the proper Hebrew words included. Genesis 11:1 reads...

"And the whole earth was of one language (sepet – language), and of one speech (dabar – religion)."

Genesis 11:6-9 reads...

"And the Lord said, Behold, the people is one, and they have all one language (sepet – language); and this they begin to do: and now nothing will be restrained from them, which they have imagined to do. Go to, let us go down, and there confound their language (sepet – language), that they may not understand one another's speech (sepet – language). So the Lord scattered them abroad from thence upon the face of all the earth: and they left off to build the city. Therefore is the name of it called Babel; because the Lord did there confound the language (sepet – language) of all the earth: and from thence did the Lord scatter them abroad upon the face of all the earth."

We see that the people of Earth, before God scattered them, were of one language and of one thought pattern, belief system, motivational direction, inspirational purpose, or what I would call, religion. Nimrod was their ruler and commissioned the people to gather together and build a tower. This was the attempted formation of a one-world government and a one-world religion. Further evidence of the attempted formation of a one-world religion can be found by taking a closer look at the tower of Babel. Genesis 11:3-4 reads...

"And they said one to another, Go to, let us make brick, and burn them thoroughly. And they had brick for stone, and slime had they for morter. And they said, Go to, let us build us a city and a tower, whose top may reach unto heaven; and let us make a name, lest we be scattered abroad upon the face of the whole earth."

We see an interesting possibility of translation when we look back to the Hebrew language. In this passage, the word *"top"* comes from the Hebrew word *"ros"* which is defined as *"to shake; the head"* and can mean *"captain, chief, every man, high priest, ruler"* as well as others. We can see that it is possible the *"top"* wasn't the literal top of the tower but may have been the *"top"* authority, such as the hierarchy of leaders within their religion or even Nimrod himself.

The word *"heaven"* comes from the Hebrew word *"sameh"* meaning *"to be lofty; the sky (as aloft; the dual perhaps alluding to the visible arch in which the clouds move, as well as to the higher ether where the celestial bodies revolve)"*. We can see another interesting possibility present itself. The *"heaven"* they were trying to reach may not have just meant the sky. This use of the word *"heaven"* could have been referring to the second heaven which is the place where the fallen angels reside.

The word *"abroad"* as used in Genesis 11:4 is a different Hebrew word than what is used later to describe God confusing the peoples' language and spreading them around the earth. The Hebrew word *"parat"* meaning *"to scatter words"* is what is used for the word *"abroad"* in Genesis 11:8-9. In Genesis 11:4, however, the word for *"abroad"* comes from the Hebrew word *"pus"* meaning *"to dash in pieces"*. I believe these definitions show a possibility that the people of Earth built the tower partly because they were afraid of God destroying them.

Putting all this together, we can see a possible translation of the text that fits right in with the idea that Nimrod had the spirit of antichrist. It is possible that the problem was not the height of the tower. We know from Genesis 11:2 that the people settled on a plain in the land of Shinar. The word *"plain"* comes from the Hebrew word *"biqa"* meaning *"a split, i.e. a wide level valley between mountains"*. The tower of Babel must not have been built just for height if they were building it in a valley between mountains. If it were only for height, they would have utilized the height of the surrounding mountains and found

343

higher ground to build. The tower was built for a different purpose than height. After all, we have had many tall towers built all throughout history that haven't made such an impact on God.

I believe it is possible that the *"top"* of the tower was actually Nimrod and the religious leaders, or priests, and *"heaven"* was actually the second heaven where the fallen angels reside. When we string all of these possible translations together, we get a very different account than what is traditionally taught of the tower of Babel. Though this account is different, I believe it to be the truth.

Sometime after the flood, all of the people of Earth gathered together in a valley between the mountains in the land of Shinar. Somehow, either from their own fearful hearts or, more likely, from a lying and deceptive spirit (possibly even Nimrod himself), the people started to believe that God was going to kill and destroy them. After this fear was spread around to all of the people, Nimrod commissioned them to build a city and a tower. At some point, a type of government was put in place with Nimrod as their king. There were possibly other officials, such as priests, that were directly under Nimrod in authority.

Nimrod, the priests, and possibly all the people of Earth came to a conclusion on how to save themselves from God.

Looking at the genealogy of Noah in chapter 10 of Genesis, we discover that Noah was actually Nimrod's great-grandfather. Nimrod's father was named Cush. Cush's father (Nimrod's grandfather) was Ham, whose wife could have carried the Nephilim gene. Ham's father (Nimrod's great-grandfather) was Noah. This means that Nimrod would have heard stories, handed down by Noah, of the pre-flood world, fallen angels, the Nephilim, the flood, and God's judgment. It is possible that, if Nimrod didn't twist these stories around by himself, Ham may have twisted the oral traditions out of resentment because of Noah cursing his other son, Canaan (Genesis 9:25). This could be why God was looked at as a heartless killer by the time Nimrod rose to power.

Nimrod probably passed these stories down to his priests and the people of Shinar. Since their view of God was flawed and they saw Him as a major threat, they only had the fallen angels left to call on. Of course, they would not have thought of them as fallen angels but as heroes. They decided to take action and do something to bring these "heroes" back to Earth to save them from God's utter destruction. They knew how to do this, either from oral tradition, demonic inspiration, or from channeling the knowledge of the spirit of antichrist. Whatever the process actually was, they knew what they wanted to do and how to do it, and so they began to build.

All the people of Earth that were gathered in Shinar contributed to the building of the city and the tower. Nimrod and his priests were going to use this tower as a place they could come together and somehow attempt to open a doorway to the second heaven. There are two reasons I can see for them wanting to do this. First, they may have wanted to allow the fallen angels to return to Earth for protection. Second, they may have wanted to enter Heaven to dethrone and destroy God. Given the deception and the mind frame of Nimrod, the priests, and the people, either of these reasons would fit in.

Whatever the reason, they clearly had the ability to open the doorway between dimensions to allow the fallen angels easy access to Earth. The proof of this is in God's words and actions. In Genesis 11:6, God was obviously concerned about what the people were doing. He knew if He did not take action, they would be able to reach their goals and nothing would *"...be restrained from them, which they have imagined to do..."* which must have been pretty bad for God to do what He did.

At some point during their preparation of the city and the tower, God noticed what they were doing, why they were doing it, and what they intended the end-result to be. It was then that God decided to give everyone different languages, group them together based on their new languages, and spread them all throughout the lands of the world. Nimrod continued his evil deeds all throughout his life, as did the priests and at least some of the people, evidenced by the number of religions that still worship false gods and deities today.

I know this seems like a lot of speculation based on very little information, but the story lines up with scripture when we compare the Babel account with the spirit of antichrist. We can see that Nimrod had all the people of Earth gathered in one place where he tried to build a city, his first kingdom, which he would rule as king, and a tower for their religious activity. The city was Nimrod's attempt at a one-world government and the tower was his attempt at a one-world religion. The spirit of antichrist got a hold of Nimrod in order to bring these things to Earth. God had to

347

put a stop to it because it was not yet time for those things to come to pass.

According to the book of Revelation, this is what the spirit of antichrist does. It shows how powerful and incredibly deceiving it is. All throughout history, it has been trying to bring about the actual Antichrist and his rule. The biblical account of Babel was the first time the spirit of antichrist made a real attempt to form a one-world government and a one-world religion. We find even more interesting facts contributing to this theory when we look at what the Bible says about who and what Nimrod actually was.

The description of Nimrod in 1 Chronicles is extremely similar to the Genesis account. 1 Chronicles 1:10 states...

"And Cush begat Nimrod: he began to be mighty upon the earth."

Going back to the description of Nimrod in Genesis 10:8-9, we read...

"And Cush begat Nimrod: he began to be a mighty one in the earth. He was a mighty hunter before the Lord:

wherefore it is said, Even as Nimrod the mighty hunter before the Lord."

The word *"began"*, as used here, comes from the Hebrew word *"halal"* defined as *"to bore, i.e. to wound, to dissolve, to profane, to break (one's word), to begin (as if by an "opening wedge")"* and, as well as *"begin"*, can mean *"defile, pollute, profane self, prostitute, wound"* among other things.

The word *"mighty"* comes from the Hebrew word *"gibbor"* meaning *"powerful; by implication warrior, tyrant"* and also *"giant"*. This is the same word used in the Genesis account of the Nephilim when they are described as *"mighty men"* (Genesis 6:4). This is extremely interesting when paired with the previous word *"began"*.

The word *"hunter"* comes from the Hebrew word *"sayid"* meaning *"the chase; also game; lunch: - catcheth, food, hunter, hunting, that which he took in hunting, venison, victuals"*. This has a wide variety of possible definitions and is important in its usage depending on the interpretation. Again, this is interesting when added to the previous words.

Looking at Genesis 10:8-9 again, with the translations added, it could read…

"And Cush begat Nimrod: he began (halal - polluted or profaned himself) to be a mighty one (gibbor – Nephilim) in the earth. He was a mighty (gibbor - Nephilim) hunter (sayid – catcher for game or food) before the Lord: wherefore it is said, Even as Nimrod the mighty (gibbor – Nephilim) hunter (sayid – catcher for game or food) before the Lord."

This seems to be saying that Nimrod did something to himself that allowed him to become a Nephilim. Once that happened, Nimrod became either a Nephilim *and* a hunter for sport or for food, or Nimrod himself hunted Nephilim for sport or for food. It could be either one, depending on interpretation, but I lean toward the latter. Once again, I know this is highly speculative but to support that interpretation, I point to Numbers 13:32 which reads…

"And they brought up an evil report of the land which they had searched unto the children of Israel, saying, The land, through which we have gone to search it, is a land that eateth up the inhabitants thereof; and all the people that we saw in it are men of a great stature."

Here is the evidence that the Nephilim, at least in part, had cannibalistic tendencies. We are not told in the Bible if this was purely for sustenance, religious rituals, or just to strike fear in their enemies. Whatever the reason, we are told that it happened in a very real and literal way. The Nephilim were cannibalistic. Given that, I believe if Nimrod had become a Nephilim, he would have adopted the cannibalistic practices as well.

We are not told what Nimrod did to actually become a Nephilim. If the timeline of the description of Nimrod in the book of Genesis is linear, we can at least map out when it happened. Genesis 10:8-10 gives us Nimrod's timeline. First, Nimrod was born. Next, Nimrod somehow turned into a Nephilim. After that, Nimrod began catching, killing, and eating other Nephilim, possibly for religious purposes. Lastly, Nimrod set up the city and tower of Babel, the beginning of his kingdom, and attempted to open a passage to the second heaven.

I believe Nimrod was completely unique in his time and the first of his kind. I believe he was possibly the first human being to become a Nephilim through artificial means. I believe the Nephilim before that time were mainly products of human women mating with fallen angels.

351

Nimrod had human parents and began as a human himself. Then something completely unique and original happened to transform the human Nimrod into the Nephilim Nimrod.

I believe this is what gave him the ability to rise to power and have so much control over all the people of Earth. In Nimrod's day, the people, priests, and probably even Nimrod himself, would have considered the fallen angels to be gods. The people of Earth would have even worshipped the fallen angels as gods. The fallen angels knew this and they knew the kinds of creatures that were born from them mating with human women. The Nephilim were brutish, tyrannical, and downright evil. The Nephilim were feared by man. I believe the fallen angels wanted to create something that would be easier for the people of Earth to accept as their leader. I don't know exactly how it happened, but I believe the fallen angels did something to allow Nimrod to become a special, new kind of Nephilim that was more powerful than the original. Nimrod proved this by hunting out, killing, and sometimes even eating the original Nephilim. To the people of Earth, Nimrod was part god and part man. Nimrod would have been their link to the gods and to the heavens. The people of Earth would have worshipped Nimrod. This authority and power was what Nimrod needed to become the world's first leader. He denied the one true God, as proven through his actions, and attempted to establish a one-world government and a one-world religion. Nimrod was set up as king and then he tried to either bring the fallen angels into physical existence, enter into Heaven to kill God and usurp His throne, or both. That is when God stepped in and defeated Nimrod by scattering the people all over the earth. This stopped the attempts of Nimrod and the spirit of antichrist.

Again, I acknowledge that much of this is speculative. The reason I put so much importance on knowing these theories is because of what it means if it is true. There are a lot of things happening in the world today that can be compared with the interpreted account of Nimrod that I presented to you.

We have things like alien abductions which, from a biblical viewpoint, look more like fallen angel activity. We have reports of alien/human hybrids being created which can be compared to the fallen angels mating with humans and creating the Nephilim. We have alien implant prototypes that seem to have the capability to change a person's DNA, which can be compared to the mark of the beast in the book of Revelation and the account of Nimrod turning from human into Nephilim. We have people in our world today trying to bring about the age and rule of the Antichrist from the book of Revelation, which was first attempted by Nimrod with the city and tower of Babel.

Even though these may just be all claims and reports, even if they do not resonate with you in a personal way, even if you don't believe them to hold any ounce of the truth, these are still all things you, as well as all of us, need to be aware of in case they show themselves to be true. We do not want to be deceived. We have to want to stand with God against our enemy, even if it means setting aside our own pride, ego, and sense of needing to prove ourselves to be right.

PHARAOH

I won't spend as much time describing Pharaoh's relationship to the spirit of antichrist as I did with Nimrod. Pharaoh's account is much more detailed and extensive in the Bible, is easier to understand, and there are already many teachings on the topic. I do believe it is worth mentioning, however, because there are a lot of parallels between Pharaoh and the Antichrist of the book of Revelation. Understanding that Pharaoh was led by the spirit of antichrist will give us more information to identify antichrists in our lives as well as the final Antichrist of Revelation.

Within the first chapter of Exodus, we read that the king of Egypt sent forth an order to kill all the newborn sons of the children of Israel. This was done out of the king's fear of the children of Israel someday rising up and overtaking him. We see the same thing in Herod as described in the book of Matthew. Herod had all the newborn males up to two years of age killed. Herod did this out of fear that the Messiah would someday overthrow him. We see the same parallel with the Antichrist of the book of Revelation. The spirit of antichrist has been leading people to slaughter God's children for all time, starting back in Genesis when Cain killed Abel.

Next we read of another telltale trait of the spirit of antichrist. Exodus 5:1-2 reads...

"And afterward Moses and Aaron went in, and told Pharaoh, Thus saith the Lord God of Israel, Let my people go, that they may hold a feast unto me in the wilderness. And Pharaoh said, Who is the Lord, that I should obey his voice to let Israel go? I know not the Lord, neither will I let Israel go."

This is Pharaoh's denial of God. Pharaoh decided to not recognize God's power and authority. Instead, he decided to lift himself above the God of Israel, deny God's command, and hold to his own. This is a classic sign of the spirit of antichrist.

In chapter 7 of Exodus, we read that Moses confronted Pharaoh again, this time showing a miracle of God. Moses and Aaron threw their rods on the ground in front of Pharaoh. The rods then turned into snakes. Pharaoh did not seem impressed when he saw this, though, and brought out his magicians. Pharaoh's magicians were able to perform the same miracle with the exception being that when the magicians' rods turned into snakes, the snakes from Aaron's rod swallowed the snakes from the magicians (Exodus 7:10-12). This shows that the spirit of antichrist can come with miracles, signs, and wonders but, since they are of Satan, they are not more powerful than God's miracles. We can see how Satan can imitate the miracles of God, a fact we need to be aware of so if we see it happen, we will not be deceived.

While there are similarities between the ten plagues of Egypt sent by God and the various judgments in the book of Revelation, our main focus here is the spirit of antichrist and its traits. The main trait we can see coming from the spirit of antichrist in Pharaoh and the Antichrist of Revelation is the reaction to the judgments. Pharaoh continually lied to Moses, saying he would let the children of Israel go, only to change his mind and continue to defy God until he was finally defeated (Exodus 7:14-14:30). We see the same parallel in the book of Revelation. The Antichrist, as well as the rest of the world who are not children of God, go through horrible and horrific judgments but they do not change their ways. The Antichrist and his followers continue to defy God (Revelation 9:20-21).

This section is, by far, not an exhaustive study of the relationship between Pharaoh and the Antichrist through the spirit of antichrist. I only included a few key points to help us realize what John was talking about in his epistle when he spoke of the many antichrists. There are antichrists that hold power in the world and there are antichrists that are everyday people in our lives. The spirit of antichrist can attach itself to anyone who allows it. We can identify this spirit by the various traits that are manifested through it. The biggest and most telling trait of the spirit of antichrist that can manifest in a person is the denial of God and Jesus the Messiah.

HAMAN

The book of Esther tells of an enemy that wished for the annihilation of all Jews. Esther 3:13 reads...

"And the letters were sent by posts into all the king's provinces, to destroy, to kill, and to cause to perish, all Jews, both young and old, little children and women, in one day, even upon the thirteenth day of the twelfth month, which is the month of Adar, and to take the spoil of them for a prey."

This alone shows an obvious tie to the spirit of antichrist because one major trait of the spirit of antichrist is the desire for the destruction of the Jewish people. Though this would be enough evidence to show Haman as a physical embodiment of the spirit of antichrist, there is also a prophecy hidden within the original texts.

The Bible tells of the Jews' victory over Haman and his ten sons in specific detail, which is where the hidden prophecy can be found. Esther 9:5-14 reads...

"Thus the Jews smote all their enemies with the stroke of the sword, and slaughter, and destruction, and did what they would unto those that hated them. And in Shushan the palace of the Jews slew and destroyed five hundred men.

And Parshandatha, and Dalphon, and Aspatha, And Poratha, and Adalia, and Aridatha, and Parmashta, and Arisai, and Aridai, and Vajezatha, The ten sons of Haman the son of Hammedatha, the enemy of the Jews, slew they; but on the spoil laid they not their hand. On that day the number of those that were slain in Shushan the palace was brought before the king. And the king said unto Esther the queen, The Jews have slain and destroyed five hundred men in Shushan the palace, and the ten sons of Haman; what have they done in the rest of the king's provinces? now what is thy petition? and it shall be granted thee: or what is thy request further? and it shall be done. Then said Esther, If it please the king, let it be granted to the Jews which are in Shushan to do to morrow also according unto this day's decree, and let Haman's ten sons be hanged upon the gallows. And the king commanded it so to be done: and the decree was given at Shushan; and they hanged Haman's ten sons."

To minimize confusion, let's break this passage down in order of prophetic importance and first mention.

We are first told that the Jews defeated their enemies which totaled to five hundred men (Esther 9:5-6). Next, the names of Haman's ten sons are listed and we are

359

told they were defeated as well (Esther 9:7-10). We are then told that the king was informed of the number of those defeated (Esther 9:11). Next, the king asked Esther what request she had and promised to grant it to her (Esther 9:12). Lastly, and quite strangely, Esther requested that *"to morrow…let Haman's ten sons be hanged upon the gallows"*, to which the king made good on his promise by commanding it to be done, and so it was (Esther 9:13-14).

The word *"morrow"*, in Esther 9:13, comes from the Hebrew word *"mahar"* and can mean either *"tomorrow"* or *"time to come"*. Queen Esther may not have been making this request for the following day but may have been making a prophetic statement. We have two possibilities. Either Queen Esther wanted to wait until the following day and rehang the corpses of Haman's ten sons for some strange reason, or she was prophesying that this same thing would happen again at some point in the future, or the *"time to come"*. I lean toward the latter for obvious reasons.

We can find further evidence of this by looking at the original Hebrew texts and how the names of Haman's sons were listed out in Esther 9:7-9. There are four Hebrew letters that stand out in the list of the names of Haman's ten

360

sons.[1] Three of the letters are noticeably smaller than normal whereas one is larger.[2] The three Hebrew letters that are smaller are the *"taf"* in *"Parshandatha"*, the *"shin"* in *"Parmashta"*, and the *"zayin"* in *"Vajezatha"*.[3] The larger Hebrew letter is the *"vav"* in *"Vajezatha"*.[4]

In the Hebrew language, each letter of the Hebrew alphabet has a numeric value.[5] The study and calculation of these numeric values to gain deeper insight is called *"Gematria"*.[6] When we add up the numeric values of the four Hebrew letters that were unusually-sized in the original text of the list of Haman's sons, we come up with the number 5707, which corresponds to a Hebrew calendar year.[7] The year 1946 A.D. would be the same as the Hebrew year 5707 according to the Hebrew calendar.[8] It seems, through this revelation, we are given a year for the judgment of Haman's future sons.

The seventh day of Sukkot, or the Feast of Tabernacles, is called *"Hoshana Rabbah"*.[9] Interestingly enough, *"Hoshana Rabbah"* is the last of the Days of Judgment. The Feast of Tabernacles is outline in Leviticus 23:33-44. Going along with this trend in the Days of Judgment, this gives us an exact date of the judgment to be carried out. The seventh day of the Sukkot in the Hebrew year 5707 would equate to October 16th, 1946.[10]

The amazing thing is that on October 16th, 1946, ten leading Nazis were hanged in Nuremburg, Germany for their crimes against the Jewish people.[11] There were originally twenty-three that were on trial, eleven were sentenced, and one committed suicide before the sentencing was carried out, leaving ten that were hanged.[12] Even though the sentencing was carried out by a military tribunal, they did not end up choosing a normal form of execution, such as by firing squad. Instead, they chose for the execution to be done by hanging, fitting right in with Queen Esther's request.[13]

It is traditionally believed that the German Nazis were of direct descendants of Amalek, thereby making them literal and biological *"sons of Haman"*.[14] This could be the case and is definitely a valid viewpoint. Even if this is not the case, the ten executed Nazis still could have been considered as *"sons of Haman"* because they were clearly tied in with the same spirit as the original ten sons of Haman.

This amazing and in-depth prophecy shows us a clear link between Haman's ten sons and the Nazi regime

362

as well as establishes the legitimacy and accuracy of the Bible. Haman's ten sons and the Nazi regime were both led by the spirit of antichrist. The evidence of this is not only found within the Esther prophecy. Further evidence can be found by merely looking at the actions of Haman's ten sons and Hitler's Nazis. Both wanted the utter destruction of the Jewish people and attempted to carry this out within their own time period. Hatred of the Jews is a clear characteristic of the spirit of antichrist.

NEBUCHADNEZZAR

The book of Daniel makes it clear that King Nebuchadnezzar wrestled with the spirit of antichrist throughout most of his life. We read about how, time and time again, he would go against God, receive a judgment, come back to God, only to fall away from Him again. In his time following false gods, Nebuchadnezzar displayed clear characteristics of the spirit of antichrist.

In the account of the fiery furnace (Daniel chapter 3), during a time of worshipping false gods, King Nebuchadnezzar had a golden image built for the people of the land to worship. The command went out that whoever did not worship the image would be executed by being thrown into the fiery furnace. This already parallels the Antichrist of the book of Revelation when he sets up an image for the world to worship. Those who choose to not worship the image will be killed (Revelation 13:14-15).

Next, we can find some parallels within certain numbers used. Daniel 3:1 reads…

"Nebuchadnezzar the king made an image of gold, whose height was threescore cubits, and the breadth thereof six cubits: he set it up in the plain of Dura, in the province of Babylon."

Later, we read in Daniel 3:5…

"That at what time ye hear the sound of the cornet, flute, harp, sackbut, psaltery, dulcimer, and all kinds of musick, ye fall down and worship the golden image that Nebuchadnezzar the king hath set up."

From where we left off in the book of Revelation, the very next event to take place is the setting up of the mark of the beast which is described as involving the number 666 (Revelation 13:16-18). We can see the timeline of events to take place in the book of Revelation concerning the false worship of the Antichrist and the mark of the beast is mirrored from this account of Nebuchadnezzar and the image of gold.

In the Daniel passages, we read that the image was sixty cubits tall and the breadth was six cubits. Next, we read that the image was to be worshipped at the sound of six different instruments. These three number six references give us a parallel to the mark of the beast, the number 666.

In both accounts, we read that an image for worship was set up, whoever did not worship the image would be killed, and there are common threads to the number 666. We later read, in true spirit of antichrist fashion, that King Nebuchadnezzar tried to kill the Hebrews Shadrach, Meshach, and Abednego for not worshipping the golden image. This was attempted by throwing them into the fiery furnace (Daniel 3:14-23). Nebuchadnezzar's plan was foiled by God, who miraculously saved Shadrach, Meshach, and Abednego from the heat of the furnace (Daniel 3:24-28). This is a parallel of how, after the terrible reign and persecution brought about by the Antichrist, Jesus will come back to Earth to rescue all of His beloved children throughout the world.

CONCLUSION

History repeats itself, plain and simple. It is important to be aware of these things because of the possibilities they hold. We need to understand what happened in our past so we can understand the things we are dealing with today. In some ways, we can learn the end from the beginning. Ecclesiastes 1:9 states...

"The thing that hath been, it is that which shall be; and that which is done is that which shall be done: and there is no new thing under the sun."

This is basically saying that everything that was will be again, everything that has already been done will be done again, and nothing is truly new. Everything that will happen has already happened in some form or another. If we want to know and be prepared for things that are going to happen in the future, we must look to things that have happened in the past. We have to at least be open to the possibility, even if we choose not to believe it, so in case we're wrong and it does happen, we can remember and be prepared for it.

Someday, the events of the book of Revelation are all going to take place and we need to be aware of where we have been in history, where we are presently, and where we're going prophetically. This awareness must be attained under the authority and accuracy of the Bible. God gave us the knowledge so we won't be destroyed (Hosea 4:6). Let's not waste the gifts God has given us. Let's learn as much as we can and hear out every possibility that lines up with scripture. Let's make sure we have as much information as possible so we won't be deceived when Satan makes his next move. Make no mistake about how deceptive Satan can be. The spirit of antichrist, as laid out within this chapter, is incredibly subtle and cunning. The spirit of antichrist makes things like a one-world government sound like a good thing. Consider this quote by Walter Cronkite which was said during his acceptance speech of the Norman Cousins Global Governance Award from the World Federalists Association in 1999...

"Pat Robertson has written in a book a few years ago that we should have a world government, but only when the Messiah arrives. He wrote, literally, any attempt to achieve world order before that time must be the work of the devil. Well, join me. I'm glad to sit here at the right hand of Satan."[15]

This is the reality of the time that each and every one of us has to live in and deal with on a daily basis. We live in a time when something like this can be said, accepted, received as inspiring, and applauded. We have to be open and watchful for these kinds of things so we don't become deceived by a lie and choose to forsake the truth that God has provided for us.

The choice is ultimately ours and, though they can be deceptive and convincing, people and spirits cannot force us into a decision. When the time comes, if we choose to deny the truth and believe a lie, God will send us a strong delusion and, by then, we will be past the point of no return and beyond hope (2 Thessalonians 2:11). However, if we choose to lift God above our own logic, reason, and supposed intellect and give His Word the ultimate authority in our lives, God will gladly and proudly direct us out of deception and guide us to claim the ultimate victory over our enemy.

Chapter 15

REVELATION AND BEYOND

Possibly the most talked about, commented on, debated, questioned, and discussed book of the Bible is the book of Revelation. There is no part of the book of Revelation that is not a subject of controversy within the Christian Church. There are even Christians out there who won't bother to read it due to its seemingly complicated details. Just about every part of the book is open to interpretation. It seems when you think you get a handle on it, some other theory or interpretation comes along that makes you rethink the whole thing. I used to look at that fact as a source of frustration but now I see it as a blessing.

For me, the book of Revelation has always been the most intriguing. I always loved the prophecies even when I couldn't understand them. I loved the order of events even when I couldn't configure them. I loved the signs and symbols even when I couldn't decipher them. It was when I would find myself most frustrated that I discovered my blessing. It taught me to study and pray. It was causing me to pray more, usually to ask God for understanding. It was flaring up my curiosity in a way that was causing me to study other parts of the Bible for comparison. It taught me how to compare scripture with scripture.

At this current point in my life, I'm not sure how much closer I am to understanding the truths found in the book of Revelation, but I do have a lot more theories and possible scenarios to consider. I have an understanding of a wide variety of interpretations that all conceivably line up with scripture and any one of them could prove to be correct. The majorly known interpretations have already been well established and written about time and time again. Here, in this chapter, I want to present some of the lesser known and lesser taught interpretations. These interpretations do not conflict with scripture and should be considered as possibilities of truth.

THE GREEN HORSE

The four horses and their riders are outlined in Revelation 6:1-8. John had already been taken up to Heaven and is now seeing visions of prophetic events. He sees Jesus holding a scroll with seven seals. Each time Jesus breaks a seal, a prophetic event takes place. For example, when Jesus breaks the first seal, John sees a white horse. Then Jesus breaks the second seal, and John sees the red horse. The third seal is the black horse and the fourth seal is the pale horse. These are what are sometimes known as the Four Horsemen of the Apocalypse.

People have been debating for years as to what these horses, their colors, and their riders represent. There is a wide variety of thought here but there are also a couple of details not commonly discussed. Usually with things like this I like to compare scripture with scripture when at all possible. Years ago, I did not believe there was another place in the Bible which spoke of the horsemen or their horses. Needless to say, I found it incredibly interesting when I was made aware of another place in the Bible that actually does make reference to these horses.

In the book of Zechariah, we see chariots of horses described very similarly to those of the book of Revelation (an interesting thing to note here is, in both books, the descriptions of these horses are found in chapter 6 verses 1 through 8). Zechariah 6:1 reads…

"And I turned, and lifted up mine eyes, and looked, and, behold, there came four chariots out from between two mountains; and the mountains were mountains of brass."

We see here the number four in relation to the chariots. The four chariots came out from between two mountains made of brass. The mountains could signify nations. The fact that they are made of brass may allude or connect to other times that brass is mentioned in the Bible, such as the belly and thighs of brass in Nebuchadnezzar's dream (Daniel 2:32), the brass nails of the fourth beast of Daniel's vision (Daniel 7:19), or even the vehicles of the four living creatures (Ezekiel 1:7).

Next we come to the horses themselves. This part can get a bit involved and deep, but I think it's important to have this information and at least consider the possibility of different interpretations. Zechariah 6:2-3 reads…

"In the first chariot were red horses; and in the second chariot black horses; And in the third chariot white horses; and in the fourth chariot grisled and bay horses."

Here we have three of the four colored horses mentioned in the Revelation 6 account. There are red, black, and white mentioned here in Zechariah. However, instead of pale, there are grisled and bay horses. The word *"grisled"* comes from the Hebrew word *"barod"* meaning "spotted (as if with hail)", probably meaning hail-colored, such as off-white. The word *"bay"* comes from the Hebrew word *"amos"* meaning *"of strong color i.e. red"*.

The color red is important to make special mention here because we are dealing with three different shades. The first chariots in Zechariah 6:2 were red horses, and the word there means a ruddy color, such as the darker red of blood. This is the same color mentioned in Zechariah 1:8. The next shade, called bay, is a stronger bright red. The last red, mentioned in the Revelation 6 account of the red horse, is more of a fiery red.

Looking back to Zechariah chapter 1 we can gain some more insight as to what these horses are and what their purpose is. Zechariah 1:8-11 reads…

"I saw by night, and behold a man riding upon a red horse, and he stood among the myrtle trees that were in the bottom; and behind him were there red horses, speckled, and white. Then said I, O my lord, what are these? And the

angel that talked with me said unto me, I will shew thee what these be. And the man that stood among the myrtle trees answered and said, These are they whom the LORD hath sent to walk to and fro through the earth. And they answered the angel of the LORD that stood among the myrtle trees, and said, We have walked to and fro through the earth, and, behold, all the earth sitteth still, and is at rest."

The horses here were red (ruddy), speckled (Hebrew word *"saruq"*, meaning bright red i.e. bay), and white. Next we are told that they were sent to walk to and fro through the earth and in doing so the earth was at rest. This is confirmed in Zechariah 6:5-7 where we are told the four chariots are four spirits of the heavens (possibly the same as the four living creatures of Ezekiel chapter 1). We learn that the black horses go into the north country and the white follow them. Then we learn the grisled (spotted off-white) horses go into the south country. Next, in verse 7, we are told the bay (bright red) horses walked to and fro the earth.

Here I want to mainly focus on the grisled and bay horses, that is to say, the spotted off-white horses and the bright red horses. These horses are grouped together in the fourth chariot, signifying they work together for a common purpose. We see that the bright red horses' purpose is to walk to and fro the earth to keep the earth still and at rest. We learn the spotted off-white horses go to the south country for an undetermined reason. As the horses are described here, they were sent by God from Heaven and are fulfilling God's purposes.

Next, let's look at the Revelation 6 account of the horses. The red horse is of a different shade altogether from Zechariah's description. The red of Zechariah was either ruddy or bright red. The red horse of Revelation is fiery red. This could be similar to the bright red of Zechariah but it is not exactly the same. We see these horses of Revelation bring all different kinds of devastation upon the world, whereas the horses (at least the red and the white) of the book of Zechariah were meant to keep the earth still and at rest. For everything God has, Satan has an evil and inferior duplicate. I believe we are seeing an example of this here. Zechariah's horses were of God. Revelation's horses seem to be more demonic in nature. To confirm this, we only need to compare the descriptions of the purposes of the horses. We read the red horses of Zechariah were to keep the earth still and at rest whereas the fiery red horse of Revelation takes peace from the earth (Revelation 6:4). We really see something interesting when we compare the grisled and bay horses of the book of Zechariah with the pale horse of Revelation.

The English word for *"pale"* used in the Revelation 6 account is translated from the Greek word *"chloros"* meaning *"greenish-green, pale"*. It is the same word used to describe the color of the grass in Revelation 8:7 and the *"any green thing"* in Revelation 9:4. There is a compelling theory that the green color signified here is that of Islam, being that the official color of Islam is green. This horse, from the Greek word used, can be defined as green and/or pale. Pale can really be just another way of saying off-white, or hail-colored, such as the grisled horses of the book of Zechariah. So instead of having a mixture of multiple red and off-white (or pale) horses, we have a single horse where the off-white (or pale) is the same but the red has been replaced with green. That means this horse does not take the God-given job of the red horse from Zechariah, which was to walk to and fro to keep the earth still and at rest, but it still holds that of the off-white (or pale - grisled), saying that it went forth toward the south country.

If the color green here is used to symbolize Islam, then we have hit upon something very prophetic and important. Now, when I make mention of Islam here, I am speaking of the radicalized Islamic community. These are the people in the middle-east that believe if they kill themselves while killing Christians or Jews in the name of Allah they will be rewarded in the afterlife. I am not necessarily speaking of what is known as "Americanized Islam", meaning people that follow the Islamic religion in a peaceful way and have no interest in hurting anybody.

I believe the *"pale horse"* of Revelation could be referring to Islam. First, we see that the God-purposed red of the horses in the book of Zechariah is replaced by the color green, the established color of Islam, a religion that worships Allah. Here we can see how God (red) has been replaced by Allah (green). In the book of Zechariah, the red horses and the pale-spotted horses are separate entities that are working together. In the book of Revelation, there is one horse signified by both the green and the pale. Comparing with Zechariah, it is probably a green horse with pale spots since the pale color in Zechariah is spotted. The flag of Saudi Arabia, which is south of Israel, is a green background with a pale emblem. Islam also began in Saudi Arabia, where their prophet Muhammad was born,

377

lived, and died.[1] The present flag of Islam is a solid green color with a pale crescent moon and five-pointed star. This is the flag used nowadays but has not always been the official Islamic flag.[2] I believe the south country that the grisled (or pale-spotted) horses traveled to in Zechariah 6:6 is actually Saudi Arabia, the birth-country of Islam.

Given this in-depth look at the horses of Revelation and comparing them with the horses of Zechariah, I believe the pale horse mentioned in the book of Revelation does signify radical Islam. We can see further proof of this in the description of the rider of the pale horse of the book of Revelation. We read that the rider's name is *"Death"*, Hell follows him, and he has power over a fourth of the earth (Revelation 6:8). Radical Islam is a religion of death, as their main goal is *jihad*, meaning to die in the name of Allah, usually by taking out Christians and/or Jews in suicide bombings.

If a person involves themselves in *jihad*, they are clearly not a follower of Jesus Christ, the only way to eternal life. This would mean the only place left for them to go when they die is Hell. First death, then Hell follows. Also, as it stands now and depending on what statistic you look at, roughly a quarter of the world's population follows the Islamic religion.[3] *"And power was given unto them over the fourth part of the earth…"*. It never ceases to amaze me how accurate and reliable Bible prophecy is.

DAMASCUS

The book of Revelation is full of unfulfilled prophecies, though many Christians debate how much, if any, are already fulfilled. There are, however, other prophecies throughout the Bible that are lesser known, are still unfulfilled, and could happen at any time. For example, Isaiah 17:1 states…

"The burden of Damascus. Behold, Damascus is taken away from being a city, and it shall be a ruinous heap."

Damascus is a city in Syria and is one of the oldest in the world. Throughout all of history, Damascus has never been destroyed the way that Isaiah chapter 17 describes.

With all of the tension around the Middle East and Syria's continued involvement, many believe the same as I, that the day of the destruction of Damascus is coming soon. I hope I am wrong, as it would grieve me deeply to know of all the lives that would be inevitably lost in such an immense destruction. However, I do believe Bible prophecy is inevitable. At the very least, it would be another fulfilled prophecy that could provide the proof needed for more people to turn to God and accept Jesus as their savior.

THE PSALM 83 WAR

Another prophecy, which is open to interpretation, is Psalm 83. The prophecy is usually known as the Psalm 83 War. There has been some debate as to the timing and fulfillment of this prophecy of war. Some say that this has already occurred, most likely during the six day war, directly after the Jews regathered, Israel became a nation, and Jerusalem became the nation's capital again. Others say this war is still to come, probably before the Ezekiel 38 war. While it is not fully known and universally accepted as to when this war will take place, if it hasn't already, it is still a very interesting prophecy that bears importance and consideration. I personally believe that the Psalm 83 war has not happened yet and we will be seeing it before the Ezekiel 38 war. There is one verse specifically that sticks out to me. Psalm 83:4 reads...

"They have said, Come, and let us cut them off from being a nation; that the name of Israel may be no more in remembrance."

Of course, this could be describing the motivation behind the six day war, but this also sounds eerily reminiscent of what is reported today in current events. The Psalm 83 war is about utter destruction of the nation of Israel which is what surrounding nations, especially Iran, are threatening today. The Ezekiel 38 war seems to be more about stealing goods, or *"spoil"* as it is worded in the Bible. I believe we are closer to seeing the Psalm 83 war before the Ezekiel 38 war, but only time will tell us for sure. This is why it is important to stay open to both possibilities.

AMERICA

Something else interesting to consider is the question of America in Bible prophecy. Many people wonder why America doesn't seem to be anywhere in prophecy. Some even worry that it may be because we are destroyed, absorbed into another country, or lose our place as one of the major superpowers of the world. I believe America is in Bible prophecy. In Daniel chapter 7, we read of a vision Daniel had concerning future nations. These nations are represented by animals. The animals conform to animals used today to represent nations. For example, a bear is used to represent Russia. To prove this further, we can look at Daniel 2:4 which states...

"The first was like a lion, and had eagle's wings: I beheld till the wings therof were plucked, and it was lifted up from the earth, and made stand upon the feet as a man, and a man's heart was given to it."

The animal that currently represents America is an eagle. The animal that represents England is a lion. Our country began by people breaking off from England and coming to America to start a new nation. This prophecy of Daniel tells this story in stunning detail. Seeing that an eagle, especially the wings, in Bible prophecy represents America, we can find it in other passages. Revelation 12:14 reads...

"And to the woman were given two wings of a great eagle, that she might fly into the wilderness, into her place, where she is nourished for a time, times, and half a time, from the face of the serpent."

In this prophecy, the woman is Israel, the eagle's wings are America, and the serpent is Satan. It seems that, reading through this chapter, Satan is going to lead an attack of some sort against Israel and America is going to assist for three and a half years. This is widely accepted as being the last three and a half years of the seven year tribulation.

THE ISAIAH 11 PROPHECY

Another very interesting prophecy is found in Isaiah 11:14 which reads...

"But they shall fly upon the shoulders of the Philistines toward the west..."

There are a couple different views to this passage. The main view is that it is referring to the regathering of the Jews to Israel. This seems to be the correct interpretation when you read the surrounding verses. The view is that this is showing that the Jews would be returning by way of airplanes, which in itself is an amazing prophecy. Even the Septuagint (the translation of the Hebrew old testament to the Greek language) says it as *"...And they shall fly in the ships of foreigners...".*[4] Another interpretation says that this verse is explaining a still unfulfilled event where the Israeli air force will come against the Gaza Strip and defeat it.[5] This is an interesting interpretation, especially with all the attacks against Israel from Hamas in the Gaza Strip.

SIMPLE AND LITERAL

As it is important to compare scripture with scripture, it is also important to take the prophecies of the Bible for their simple meanings and not overcomplicate, allegorize, or spiritualize them. When we look at all of the Old Testament prophecies concerning Jesus, they were all fulfilled literally and simply, just as they were written. Why should the rest of the Bible be any different?

For example, when the Bible makes mention in the book of Revelation of a rebuilt temple, the third of its kind in Israel, and even gives its dimensions, it means there will be a temple rebuilt in Israel at some point in the future. It does not mean that when the book of Revelation says *"temple"* it really means our bodies because now we are the temple of Christ and the antichrist will take place of God in our hearts. If that were true, why would it give the dimensions and even go as far as to say that the outer court is for the Gentiles?

This is what happens when we try and spiritualize scripture that we either don't understand or think will never happen. Before we know it, our spiritualized interpretations don't fit other aligning scriptures, and we have to twist scripture more and more to fit until nothing makes sense. Impossible as it may seem due to the unrest in the Middle East and the controversy a rebuilt temple in Israel would cause, the Bible says a third temple will be built, so we must have faith in that. There are things that are symbolic in Bible prophecy but those things are stated and made quite clear. There is no need to overcomplicate the Bible. Doing so will only end up turning people away from the Bible.

Even Isaac Newton understood this concept as he believed in the simple and literal interpretation of Bible prophecy.[6] Nahum 2:4 states…

"The chariots shall rage in the streets, they shall jostle one against another in the broad ways: they shall seem like torches, they shall run like the lightnings."

Isaac Newton believed in the simple and literal interpretation of this verse. He believed there would come a day when people could travel faster than even forty miles an hour, an impossible speed in his day. Voltaire, a well-known skeptic of Christianity, scorned Isaac Newton for this and said *"See what a fool Christianity makes of an otherwise brilliant man, such as Sir Isaac Newton! Doesn't he know that if a man traveled forty miles an hour, he would suffocate and his heart would stop?"*.[7] Well, of course, Isaac Newton was right and Voltaire was wrong. We have today many types of vehicles that can travel much faster than was believed possible in Voltaire's day. Nahum 2:4 is more than likely describing our modern-day automobiles.

CONCLUSION

Though the book of Revelation is the most recognized book of prophecy in the Bible, there are many prophecies found in other books throughout the Bible that have yet to be fulfilled. It is good for us to pay attention to these prophecies and watch the events of our day. We need to understand the prophecies so we can accurately gauge where we are within the timing of events in the Bible. If we understand what is ahead, we have a greater chance at being able to accurately prepare for it.

This is also why we should not engage in overcomplicating or spiritualizing the prophecies of the Bible. All this will do is lead us astray. We should look at Bible prophecy and the interpretations as they are meant to be viewed. The best way to know how these prophecies should be interpreted is by looking at the ones already fulfilled. They have been fulfilled simply and literally by the plain sense of the text. We need to take this approach when it comes to future prophecies. As the saying goes, when the plain sense of the Bible makes common sense seek no other sense or you'll be left with nonsense.

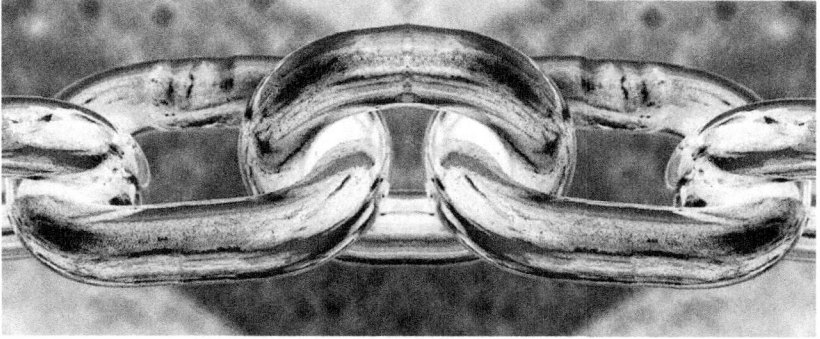

Chapter 16

THE FINAL DECEPTION

I could have just as easily called this chapter *"What Satan Doesn't Want You to Know"*. In the writing of this entire book, especially these last few chapters, I have never been through so much spiritual attack in my life. I have dealt with increasingly difficult and distracting problems with physical pain, family members, friends, emotional pain, sickness, spiritual doubt of others, demonic manifestations, and satanic attacks in my household. I don't list these things as a victim, but as an overcomer. All these attacks from the enemy have added to my testimony and even confirmed God's will. God has brought me, my wife, and my daughter through each and every attack the enemy has thrown at us.

These things are to be expected if you are doing the will of God. The enemy wants to destroy. They will even settle with distracting if that's all they can manage. If you are in the will of God, the enemy will be throwing attacks of various kinds at you. It is when they leave you alone completely that you have to start wondering. If Satan doesn't attack us at all, it is showing that we are not a threat. Of course, God uses His grace and mercy to keep the enemy away from us sometimes too, but there is a big difference between that and not being in the will of God. The difference is usually detectable if we are willing.

The various forms of attacks really began to increase when I started studying things concerning what the Bible says about the Nephilim, extraterrestrials, and the alien deception. The enemy was angry about the exposure and it clearly showed. It wasn't as if I was studying something heretical that opened a door for the enemy to enter my life because, in situations like that, they want you to continue what you are doing. The enemy was actively trying to get me to stop what I was studying, usually by distracting me with other terrible things coming into my life, or sometimes by even manifesting and showing me their anger pointblank. In a way, there was a sense of importance put on my research through the fact of the attacks. Despite what the enemy was trying to do, they only confirmed for me that I was on the right track.

This chapter is going to deal with some possible scenarios that might play out in the future. There are many things here that have been widely researched and discussed by other authors. I have provided information of these other authors and researchers in the bibliography for your benefit, so you may seek out their research as well. Because there are so many out there, I only had room to mention a few. I highly recommend everything I have listed in the bibliography, especially for this chapter, and would greatly encourage you to seek out the other works of these authors and researchers, as well as other authors and researchers not listed here. There are many talented and brilliant individuals with excellent and informative materials out there (such as Rob Skiba, Doug Hamp, L.A. Marzulli, etc.). The more information we have, the better prepared we will be. Just remember, as with everything else, test everything against scripture before making a final decision as to what you will accept as truth. This chapter deals with things that Satan may do to deceive the world. We need to be aware of these things so, in case they happen, we will remember and not be deceived.

There is a final deception coming. Paul called it a *"falling away"* (2 Thessalonians 2:3). Something is coming that will deceive the whole world, be incredibly difficult to resist, and will somehow usher in the reign of the antichrist. What could possibly be that powerful? What could have the ability to deceive the entire world? What on Earth could do that?

APOSTASY

We, as Christians, have a powerful enemy named, among other things, Satan. We know his power is limited as he is not equal with God but we don't know exactly what all of those limits are. We know he was able to deceive Adam and Eve at a time when they only knew the truth and love of God while living in a perfect world. If he was able to deceive them, how much more is he able to deceive us, who live in a broken world full of lies, doubt, and unbelief?

The Bible makes mention of a falling away from Christianity in the last days. 2 Thessalonians 2:3 reads…

"Let no man deceive you by any means: for that day shall not come, except there come a falling away first, and that man of sin be revealed, the son of perdition;"

The word for *"falling away"* used here is the Greek word *"apostasia"* meaning *"defection from the truth"*. This is where we get our English word *"apostasy"* from. For one to deny, or fall away, from the truth, one must first have knowledge of the truth. Here, Paul is giving a prophecy, saying that at some point in the last days, before the antichrist is revealed, there will be Christians turning away from the truth.

The thing we have to realize is that there has always been apostasy in the Church. There have always been people who know God but turn from Him in pursuit of other religions or carnal lives. For Paul to make special mention of apostasy in the last days, it has to be something much bigger than what normally occurs.

This last-days apostasy would be something outside of the normal decline in belief and faith. It could not be merely gradual. It could not mean that there will only be an increase in percentages of Christians falling away, as that is something that has been continually happening since the Church began.

393

This also could not be something localized within one area because this is a prophecy for all of us to be looking for in the last days. This apostasy would have to be immediate and worldwide. This would have to be something that the majority of Christians would not expect because if they knew ahead of time, they would not be deceived (Hosea 4:6).

Something massive is going to occur that will change people's worldview immediately. Something is going to happen that will be global and will turn people away from God and the Bible. There is a final deception coming. Satan knows this is his last chance to deceive the world and he isn't going to hold anything back.

ANGELS OR ALIENS

Within the past few decades, there has been an explosion of people claiming to witness and interact with extraterrestrials and alien activity. From a biblical worldview, there are three main ways to interpret this phenomenon.

1. They are all lying or mistaken.

2. There really are life-forms on other planets and they are interacting with us.

3. It is some kind of satanic deception.

If the reports of these experiences were few and far between, I might be able to accept that the witnesses might be confused or are just lying. The fact is, the reports are increasing and are becoming more convincing. The reports usually range anywhere from UFO sightings to alien abductions. There are reports made from all over the world. Reports are made from all types of people, from regular and everyday people to politicians, leaders, and even astronauts. The statistics concerning these reports are pretty amazing as they show about six percent of the population has sighted a UFO and between two and four percent of the world's population claims they were abducted by aliens at some point in their life.[1]

There is a wealth of documentation from eye-witness accounts to photographs to videos. Of course, there have been some proven to be faked but there are others that have been tested to show otherwise. Statistics show that at least 75% of UFO sightings remain probable after exhaustive study.[2] Reported UFO sightings are definitely increasing. In 1998, the number of reported UFOs was in the double-digits, between 70 and 90, but now the number is nearly in the thousands.[3] Something huge is going on here.

The UFO and alien abduction phenomenon has even been a major source of creative inspiration in our culture through television shows, movies, books, advertising, and many others. There are people who dedicate their lives to discovering more about what they see as truth. We can't just brush this under the rug by saying all of the witnesses are lying or mistaken, all the documentation is in error, and all of the visual proof is fraudulent. There is something deeper going on here.

Most people who accept the reports and eyewitness accounts believe there is life on other planets and we are being visited. From a biblical standpoint, either side could be argued. The fact is that the Bible does not clearly state if there are planets with intelligent life or not. In cases like this, we must look at what the Bible does state as opposed to what it does not.

We do know the Bible speaks of intelligent beings other than mankind. The argument has gone out that, since they are intelligent beings that are technically outside of our world, they can be called extraterrestrials. I tend to stay away from that term as it causes confusion and makes it sound like we are talking about alien beings from other planets. In the Bible, the intelligent beings outside of mankind are referred to as angels.

We know that angels are incredibly intelligent, understand the mysteries and technologies of Heaven, and seem to have access to vehicles that transport them between dimensions and throughout space and time, as described in chapter 1 of the book of Ezekiel. Some angels are on the side of God and some are not. The angels who are on God's side, working in accordance to His will, reside in Heaven with God and do not cause problems or harm to the people of Earth that is outside of God's will.

We know the angels who aren't on the side of God fell from their original habitation and, as it seems now, reside somewhere between Heaven and Earth (sometimes referred to as the second heaven). We also know that, at least once before, the fallen angels mated with humans and had offspring known as the Nephilim. After the second influx of the Nephilim was wiped out, it seems Satan and his angels have decided to change their strategy slightly. When they tried creating Nephilim on the earth, God intervened and made sure they were destroyed. Is it possible Satan and his angels are trying to perfect their attempts? If they can't create these beings on the Earth, is it possible they are trying to create them somewhere above the Earth? After all, we are told in the Bible that Satan is the prince of the power of the air (Ephesians 2:2).

Nowadays, we are seeing unearthly vehicles in the sky that seem to maneuver in ways defiant to our known laws of physics. There are various eyewitness accounts, pictures, and videos recorded as proof. People are reporting being abducted from their homes, against their will, and transported into these vehicles, nowadays referred to as UFOs. The appearance of the beings in these vehicles are usually described as either grey-skinned (known as they Greys), lizard-like (known as the Reptilians), or human-like (sometimes known as Nordics).[4]

These beings, usually referred to as aliens, perform various medical examinations, tests, and extract DNA samples from various parts of the body, but especially those essential to procreation (such as sperm or ovum).[5] The victims of these experiments sometimes report seeing various types of large tubes or containers where humanoid beings are being grown.[6] The humanoid beings are reported as being a genetic cross between humans and aliens.[7] There are even reports of women being artificially impregnated by these beings only to be abducted again, sometimes months later, to have the fetus removed.[8]

The aliens then tell the abductee that they are creating a superior race. They say they are doing this in order to usher humanity into a new era of peace and prosperity. They say the time is coming soon when they will reveal themselves fully to the world and guide us on the path of enlightenment. They say they are beings from another planet in another star-system. They also state that there are many such planets throughout the universe and that Earth is not alone. At first, all of this may seem wonderful, and I suppose it would be if it were true. Well, there's more.

DECEPTION

What is really strange is that these "aliens" say there is no kind of personal God and they deny the divinity of Jesus. They say that they created us, seeded us on Earth, and deny the involvement of the God of the Bible. They claim that our notion of God is flawed and that God is really just the completely impersonal power of the universe. They claim that we can tap into this power and become our own gods, much like what the New Age movement teaches, and they are here to show us how.

They sometimes claim that Jesus was an alien like them and they sent him here to try and guide humanity for their purposes. They say that Jesus was not the son of God and, depending on which alien is talking, they will say either he did not die on the cross or that he was crucified but was never resurrected. Sometimes they even claim they took the body of Jesus out of the tomb before anyone saw the stone rolled away.

All of these things, of course, go directly against the teaching of the Bible and the basic doctrines of our faith. The sad thing is people will believe these supposed aliens instead of the Bible. Sometimes, Christians will even try and marry the Bible with what the aliens teach. Other times, Christians will just abandon the Bible altogether.

These beings, these liars, are not aliens from another planet. They are malevolent entities from another dimension. They are the very fallen angels mankind has had to contend with since the very beginning. Nothing has changed, only the packaging. The followers of Satan are selling us the same lie that caused Adam and Eve to rebel against God. They are telling us we can be gods ourselves. Everything they say goes against the teachings of the Bible.

Does it make sense that aliens would travel millions of light years just to tell us that God isn't real? If they were here to usher in peace and freedom, why is it only by their lead, under their control? It is because they don't want to show us how to live in peace with each other. They want to show us how to live under their rule. This is the very thing Satan has wanted from the time he fell with a third of the angels of Heaven. These are the very events that are described in the prophetic books of the Bible, such as the book of Revelation. The fallen angels and these supposed aliens are one in the same.

HYBRIDS

Witnesses claim that the aliens are combining human DNA with their own to create human/alien hybrids in order to usher humanity into a new age of enlightenment. In reality, it seems that these human/alien hybrids are nothing more than modern-day Nephilim. I believe they are taking the genetic route this time, instead of mating, so they can control the genes of the Nephilim. This way, they can make them look and act more human while still being demonically enhanced.

If we had giants on the Earth again, it would be too obvious for many Christians and it would be more likely the giants would be feared instead of revered. All throughout the Bible, the Nephilim were frightening to those who saw them and there was nothing seemingly intelligent or peaceful about them. Also, brute force was the way of dominance in the ancient world, but nowadays it is information. This time around, Satan and the fallen angels want to create a more advanced version of the Nephilim, with the appearance of a human but the intelligence and power of a fallen angel. It is the biblical account of Nimrod all over again, only this time in our modern day.

To see the purpose of these modern-day Nephilim from another angle, let us go back to the origin of demons theory. If demons and evil spirits really are nothing more than disembodied spirits of the Nephilim, it is possible that the fallen angels are now creating these hybrids as empty shells. This would be a way for the dead Nephilim to be able to operate within our physical existence. The fallen angels could even be creating new Nephilim spirits within the empty-shell bodies, thereby increasing the number of Satan's army. We know demons can possess animals but this is not preferable to them (Matthew 8:28-34). They want the highest class of physical body they can attain. I believe this is why they will possess humans from time to time.

We know from the book of Revelation that Satan took a third of the angels with him when he fell meaning he is outnumbered two to one. If Satan wanted to best utilize what he has at his disposal, it would make sense, if he is able, to create cloned bio-suits for the disembodied spirits of the Nephilim to inhabit. This is speculation but it would explain certain trends found within supposed alien abductions.

I believe a time is coming very soon when the fallen angels are going to reveal themselves around the world as aliens and UFOs as their spacecraft. I believe they will say they are here to advance us as a species. What would the world think if a third of the skies of Earth were covered with these UFOs and a message was sent, from them to us, about their seemingly peaceful purposes? The worldview of every man, woman, and child who is not deeply rooted in the Word of God would be changed in that instant. I believe this is what will happen when the Restrainer is let loose. This is what will cause the apostasy Paul warned us about. This will usher in the reign of the Antichrist, the one-world governmental system, and the one-world religion. It will happen exactly as the book of Revelation tells us it will. It will all be done under the authority of Satan, the fallen angels, and the new, modern-day race of the Nephilim.

IMPLANTS

There have been reports of abductees being implanted with some kind of chip. The fascinating thing is that these implants have actually been surgically removed and scientifically examined. The results of the tests performed are amazing. The implants have been shown to be made of materials not found on Earth, be manufactured with nanotechnology, run at clock speeds incredibly faster than anything we have on Earth, be powered by being attached to a nerve ending and absorbing the biological sustenance of the host, be protected by a membrane that ensures it will not be rejected by the host's body, and have incredible endurance and strength, demonstrated by the fact that they cannot be cut with a surgical scalpel.[9] It has been discovered that these implants would be impossible to replicate on Earth as we do not have anywhere close to the level of technology needed.[10]

It has also been theorized by Dr. Roger Leir (best known for the removal and study of the alien implants) that the purpose of the implants is to eventually change the DNA of the human host.[11] The implants we are seeing today might be a prototype for something that is in the testing phase now, evidenced by the fact that the removed implants seem to be getting more complex in design.[12] The implants even seem to have a type of artificial intelligence. Dr. Roger Leir reported that an implant had the ability to move underneath the skin of an abductee.[13] The implant even followed his finger once the skin became accustomed to his finger movements.[14]

There is the physical proof. The implants have been scientifically and medically tested. Of course, because of the world we live in, the reality of these implants is still met with a high level of scrutiny and a low level of exposure. We need to reverse that trend with issues like these, stop trying to brush them under the rug, and take these issues very seriously. These beings are getting more courageous and comfortable in our realm. They are leaving behind physical proof that they exist. The problem is the world recognizes them as aliens, when the reality is that they are highly deceptive fallen angels.

It may seem fantastic and unbelievable now, but consider the facts of the days we live in. Weigh out the possibilities. Ask yourself the important questions. What if this did happen? What if the Ezekiel 38 war took place? What if the aliens came afterward saying they want to help us to ensure we would never have another war like that again?

What would you do if they offered you an injection or chip that could cure diseases, reduce pain, make you superhuman, provide you with a type of immortality, and all you had to do was pledge allegiance to their system and claim them as your spiritual rulers? Consider these Bible verses. Revelation 13:16-17 reads…

"And he causeth all, both small and great, rich and poor, free and bond, to receive a mark in their right hand, or in their foreheads: And that no man might buy or sell, save he that had the mark, or the name of the beast, or the number of his name."

As a quick side-note, I find the way that verse is worded interesting. It says the mark will be *"in"* the right hand or forehead, such as with an injection or implanted chip of some kind. It does not say *"on"*, such as would be with a tattoo of some sort. Moving on, Revelation 9:6 reads…

"And in those days shall men seek death, and shall not find it; and shall desire to die, and death shall flee from them."

Keep in mind that for everything God has, Satan tries to duplicate. We know that in the resurrection we will have brand new, disease-free, pain-free, immortal bodies. I believe Satan will try to create his own version of an immortal body and make it available to the people of Earth. I believe he will do this by creating a chip or injection of some sort that can be implanted into our hand or forehead and that will change the DNA and physiology of our bodies in a seemingly beneficial way. The only catch is, according to the Bible if you accept the implant, or mark of the beast, you are ensuring your own eternity in the lake of fire.

What if the aliens showed the world video recordings, or even holograms, of biblical accounts that play out different than what the Bible says? What if they showed a UFO parting the Red Sea, or showed Jesus being beamed out of the tomb by a UFO, or showed the aliens creating humanity and seeding Earth? Would you believe the physical proof right before your eyes, or would you still be able to accept the Bible as truth? Consider these Bible verses. Revelation 13:13-14 reads…

"And he doeth great wonders, so that he maketh fire come down from heaven on the earth in the sight of men, And decieveth them that dwell on the earth by the means of those miracles which he had power to do in the sight of the beast; saying to them that dwell on the earth, that they should make an image to the beast, which had the wound by a sword, and did live."

2 Thessalonians 2:9 reads…

"Even him, whose coming is after the working of Satan with all power and lying wonders,"

What if the aliens tried to advance humanity by teaching us their ways and doctrines? What if the people opposing their system were looked at as enemies of enlightenment and as getting in the way of the advancement of the entire human race? What if it was decided that, for the benefit of humanity, these seemingly rebellious people needed to be put to death? What if the aliens and their followers started killing Christians who would not take their mark and pledge allegiance to the leader of their system?

What if, after all this, the rapture had not yet taken place? Would you still stand by God or would you find it easier to succumb to the pressures of the world? Would it be easier to assume that since the rapture had not come, either the implanted chip was not really the biblical mark of the beast, or maybe God really isn't real and the aliens are telling the truth? Would you be able to sacrifice your own life instead of taking what the aliens have to offer? Consider these Bible verses. Luke 9:24-25 reads…

"For whosoever will save his life shall lose it; but whosoever will lose his life for my sake, the same shall save it. For what is a man advantaged, if he gain the whole world, and lose himself, or be cast away?"

Revelation 14:9-11 reads…

"And the third angel followed them, saying with a loud voice, If any man worship the beast and his image, and receive his mark in his forehead, or in his hand, The same shall drink of the wine of the wrath of God, which is poured out without mixture into the cup of his indignation; and he shall be tormented with fire and brimstone in the presence of the holy angels, and in the presence of the Lamb: And the smoke of their torment ascendeth up for ever and ever: and they have no rest day nor night, who worship the beast

and his image, and whosoever receiveth the mark of his name."

The time is coming for these things to become a reality and not just an idea of the future. There will be a time when these Bible verses become very relatable to the time we'll be living in. The problem is, by then there will be so much deception in the world, it will be too late to really get a hold of all this information. The roots of faith and truth need time to grow.

MARTYRDOM

Most of us have never had to make a choice between death and our belief in God, Jesus, and the Bible. It is difficult for any of us to say with any degree of accuracy how we would handle something like that. We'd like to say we would gladly die before denying God, but when faced with that choice, how easy would it be to fall into our own human justifications? How easy would it be to just "lie", and say we believe in something other than God to save our lives, but secretly justify it by thinking that God knows our heart and we still love Him? There are

Christians in the world who have to deal with these decisions and choices right now.

Today, radicalized Islamic terrorist groups are killing Christians because of their faith in Jesus. Sometimes, if they aren't killed instantly, Christians are told to worship and pledge allegiance to Allah and their lives will be spared. Many choose to be killed instead of saying "Praise Allah", even if it would be a lie. They are making the right choice.

Jesus never told us to lie or justify ways around it. We are never told it is acceptable for us to save our lives by denying Him. We have to accept the fact that we are living in the end times and we are right on the edge of all of the prophecies coming to pass. We have to not only accept, but expect that there may come a day when we will have to choose Jesus or physical life.

People in the world and all throughout history have had to make that choice. The people who truly loved Jesus chose death. There have even been Christians in America in our time that have had to make that choice and still chose death. Just because it hasn't hit our country in the extreme way it has hit the Middle East doesn't mean it never will. In fact, the Bible promises it will someday. Given all of the prophecies that have already been fulfilled and what Jesus says about our generation, it is apparent that day is coming sooner rather than later.

I don't say these things to make you fearful. I want you to be informed properly so you can make your own choice as to what you are going to believe. Remember that we were not given a spirit of fear, but of power, love, and a strong mind (2 Timothy 1:7). Also, remember that a lack of knowledge will bring our destruction (Hosea 4:6). Lastly, remember that God tells us things ahead of time, so that when they do happen, we will believe Him (John 14:29).

TRANSHUMANISM

There is a temptation that is being fed to our generation that originated from the serpent in the book of Genesis. The temptation is that we can be like gods. It was the believing and following after this false promise of immortality, power, and knowledge that resulted in the expulsion of Adam and Eve from the Garden of Eden. Genesis 3:4-5 reads…

"And the serpent said unto the woman, Ye shall not surely die: For God doth know that in the day ye eat thereof, then

412

your eyes shall be opened, and ye shall be as gods, knowing good and evil. "

This lie of the serpent is still being told to humanity today.

There are people today who are putting their resources, money, and energy into a cause to improve humanity. Their goal is to use various genetic engineering methods to improve the biology of man through a process called "guided evolution". These people are most often referred to as "transhumanists". There is a wealth of information out there concerning the transhumanist movement and the dangers of guided evolution so I won't spend much time on it here. For more information, I would highly suggest looking into the materials provided by author and researcher Tom Horn concerning the topic of transhumanism.

The basic idea is that through genetic tampering, the transhumanists believe they can cure all diseases, provide special abilities, and even abolish death itself. They do this through a variety of genetic methods, such as implementing cloning techniques, combining animal and human DNA, and manipulating existing DNA within a human host's body. I do not believe the transhumanists are doing this for intended malevolent reasons. I believe they truly want to help humanity. The problem is, according to the Bible, this is not the way to do it.

Any promise of escape from death apart from Jesus Christ is a false immortality. Remember what the serpent said to Eve, *"Ye shall not surely die"*. The serpent promised Eve something he had no right to promise. The serpent lied. Eve rebelled against God and eventually died. As for mixing human and animal DNA, this is also a forbidden practice according to the Bible. God put barriers up between the species so every animal can only naturally reproduce after its own kind (Genesis 1:11-25). As Bible-believing Christians, we must trust that God knew what He was doing.

Going back to the Genesis chapter 6 account, we read that all flesh was corrupted (Genesis 6:12). This would include animals as well. I believe when God tells us something through His Word, we can take it for exactly what it says. If the Bible says that all flesh was corrupted, it means that all flesh, man, animal, and perhaps even plant-life, was corrupted.

As stated before, I do not believe the corruption of animal flesh happened in the same way as the corruption of human flesh. I believe that when the angels fell from

414

Heaven, they brought the knowledge of the technology of Heaven with them. I believe it is possible that the fallen angels had knowledge of genetics and were able to manipulate them to create various animal hybrids, including animal/human hybrids. I believe this could have been the origin of ancient myths of the various gods in antiquity. If we look at these various characters and gods of the ancient cultures, such as Egyptian and Greek, we see many animal and animal/human hybrids. We have certain animal/human hybrids today, such as pigs with human hearts, and I believe this is an example of what the book of Ecclesiastes states about history repeating itself. If it is happening now, we can be sure it has happened before.

It is possible that this could all tie in with the mark of the beast. We know that, according to the book of Revelation, anyone who accepts the mark will have no chance of redemption and will be cast alive into the lake of fire. We also know that the Nephilim have no chance of redemption and are possibly walking the earth today as disembodied spirits. I believe it is possible that there is a connection.

The mark of the beast could be something, as we discussed earlier, that changes our genes in a way that transforms us to what the Bible would call Nephilim. We can look back to Nimrod as an example of this. We also know that whoever accepts the mark will not be able to die (Revelation 9:6). This false immortality is the same thing the transhumanists are trying to accomplish.

There could be a variety of ways that the enemy could implement this and make people want to take it. There could be a worldwide epidemic of a disease that ravishes the world. The fear of contracting this deadly disease could be what the enemy will use to make it easier for us to accept something that promises to cure all diseases and provide hundreds of years of additional life on Earth. It could also come in the form of an implant that is a gift from supposed extraterrestrials, as we discussed earlier. It could even come in the form of a liquid injection containing something that rewrites DNA. Whatever the case, anything that promises to change our genes, cure all or many diseases, and provide immortality, we should be incredibly weary of and not accept. We do not want to follow the example of Nimrod.

This hits close to home for me personally. I have an extremely rare and incurable bone disease, known as Trevor's Disease, which causes a lot of pain, limited mobility, and abnormal bone growth on my right hip, knee, and ankle. The disease itself is not life-threatening, but can be incredibly debilitating. The idea of this degenerative bone disease being cured is absolutely wonderful to me. I can understand how tempting something like a simple injection could be and how innocent it could seem.

As much as I would love to be cured, however, I love God more. If I am to be cured, it will be by the hand of God, not by the hand of Satan. I am not saying all practices of medicine are tools of Satan. I only believe the ones clearly outlined, described, and spoke against in the Bible are. When we start tampering with God's creation, mixing animals, plants, humans, and machines such as with injected nanotechnology, changing our DNA, and doing things to try and improve on His design, we have crossed a line we were never meant to cross. For me personally, as much as I would love to have even one day completely free of pain, it is not worth going against God. It is not worth losing the love of God over. It is not worth the risk to my soul or eternity. I have faith in God and His power. If He wishes to heal me, then He will in His perfect timing.

All of these things we are doing now, mixing DNA, gene manipulation, genetic engineering, were already done once before in the pre-flood world. These were the days of Noah. As Jesus said in Matthew 24:37...

"But as the days of Noe were, so shall also the coming of the Son of man be."

We have to be aware of what we are putting in our bodies and not be afraid to say no to something. We have to realize the times we are living in. We have to wake up.

We can't just stay asleep anymore. We can't deny the truths of the Bible just because they are unpopular or not commonly believed in or taught. Jesus never gave us permission to bury our heads in the sand. We have to accept God's Word for what it is and receive the teachings it has for us. We have to be aware of current events and be prepared for the things the world is going to throw at us. We have to keep our minds open to new ideas and possible beliefs as long as they line up with the Bible. Ignorance is not an excuse and doubt is not an option.

ROSWELL AND FATIMA

No one knows for sure how everything will play out but one day we all will. As for now, God has provided us with some clues in the Bible, but we do not know the truly exact and full interpretations of all the biblical prophecies. Truthfully, I'm not even sure if Satan fully knows. I believe he has a lot of different plans but might be in the dark, as we are, concerning much of the meaning to certain biblical prophecies. If Satan knew the true outcome and fulfillment of all Bible prophecy, he never would have worked so hard to get Jesus crucified. Before the crucifixion, Satan probably thought as Jesus' followers did, that He had come to free them from the Romans and to set up His Kingdom on Earth. Satan clearly knows the Bible and what it says but, like us, has a limited understanding of the meaning of everything contained.

I believe it's possible that Satan has been setting up certain tests to see how we will react to things and what will deceive us the most. It is possible that the whole Roswell spacecraft crash could have been an elaborate hoax by the fallen angels to see how humanity would react to the thought of alien life interacting with us. With everything in the media that exploded from the Roswell UFO crash and all of the deception surrounding it, there is no wonder Satan seems to be running with that one.

I think the Fatima apparition was another demonic hoax to test people's reactions. The thing that really stands out to show that it was not of God was that the supposed apparition of Mary said it would be back at a certain time and it was an hour late.[15] Aside from that, reports say that people were worshiping and praying to this thing, the apparition did not rebuke this behavior, and Fatima became a place of Marian worship.[16] According to the Bible in the book of Revelation, any angel of God would have immediately rebuked behavior such misplaced worship.

I believe it is possible that a fallen angel took the form of Mary (remember that even Satan can appear as an angel of light, according to 2 Corinthians 11:14) to see how people would react and if they would be deceived. Clearly they were. It is possible this was another test of the enemy to find out what deception works best toward their advantages and goals.

The Fatima apparition was reported to give three prophecies. Apparently, two were fulfilled but mysteriously, the third one is controversial. The Vatican got a hold of the third prophecy and did not release it when the apparition meant it to be released.[17] When the third prophecy was finally released, many people believed it was a fake.[18]

There is now so much controversy surrounding the third prophecy of the Fatima apparition that no one really knows what to think. Personally, I believe the original third prophecy that the apparition gave could have proved to be inaccurate. This may not answer all of the controversy surrounding the third Fatima prophecy, but again, it is only a theory. If the prophecy did not end up coming to pass exactly as described, it would mean it was a false prophecy. Since this prophecy came from an agent of Satan, I believe there may have been misinformation that was either purposely or mistakenly added. It is possible that if there was misinformation contained in the third prophecy, it did not come to pass as the apparition said it would.

Now, I do not say this to criticize, demean, or insult the Catholic church in any way, but I believe it may have been at this time that the Vatican covered up the third prophecy so as to not admit fault in the involvement of a false prophecy. This is highly speculative, of course, but I believe they may have done this because, by that time, there were countless believers and followers of the Fatima apparition. If the misinformation was planted in the

421

prophecy by the apparition on purpose, I believe it was because Satan wanted to see if he could deceive and manipulate the Vatican to cover up his dirty work, thereby leading people away from the truth. Again, I understand and fully accept that this theory is highly speculative, which is why it is only a theory. I believe it is possible this was another test from the enemy to see how people would react to a spiritual manifestation.

Nowadays, we have the apparition of Mary showing up over mosques and Coptic churches in the Middle East with Christians and Muslims praising and worshipping it together. A witness of one of these Marian apparitions in Egypt was quoted as saying...

"...There were Muslims and Christians, and everyone was as one, one religion together..."[19]

I don't know if these Marian apparitions will have anything to do with Satan's final deception or not. I do believe, however, that Satan is testing the waters to see what he can get away with, what people will accept, and what will best deceive humanity.

CONCLUSION

I don't know if this alien deception is going to be the scenario that will play out or if it will be something else. I feel there is a lot of evidence for the alien scenario and, if Satan is able to, it seems to be the deception he would choose as it the one most likely to deceive the whole world. I believe he is already setting the stage for this by indoctrinating us with his lies through various forms of media. There has been a major increase of movies, books, and television shows about things like aliens, vampires, werewolves, ghosts, demons, and super-humans.

There is an unbalance in most Christian lives. On average, we tend to spend four to five hours a day watching television but only an hour per week learning about God. Even when we do take the time to learn about God, it is usually confined to a church. We usually bring none of what we learned home with us to apply to our daily lives. I am not saying it is bad to be entertained once in a while, but I do believe these things are set in place to make it easier for the world to accept the lies when the final deception actually happens. But, as I said, I don't know for sure which route Satan will end up taking.

If not the alien scenario, maybe a different deception will play out, such as a worldwide acceptance and following of Islam, the transhumanist movement, or some other false teaching. The final deception may have nothing to do with aliens. What I do know is there is a lot of deception in the world and Satan has his hands in a lot of different things. The only question is, which route will he take? Which thing will be the thing he ends up running with to deceive the world? Does Satan even completely know what he will end up doing? Perhaps it will be a combination of many different things.

I do believe, since we have the Spirit of God within us, that we can gain a deeper insight into the Bible than Satan can on his own. The problem is that whatever we know, Satan also knows. Demons and fallen angels can hear us teaching the truth and read the books we write about various biblical meanings. Satan can choose for himself what he believes about what we have to say. The same is true now as it was in Jesus' day.

Satan knows the book of Revelation but he doesn't know or understand every meaning and correct interpretation of the verses. I believe that is why he has so many deceptions and various things going on all at once.

He is waiting it out and paying attention to the events around the times we're living in. When the time comes, he will take what he thinks will oppose God and deceive us best, and use it.

Little does Satan know that despite his best efforts, he will actually be fulfilling Bible prophecy with whatever he will decide to do. Maybe he doesn't know exactly what plan he will end up going with, but he is prepared to use any one of them when the time comes for him to do so. This is why we need to be aware of all possibilities. We need to be mindful of Satan's tactics and ways. If he has a lot of plans ready to go then we need to have a lot of preparations.

As I have stated all throughout this book, we need to hear out every scenario that matches scripture, consider and plan responses for them, and wait to see what will take place. Chances are, if he can, Satan will end up running with the most unbelievable one to us, the scenario that the least people consider, the one that seems most ridiculous, the one that Christians scoff at other Christians for believing, the one scenario that seems to have the least credible proof and acknowledgement. Personally, I believe this to be the alien deception scenario, but am open to the possibility of others.

I believe that chances are, if he can, Satan and his angels will not only be spreading around the alien gospel, as they are today, but will also physically manifest and reveal themselves to the world as our alien creators. We have to keep in mind what the Bible says about things like this. Galatians 1:6-9 reads...

"I marvel that ye are so soon removed from him that called you into the grace of Christ unto another gospel: Which is not another; but there be some that trouble you, and would pervert the gospel of Christ. But though we, or an angel from heaven, preach any other gospel unto you than that which we have preached unto you, let him be accursed. As we said before, so say I now again, If any man preach any other gospel unto you than that ye have received, let him be accursed."

This passage says that even if an angel preaches another gospel, not to accept it. Angels are not always benevolent. They can lie and fall away from God. This biblical passage is speaking of the fallen angels.

Most people nowadays who hear a spirit speaking or see a spirit manifest will blindly accept and believe anything it has to say. Most never test the spirits to make sure they are telling the truth. Most don't really know how. So how can we know if a spirit is an angel of God or of Satan? If even Satan can appear as an angel of light (2 Corinthians 11:14), how can we know if a manifested spirit is bringing us the truth? We are told how to test the spirits in 1 John 4:1-3 which reads…

"Beloved, believe not every spirit, but try the spirits whether they are of God: because many false prophets are gone out into the world. Hereby know ye the Spirit of God: Every spirit that confesseth that Jesus Christ is come in the flesh is of God: And every spirit that confesseth not that Jesus Christ is come in the flesh is not of God: and this is that spirit of antichrist, whereof ye have heard that it should come; and even now already is it in the world."

Just because something spiritual might manifest to us, that doesn't mean we can believe anything it says. If we do not test the entity, then we have no idea if it was telling us the truth.

We have to test any spirit, be it of man or angel, by asking it directly if Jesus came in the flesh. If it tries to give you the runaround, then cast it out by the power of the blood of Jesus and His name. If it simply says yes, without some longwinded explanation of why it was different than what they Bible teaches, then you know it is of God and it can be trusted.

We need to test the spirits. If the manifested angel is of God, he will not be offended by you following the Bible's instruction and testing him to make sure he can be trusted. I don't know how many of you this will ever happen to, but just in case it does, we need to be prepared for it. God included it in the Bible, so He thought it was important enough information for us to know. We need to respect that and, at the very least, keep the knowledge of what to do in our minds just in case it ever happens in the future.

As for now, we do know that we are called to destroy the works of Satan (1 John 3:8), but we can't do that if we are unaware of what those works are. Since we are not plainly told every minute detail of Satan's agenda, we must consider all applicable possibilities. I have come across, believed in, thought about, considered, discussed, and debated so many possible scenarios concerning the end times and different paths the enemy might take that it is impossible for them all to be correct. The trick is to not let all of the ideas confuse you. Instead, research and study each one, rule out those which conflict with scripture, and file away the rest in your memory.

We have to learn how to apply what happens in the world with Bible prophecy. Doing so will give us a clearer picture of what the prophecies are saying. There are many things we are unaware of, many things we don't know exactly how to interpret, and many things we can't explain. When we get overwhelmed in the mysteries of the unknown, it is important to remember the things that are known. There are many things the Bible is extremely clear about. Those are the things that should make up our doctrines and foundations of our faith. Through those things, we can learn even more.

Trust in God and in His Word. He will never steer you wrong. Test everything you are told or taught against God's Word. Always be honest with yourself about your own flaws. Allow God to help you work on you flaws because Satan absolutely knows them and will try to use them against you. Lastly, stand on the promises of God. Those promises are yours to claim. You have every right to them if you love God and follow Him. We have those promises so that when the enemy attacks, we have something to fall back on and something to limit Satan's power over us. Satan can never break a promise of God in any way. There is no need to fear anything the enemy can throw at you because God promises to keep you safe. Even when you die, you are safe, because He has you and has promised to never let you go (John 10:27-30). Simply put, God loves us and all we have to do is love Him back. Through that love will come everything else.

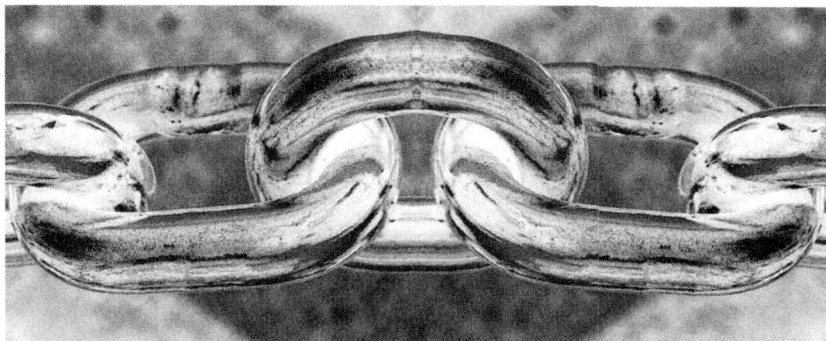

CONCLUSION

I sincerely hope this book has been a blessing to you. I pray that I have succeeded in opening your eyes, or at the very least, caused some of you to take in some new considerations. I presented these teachings to you in the way that it was presented to me by God.

This book is all about learning to see what the enemy is trying to hide and combating deception and unbelief. We learned that everything starts with salvation. After that we needed to learn how to let the Bible teach us for itself. For that to happen we had to cast aside the traditional teachings we have that conflict with scripture. Simple, recognizable, and easy to understand examples were presented to show that the Bible, in some cases, may

431

be saying something different than we are originally and traditionally taught, such as with the Christmas story centered on the birth of Jesus Christ. Then we had to make sure we were all on the same page as to who exactly Jesus is. After all, how can we trust in someone to lead us if we don't know the Leader Himself or even His nature?

Once we understood the foundational teachings, we had to learn what the Bible says about the day we live in and how to get through it. We learned the importance of the difference between forgiveness and trust so we know who we can have fighting beside us in this battle against Satan. We learned how to gain the insight to identify distractions in our lives that could pull us out of the battle, cause us to go AWOL, and sometimes even switch sides without realizing it. Then we had to learn what God says about the people who could be potentially fighting alongside us and showing that Satan does not want our army to grow. He will try to cause us to judge people for ourselves instead of leaving it up to God. We saw how, many times, we make the mistake of choosing to believe that certain people are not fit to fight in this army of God, regardless if they accept Jesus as their savior. Then we learned about the weapons we have at our disposal, both for defensive and offensive purposes. We learned that, though we all may have different weapons that God assigns us, we are all on the same side fighting for the same cause under Jesus Christ.

Last we learned how to properly draw out information from the Bible, especially concerning prophecy and the deceptions of Satan. We learned more about our enemy. We learned more about his devices and tactics. We saw how he created a faction of his army, called the Nephilim, in an attempt to destroy humanity. We learned about some of the weapons of the enemy and the types of technology they have at their disposal. We also discovered more about the spiritual side of our enemy.

We learned more about our own battle plans from our Commander and Leader, Jesus Christ. We learned about some lesser-known prophecies and how they have to do with the war we are fighting in. Finally, we learned of the potential future battle plans of the enemy, how to not be deceived, and how to fight against it when it happens.

We may not fully know exactly what the war between God and Satan will include, but we have a lot of clues pointing us to a clear direction. We are involved in this battle whether we like it or not. We must choose sides. To choose to sit on the sidelines and see how everything plays out is to allow Satan to do what he wants and not help

Jesus destroy his evil works. We need to realize and accept who we are, what we are doing here, why we were created, what this life is, and what is expected of us. We need to choose either the army of God or the army of Satan. There is no in-between.

It is no accident that you have read this book. God has a purpose for you. Now you have the information needed to execute His plans. You have the knowledge. Now you must use wisdom. You can't just sit on the information and do nothing with it, unless you are siding against God.

I don't know what God has planned for you. That is something between you and God. You must have the wisdom to allow Him to guide you and show you what He created you for. Reading this book has given you a base understanding of the war we are all engaged in, but information and understanding can only bring you so far. You must now let God take over and follow His lead. If you are willing, He will give you all that you need to fight in this war by His side. There is no greater honor. This is the call to all Christians, to give our lives to Jesus Christ, allow Him to lead us in every way, and fight together to destroy the works of Satan.

Again, I pray this book has been a blessing to you. I sincerely hope you will take the information contained in this book to heart. You should test everything against scripture and learn to do your own research into any topic that God leads you. Satan has made an incredible mess of things and there is a lot of work to be done in the world. The great news, the thing we can always hold onto, is that we serve a God who knows the end from the beginning and has revealed it to us. We know that we win the war in the end. We know that, though these battles can wound us and wear us out, they can't keep us down if we let Jesus lift us up. Satan holds no power over us because, in reality, the war was won on the cross. Now we just have to fight beside Jesus to claim the victory. Take care, God bless, and trust Jesus in all things.

NOTES

SALVATION

1. The New Living Translation of the Bible, Romans 7:17-20

PLACES AND NUMBERS

1. http://www.bible-history.com/geography/ancient-israel/bethlehem.html
2. Strong's Exhaustive Concordance of the Bible: Updated Edition by James Strong 2007 Hendrickson Publishers, Inc.
3. The Companion Bible, 1974, Appendix 179 p.200

THE HOLY TRINITY

1. Strong's Exhaustive Concordance of the Bible: Updated Edition by James Strong 2007 Hendrickson Publishers, Inc.

2. Mere Christianity by C.S. Lewis, HarperOne of HarperCollins Publishers, containing Beyond Personality by C.S. Lewis, copyright 1944 and renewed 1972, C.S. Lewis Pte. Ltd.

FORGIVENESS

1. The Freedom and Power of Forgiveness by John MacArthur, 1998, Crossway Books of Good News Publishers, page 158

DISTRACTIONS:

1. http://bible-christian.org/wine.html
2. Ibid.

GIFTS OF THE HOLY SPIRIT

1. http://www.bible-knowledge.com/gifts-of-the-holy-spirit/

NEPHILIM

1. http://www.dailymail.co.uk/sciencetech/article-2017818/Embryos-involving-genes-animals-mixed-humans-produced-secretively-past-years.html
2. http://ligerliger.com/

THE EZEKIEL PROPHECIES:

1. http://www.differentspirit.org/evidence/israel.php
2. Ibid.
3. http://www.martinfrost.ws/htmlfiles/holocaust.html #Jews
4. http://www.mfa.gov.il/MFA/Government/Speeches+by+Israeli+leaders/2010/Address_PM_Netanyahu_at_Auschwitz_27-Jan-2010.htm
5. http://www.contenderministries.org/prophecy/gogmagog.php
6. The Encyclopaedia Biblica – p.1747 Gog and Magog entry
7. Flavius Josephus, Antiquities of the Jews, Book I, Ch. 6

8. http://www.wnd.com/2012/06/ezekiels-magog-russia-or-turkey/

9. http://archives.joelstrumpet.com/?p=2681

10. http://www.cfr.org/iran/russia-iran-arms-trade/p11869

11. http://www.contenderministries.org/prophecy/gogmagog.php

12. http://www.biblicalstudies.com/bstudy/eschatology/ezekiel.htm

13. http://www.prophecyclub.com/article_2004_jan-feb.htm

14. http://www.contenderministries.org/prophecy/gogmagog.php

THE SPIRIT OF ANTICHRIST

1. http://www.shemayisrael.co.il/parsha/rosenzweig/archives/vayikra.htm

2. Ibid.

3. Ibid.

4. Ibid.

5. http://en.wikipedia.org/wiki/Gematria

6. Ibid.

7. http://www.shemayisrael.co.il/parsha/rosenzweig/archives/vayikra.htm
8. Ibid.
9. http://en.wikipedia.org/wiki/Hoshanah_Rabbah
10. http://www.shemayisrael.co.il/parsha/rosenzweig/archives/vayikra.htm
11. http://www.truecrimelibrary.com/crime_series_show.php?id=829&series_number=13
12. http://nazarenespace.com/profiles/blogs/the-prophecy-of-ester
13. Ibid.
14. Ibid.
15. http://www.wnd.com/2009/07/104399/

REVELATION AND BEYOND

1. http://www.allaboutreligion.org/place-of-origin-islam-faq.htm
2. http://www.crwflags.com/fotw/flags/isl-ori.html
3. http://www.pewforum.org/The-Future-of-the-Global-Muslim-Population.aspx
4. http://bible.cc/isaiah/11-14.htm
5. http://www.bibleprophecyblog.com/2010/08/isaiah-11.html#

6. http://www.propheciesofrevelation.org/signs10.php

7. Ibid.

THE FINAL DECEPTION

1. http://www.uforq.asn.au/articles/statistics.html

2. Ibid.

3. http://www.nuforc.org/webreports/ndxevent.html

4. http://extraterrestrials-aliens.com/new-about-aliens/2012/three-different-types-of-aliens

5. The Alien Interviews by L.A. Marzulli, Ebook, Spiral of Life 2008, page 50

6. The Alien Interviews by L.A. Marzulli, Ebook, Spiral of Life 2008, page 20

7. Ibid.

8. Ibid.

9. The Watchers DVD series, 1-5, specifically the Dr. Roger Leir interviews, produced by L.A. Marzulli and Richard Shaw, Spiral of Life/Pinlight, 2010-2012

10. Ibid.

11. Ibid.

12. Ibid.

13. The Alien Interviews by L.A. Marzulli, Ebook, Spiral of Life 2008, page 49
14. Ibid.
15. Politics, Prophecy & the Supernatural by L.A. Marzulli, Spiral of Life Publishing, 2007, page 111
16. http://en.wikipedia.org/wiki/Fatima%2C_Portugual
17. Ibid.
18. Politics, Prophecy & the Supernatural by L.A. Marzulli, Spiral of Life Publishing, 2007, page 118
19. http://www.touregypt.net/featurestories/vmary.htm - article entitled "Egypt's 1960s Remarkable Virgin Mary Sightings" by Amargi Hillier

Printed in Great Britain
by Amazon

45456585R00255